# THE EVOLUTION OF LIBERAL ARTS IN THE GLOBAL AGE

Advanced and developing countries across the globe are embracing the liberal arts approach in higher education to foster more innovative human capital to compete in the global economy. Even as interest in the tradition expands outside the United States, can the democratic philosophy underlying the liberal arts tradition be sustained? Can developing countries operating under heavy authoritarian systems cultivate schools predicated on open discussion and debate? Can entrenched specialist systems in Europe and Asia successfully adopt the multidisciplinary liberal arts model? These are some of the questions put to leading scholars and senior higher education practitioners within this edited collection. Beginning with historical context, international contributors explore the contours of liberal arts education amid public calls for change in the United States, the growing global interest in the approach outside the United States, as well as the potential of liberal arts philosophy in a global knowledge economy.

**Peter Marber** lectures on emerging markets and socioeconomic development in the Faculty of Arts and Sciences at Harvard University, USA.

**Daniel Araya** is a Hult-Ashridge Research Fellow at the Hult Center for Disruptive Innovation in San Francisco, USA.

# THE EVOLUTION OF LIBERAL ARTS IN THE GLOBAL AGE

*Edited by*
*Peter Marber and Daniel Araya*

Routledge
Taylor & Francis Group

NEW YORK AND LONDON

First published 2017
by Routledge
711 Third Avenue, New York, NY 10017

and by Routledge
2 Park Square, Milton Park, Abingdon, Oxon, OX14 4RN

Routledge is an imprint of the Taylor & Francis Group, an informa business

Library of Congress Cataloging in Publication Data
A catalog record for this book has been requested

ISBN: 978-1-138-18442-8 (hbk)
ISBN: 978-1-138-18443-5 (pbk)
ISBN: 978-1-315-64521-6 (ebk)

Typeset in Bembo
by diacriTech, Chennai

# CONTENTS

# FOREWORD

*Cathy N. Davidson*

In "Did You Know?," a popular five-minute info-video making the rounds of Twitter, we are presented with a flow of eye-popping numbers in rapid succession, all intended to remind us of how quickly the Internet is taking over every aspect of our lives. From the 1.3 billion users on Facebook to the 5.9 billion Google searches that take place every day, we are living in "exponential times," the video tells us. Indeed, this video itself is a 2014 update and remix of the 2008 original and a number of the facts stress how much faster things are now than they were way back then, six years ago. Since I'm writing this Foreword in September of 2016, no doubt this data is now practically obsolete. Two years constitute an epoch in exponential times.

So how does one learn in an era of constant change? How, as educators, do we prepare our students? As the video tells us, any student who is now pursuing a four-year technical degree is in a race against time, where half of what they are learning will be out of date before the third year of their program. "We are currently preparing students for jobs that don't exist, using technologies that haven't been invented yet, in order to solve problems we don't even know are problems yet."[1]

What form of higher education helps students today as they confront this blur of data, information, and technological change, and with it tremendous social, political, and economic upheavals too? If data is proliferating at the speed of light, shouldn't we be learning in the same lickety-split fashion? Who has time, in such an exponential world, to reflect? Predicting the "end of college" is an obsession of our era. As John W. Burgess, a professor at Columbia University, says, in frustration: "I am unable to divine what is to be ultimately the position of colleges … I cannot see what reason they will have to exist. It will be largely a waste of capital to maintain them, and largely a waste of time to attend them. It is so now."

Many would agree that traditional liberal arts colleges have no value in exponentially changing times. Except that Burgess was writing in 1884, presumably before the era in which change was exponential. College has often been under attack, it turns out, for being out of date only to weather, again and again, the technologies that themselves become outdated.

The essays in *The Evolution of Liberal Arts in the Global Age* make the case that college and the liberal arts endure precisely because they are timeless. That which is timeless has particular value at times of exponential change. In his essay "The Declension Narrative, the Liberal Arts College, and the University," Bruce A. Kimball quotes John W. Burgess and several of his contemporaries who were sure that, in the era of the telegraph and the horseless carriage, college would soon disappear. Interestingly, one could argue the opposite happened. During this era when the American college was undergoing profound change and modernization, the essential elements of general education were incorporated rather than discarded. The new forms of higher education—the land grant university, the research university, and the community college—all embraced rather than obliterated the ancient liberal arts tradition, melding general education with the vocational (whether the vocation was agriculture, K-12 education, or becoming a distinguished researcher in one's field). As Kimball shows, the research university and the community college, each with support for basics as well as for professionalism, have endured, perhaps even giving support to the distinctive, flourishing stand-alone four-year liberal arts college.

This essays in this collection show that the liberal arts college is neither archaic nor provincial. Based on the Greco-Roman notion of the *artes liberales* and the idea that free citizens need systematic training in deep, critical thinking in order to participate in a democracy, the liberal arts have, historically, provided a lesson plan for reflective, cross-disciplinary thinking about how we think as well as what we think. The ancient origins comprised both arts and sciences, with a syllabus designed to train all the five senses (sight, sound, taste, touch, and smell), and to offer rigorous understanding of grammar, logic, rhetoric, arithmetic, geometry, music, and astronomy. Together, these comprise the necessary literacies for full participation in cooperative, civil society.

In *any* era, these arrays of creative, critical, and computational skills are crucial. I would suggest, in eras of constant, disturbing, global change they are survival skills, for individuals and for society at large and, indeed, for the future of the planet. Historically, of course, the United States went its own way at the height of the Industrial Age in embracing this interdisciplinary general education approach to higher education. When Charles Eliot, then a professor of math and chemistry at Harvard, learned that his father had lost the family fortune in the Panic of 1857 necessitating that Eliot now earn a living and not simply live off his inheritance, he was sure that archaic higher education was both to blame for the Panic and could be saved in the future. He went off to Europe to study the new European research universities, especially in Germany and France, with the goal of seeing what he and others might do to modernize the Puritan college. He agreed with those who thought poor education contributed to American naiveté and that both had "caused" the Panic of 1857, the world's first global financial collapse. However, after two years in Europe, studying the systems there and interviewing both graduates and those in the general population, Eliot was sure that a third way was necessary, a hybrid of the European and American systems.

During his forty-year presidency at Harvard, Eliot worked to design the apparatus of the American research university, a hybrid that was part liberal arts college, part research university. Harvard set the standard for all of this innovation, and Eliot worked hard to join forces with many other educators and college presidents to ensure those features were institutionalized broadly. Basically, they melded the Puritan college onto the European research university, making general education not only the foundation for further preparation but a time where students could find their interests and passions, and perhaps even change direction. In Europe, students were (and still are) essentially selected for the university as early as twelve or thirteen and, at that age, were also gearing up for "reading" in a particular discipline while at university. The American system allows second chances, new options, and a broadly general education on the way to professionalism. None of the rest of the world followed this pattern, although, throughout the twentieth century, much of the world has admired it.

The essays in this volume show how that continues to be the case in the 21st century of exponential change. Even as college costs more in the US than just about anywhere else, significantly more students come to the US for college from other countries than go from the United States to earn degrees abroad. The famous Yale Report of 1828 continues to describe the American tradition of higher education: "The two great points to be gained in intellectual culture, are the *discipline* and the *furniture* of the mind; expanding its powers, and storing it with knowledge."

These essays show that in Europe (especially the Netherlands), Asia, the Middle East, and Africa and South America, more and more universities are paying attention to expanding the mind as well as furnishing it. One new form of this double focus is "design thinking," a new variation on what the Greeks called "*phronesis.*" While the "d.school" at Stanford, the Hasso Plattner Institute of Design, has practically made design thinking a brand, the essays in this collection show how more and more universities in the US and abroad are taking up the charge to "show don't tell," "embrace experimentation," and "focus on human values." Whether at St. John's College, which has never given up its Great Books focus, or Warren Wilson (based in North Carolina that focuses on experiential enhancements), more and more institutions of higher education are rushing boldly into the future by embracing and enhancing the liberal arts ideals and methods of the past.

In the magisterial essay that concludes this volume, philosopher and public intellectual Martha Nussbaum argues that you cannot live in a globally interdependent world without understanding the deep concepts of global citizenship and cultural difference as a basis for appreciation and understanding. No, the liberal arts won't stamp out evil in the world but, for those willing to listen, they offer the basis for a different, collective, humanistic way of being in the world.

These essays provide food for the soul, the mind, and the spirit in these disruptive, chaotic, often brutal and exponentially changing times. We desperately need such reaffirmation of the importance of informed citizenship in despotic times. We also need the next generation to be better educated to understand the moral, social, intellectual, and ethical dimensions of a digital age run amok. It is hardly an argument for STEM-only education or the superfluousness of college that so many of the leaders of our era were young coders who dropped out of college entirely or left college or graduate programs prematurely to found the biggest corporations the world has ever known—whether Microsoft or Apple or Google or Facebook. Perhaps with the lessons of history, attention to ethics, and appreciation of what it means to be human we would all be living in a post-Internet world where exponential change improved the human condition.

Computers are supposed to help humans, not serve to hinder us or to exploit our data. It's this human dimension that we must restore to this age. We are, all of us, more than the sum of our exponentially increasing data flows. The AlphaGo computer can now beat the world's greatest Go Master at his very human (or so we had thought) game of strategy. That same computer cannot feel empathy for this champion's very real and devastating loss to an intelligent machine.

Instead of exponentially increasing data, it is the empathy and humanness that our computational world needs. It is to the liberal arts that we turn for those consolations, insights, and abiding human powers. It is to these essays that I invite you, now, to turn and be inspired

## Note

1  "Did You Know, 2014 Remix - Stretch Your Digital Dollar." Accessed August 29, 2016. http://digitaldollar.edublogs.org/2014/07/06/shifthappens/.

# PREFACE

The phrase "liberal arts" typically conjures images of small residential colleges with ivy-covered quads in bucolic locales, or connotes a curriculum of humanities subjects like history, language, and literature commonly associated with undergraduate education in the United States. But the liberal arts are much more than a setting or a curriculum; rather, they comprise an educational *philosophy* that fosters critical thinking and rational judgment, emphasizing discursive reasoning across all disciplines. In the liberal arts tradition, discussion and debate, rather than technical or vocational training, provide the foundation for collaboration and social problem-solving.

Indeed, the *artes liberales* or "arts of freedom" grew from the Greco-Roman notion that free citizens need certain proficiencies to actively participate and cooperate within civil society. Acquiring these essential tools began with a systematic method of critical thinking derived from the five senses (sight, sound, taste, touch, and smell) through three courses known as the Trivium: grammar, logic, and rhetoric (associated with input, process, and output). These three were followed by four courses of the Quadrivium: arithmetic, geometry, music, and astronomy. Together, these seven literacies—comprising both arts *and* sciences—were seen as fundamental to basic literacy and qualified free citizens to participate in public debate, as well as serve in court and the military.

Dormant throughout Europe's early mediaeval period, the liberal arts were quietly revived in the late 8th century by a small group of Christian monks. Supporting philosophical and religious scholarship, the liberal arts provided a common language—an elite *lingua franca*—and a common cultural reference for cooperation in an otherwise politically, culturally, and linguistically fragmented world. From this burgeoning intellectual activity sprang the great universities in Bologna (1088 CE), Oxford (1109 CE), Salamanca (1134 CE), and Paris (1150 CE).

Strangely, this educational tradition withered over time as European universities largely opted for a model of specialized "reading" in a single subject (e.g., math, history, or art). Later building on the 19th-century German research model, this approach stressed focused and concentrated study within a single discipline. To be sure, higher education in Asia, the Middle East, Africa, and Latin America largely followed this mono-disciplinary track, and do so to this day.

It was only in the United States that the broad multidisciplinary liberal arts tradition would come to be a significant feature of higher education. Much of the *artes liberales* philosophy was adopted in pre-colonial America, providing many democratic precepts that, in fact, urged the fledgling republic "to form a more perfect union." Harvard College (1636 CE) and other colonial schools founded before 1776 were deliberately modeled on the ideal of liberal thought and debate. The famous Yale Report of 1828, which many consider the Magna Carta of America's liberal arts tradition, opens with words that have shaped hundreds, if not thousands, of higher educational institutions in the United States: "The two great points to be gained in intellectual culture, are the *discipline* and the *furniture* of the mind; expanding its powers, and storing it with knowledge." As the report goes on to propose, by endorsing a prescribed course of study in depth *and* breadth, the liberal arts prepare students for thinking over a lifetime rather than for a specific trade: "Our object is not to teach that which is peculiar to any one of the professions; but to lay the foundation which is common to them all."

At its core, a liberal arts education should be seen as cognitive "cross-training" enhancing the capacity to think critically and understand connections *between* interlocking disciplines. That is, the ability to *think about thinking*. And "critical" is the important word. Critical thinking uses critique to replace weak thinking with stronger thinking—*ad infinitum*. But critique alone is not enough; inherent in the ideal of improvement through critique is a tolerance for multiple and emergent possibilities, possibilities that must be continually conceived, analyzed, and critiqued anew. For without critique, there is little impetus for improvement and further progress.

Originally limited to elite males in the early 19th century, this strain of Greco-Roman liberal education has since been infused with an expanding focus on pragmatism and inclusiveness. Indeed, during the Industrial Revolution, the self-educated Abraham Lincoln transformed liberal arts education in the United States with the Morrill Act (officially, the Land-Grant College Act of 1862), endowing "a college in every State … in order to promote the liberal and practical education of the industrial classes in the several pursuits and professions in life." This transformation of the US education landscape included agriculture, the mechanical arts, and even military science. Interestingly, the bill was passed the day after Lincoln signed the Pacific Railroad Act, which promoted the Transcontinental Railroad, and just months after the Homestead Act. Alongside these two pieces of seminal legislation, Morrill helped redefine the expansion and trajectory of American liberal arts, bridging American education with the country's broader social and economic needs.

Technical disciplines needed for economic growth were blended into liberal arts and science curricula as colleges and universities proliferated throughout the 19th and early 20th centuries. This model was expanded further after World War II with Vannevar Bush's presidential report *Science, The Endless Frontier* (1945). Promoting federal funding for "basic research", the report argued for the importance of research for insuring a competitive economic future. As the report elaborates:

> Basic research leads to new knowledge. It provides scientific capital. It creates the fund from which the practical applications of knowledge must be drawn.... Today, it is truer than ever that basic research is the pacemaker of technological progress.... A nation which depends upon others for its new basic scientific knowledge will be slow in its industrial progress and weak in its competitive position in world trade, regardless of its mechanical skill.

As higher education becomes ubiquitous to our global age, more and more developing countries are embracing the liberal arts, even as many advanced countries reconsider the philosophy in order to cultivate what Peter Drucker (1969) described as a "knowledge society." This includes building a durable labor force with the capacity to learn and synthesize new ideas. In Europe and Japan, for example, where older higher education systems are dominated by single discipline specialist degrees, new liberal arts programs and schools are being launched to bolster innovation and creative thought. In industrializing countries across Asia, Africa, Latin America, and the Middle East, liberal arts training is gaining widespread attention as an economic strategy for continually improving productivity and living standards.

Oddly, it is in the United States where liberal arts education is now under pressure. Increasingly, critics contest the purpose, goals, and cost of the liberal arts model. In the wake of the Great Recession and a long decline in American manufacturing, many policymakers have begun calling for greater vocational training with increased focus on producing more STEM (science, technology, engineering, and mathematics) graduates. Rising anxiety about technology has fomented fears about structural underemployment linked to robots, automation, and the rise of the "platform" economy. However, as proponents like Fareed Zakaria (2016) contend, liberal arts education is, in fact, vital to generating the entrepreneurial and cognitive skills needed for the 21st century.

While interest in the liberal arts philosophy expands outside of the United States, so do the questions challenging its sustainability. Amid skyrocketing costs and trillions in student debt, has the tradition become available only for the few, and not the many? Can developing countries, particularly those with authoritarian governments, cultivate schools predicated on discussion and critical debate? Can entrenched specialist higher education systems in Europe, Asia, and elsewhere successfully adopt the liberal arts model? And what is the role of technology in the future evolution of liberal arts education? These are the questions put to leading scholars and senior higher education practitioners within this edited collection.

## Part I: *The American Tradition*

Part I of this volume examines the liberal arts approach amid growing calls for change in the United States. While building on an intellectual heritage rooted in Europe, the American tradition of liberal arts education has been a sustaining force in generating the leadership of the country and a vision for its future. Embedded within a unique history and culture, the American liberal arts tradition remains a pillar in the cultivation of a progressive philosophy of citizenship and cultural identity. Arguably it has made the US higher education system the world's gold standard, the benchmark for all national models.

In Chapter 1, the distinct American version of "liberal education" is introduced through an edited version of the famous Yale Report of 1828, a faculty-generated document offering startling relevance and parallels to our world today. At the dawn of the Industrial Revolution, disruptive changes were afoot. Students were entering a world far different from their parents'—technologically, economically, geographically, and demographically. American labor was transitioning away from farming toward factory and industrial work. Nearly two centuries later, the US higher education system—and the country itself—still remains globally competitive, even enviable. Creativity, critical thinking, and lifelong learning—philosophical legacies of the Yale Report and the broad adoption of a liberal arts philosophy by US colleges and universities—have never been more in demand around the globe.

Unfortunately, much of the liberal arts debate is semantic, with a variety of definitions being offered. While many critics assert that US liberal arts colleges (LACs) (based on the Carnegie Classification system) have continually fallen in number and status, Bruce Kimball points out in Chapter 2 that liberal arts programs at universities and other higher education institutions have actually *increased* in the United States, including 400 new programs since 1970. This has been the pragmatic result of a long-term upsurge in college attendance, particularly with "nontraditional" students—those older, working, married, part-time, and working-class who cannot, for various reasons, attend a traditional US LAC that is full-time and residential. In fact, the US liberal arts educational philosophy (i.e., broad subject distribution requirements, followed by concentrated studies in a major subject) has been emulated at virtually all US schools, including community colleges and larger research universities—institutions that have mushroomed in the postwar period.

In Chapter 3, a University of Iowa research team challenges the notion that classic liberal arts colleges are outdated and uncompetitive in the 21st century. While LAC-specific enrollment has declined in recent decades—partially due to rising costs and the flourishing of publicly funded community colleges and research universities—many schools have adapted by blending in vocational and professional disciplines with traditional liberal arts subjects. The authors compare learning outcomes among students enrolled in professional majors (e.g., engineering, nursing, education) with students enrolled in classic liberal arts majors. Findings suggest that a student's academic major field category—liberal arts versus professional/vocational—is not a significant predictor of gain in most LAC student learning outcomes. The Iowa research suggests that LACs should consider drafting such professional majors (or minors) into their classic liberal arts curriculum to help satisfy the growing demand for marketable skills from higher education.

Peter Marber argues in Chapter 4 that international students consider the multidisciplinary curriculum embedded in the liberal arts tradition—as well as the customary freedom to take such courses before declaring a major—a key attraction of US undergraduate programs. Over the last generation, an unprecedented number of students from Asia, Africa, Latin America, and the Middle East have opted to earn their undergraduate degrees in the United States, and that trend has accelerated since 2000. Marber surveys more than 1,200 foreign students from more than seventy countries and studying at 159 US colleges and universities. While the prestige of American degrees was found to be a key motivator, his research also suggests that learning to think broadly through a flexible curriculum—the hallmark of a liberal arts education—was the highest ranking factor in deciding to pursue a US undergraduate degree. Moreover, in investigating school motivations to attract such EM students, Marber found that the strong desire for broader opinions, perspectives, and diversity in school curriculum and culture—again, central features of the liberal arts tradition – ranked highly in qualitative findings from 33 higher education experts.

In Chapter 5, Daniel Weiss and Jesse Lytle tackle the pragmatic issues that confront classic small American liberal arts colleges. They examine the disparate pressures facing such contemporary institutions across three challenges: economic, value-related, and community-related. As they suggest, *economic* challenges stem from the resource-intensive nature of liberal arts education and how it might remain an affordable option for students. Questions about *value* relate to the real and perceived benefits of a liberal education to students and to society. And finally, ongoing changes in society at large stress the intentional *community* that is foundational to the liberal arts model. Weiss and Lytle propose new structures for sustainability in the 21st century and boldly note that such a tradition may design knowledge, incubate intentional communities, and possibly promote greater cross-border understanding amid intense economic and social globalization.

## Part II: *Liberal Arts around the World*

Part II considers the growing global interest in liberal arts institutions in Western Europe, Asia, Africa, and the Middle East. Most tertiary systems outside the United States are publicly funded, reflecting policy and planning at the national level. Amid a global economic slowdown and challenges associated with aging populations, governments within Western Europe and Japan have been challenged to reconsider liberal arts and sciences education to help resuscitate national systems of innovation. Elsewhere in emerging markets, countries not traditionally known for creativity and innovation are cultivating some of the boldest experiments in liberal education.

Kara A. Godwin opens Chapter 6 with an investigation of liberal arts college expansion outside the United States. Where does liberal education exist around the world, and how might its emergence differ from region to region? In what format are liberal arts initiatives evolving? What are the similar and diverging characteristics of programs and institutions? What are the rationales for developing new programs? Why is there growing global interest in liberal education, and why now? Godwin addresses these questions and provides a global profile, a foundation upon which policymakers, institutional leaders, and scholars might situate individual liberal education initiatives.

In Chapter 7, Marijk van der Wende follows on some of Godwin's themes by exploring the recent reemergence of liberal arts in Europe. Despite centuries of higher education in Europe, much of this study has been dominated by state institutions and mono-disciplinary courses of study—a sharp contrast to the US model. This has resulted in publicly funded, mass-scaled, and egalitarian higher educations systems that, while effective during the 20th century, may have disadvantages in generating graduates with skills relevant for the 21st century knowledge economy. As a response, many European countries have augmented their systems over the last two decades with the formation of several new America-style liberal arts colleges, several taught exclusively in English. Van der Wende highlights two driving forces behind the trend: (1) the desire to overcome the limits of early and overspecialization, as well as enhancing learning effectiveness; and (2) the search for elite education, with more selective branches of higher education focusing explicitly on excellence amid intensified global competition. She looks to the Netherlands (home of more than one-quarter of Europe's liberal arts institutions) and uses her own school, Amsterdam University College, as a case study for the future of the European liberal arts model within a global higher education context.

Charlene Tan shifts attention to Singapore's approach to cultivating its own model of liberal arts education in Chapter 8. Given the European origins of the liberal arts tradition, adopting the philosophy within Asian schools often brings its own sets of issues and challenges. While focusing on two controversies surrounding a liberal arts college jointly run by Yale University (arguably the fountainhead of the liberal arts tradition) and the National University of Singapore (NUS), Tan identifies and discusses the different conceptions and assumptions regarding "freedom of expression" and "critical thinking." Whereas critics of Yale-NUS College generally view freedom of expression as unfettered and critical thinking as adversarial, supporters of the school view freedom of expression within Asian historical realities and constraints and view critical thinking as culturally embedded and cooperative. The chapter further proposes a contextually appropriate form of critical thinking for Singapore in which participants seek to understand different perspectives empathetically while acknowledging individual bias through openness and cross-cultural dialogue.

While critics often suggest that academic freedom and critical thinking cannot be replicated outside of the United States—particularly in less democratic and authoritarian societies, in Chapter 9 Neema Noori examines the evidence in the Middle East. As he notes, across a region spanning eighteen countries, each with its own distinct economy, political system, history, and social balance, a common theme emerges: youthful populations and growing middle-class affluence are attracting many higher education institutions from America and elsewhere. Noori considers whether the expansion of Western universities in the region can accompany an earnest attempt to protect academic freedom—an integral element of the liberal arts tradition. Having taught in the region for several years, he argues that the limited curricular offerings, scarcity of tenure, and absence of faculty advocacy may restrict academic freedom in unacknowledged ways. Noori observes that the Middle East liberal arts experience, to date, has been limited to regional elite students with very little impact outside of niche enclaves.

Shifting to Africa, Grant Lilford examines the development of African liberal arts in Chapter 10. He proposes that the mixed European colonial legacies across African societies and institutions have, until recently, promoted a holistic model of higher education associated with the liberal arts. Lilford explores over-specialized postcolonial systems of higher education and makes a case for a broader paradigm for solving increasing graduate unemployment. Importantly, he showcases current African initiatives and thinkers that are supplying needed liberally educated leaders and technologists for the region.

## Part III: *Evolutions and Revolutions in the Global Age*

Part III considers the future of the liberal arts in an expanding global era. Examining new and established approaches to the liberal arts tradition, the chapters highlight the changing role of liberal arts education within the context of a global economy and the rising economic importance of creativity and innovation (Schumpeter, 1976 [1942]). What is obvious is that globalization remains a contradictory force today. On the one hand, it continues to generate astonishing levels of prosperity. On the other, it is driving a range of global crises including species extinction, climate change, and accelerating socioeconomic gaps between haves and have-nots. Can liberal arts education play a role in alleviating these tensions? Is the liberal arts tradition relevant in the face of an entrepreneurially driven knowledge economy? How might a "Western" inspired liberal arts tradition be adapted to solve locally embedded social and economic quandaries?

Part III begins with Peter Miller's thought-provoking essay on 21st-century "design thinking" and its connection to the liberal arts philosophy. He investigates Stanford University's "d.school," the Hasso Plattner Institute of Design. Whereas design schools elsewhere emphasize the design of products, Stanford's philosophy is far more integrative, equipping students with a methodology for producing reliably innovative results across fields. Born from Silicon Valley's commercial culture, design thinking is an approach to problem-solving based on a few easy-to-grasp principles that may sound like hackneyed MBA textbook slogans: "show don't tell," "focus on human values," "craft clarity," "embrace experimentation," "mindful of process," "bias toward action," and "radical collaboration." Miller argues that despite its simplicity, design thinking could be key to tackling widespread global issues that overlap poverty, scarcity, and inequality. Indeed, Miller argues that such design thinking may be valuable for all undergraduates, not only those interested in design or engineering. As he notes, "What's happening in Palo Alto right now is really about the future of the liberal arts."

In Chapter 12, Gray Kochhar-Lindgren probes similar questions in the context of Asia. He asks the following question: How might the practical wisdom or *phronēsis* and modern "design thinking" contribute to liberal arts in different parts of Asia? Working to align Hong Kong's monodisciplinary higher education model with America's multidisciplinary approach, Kochhar-Lindgren considers the future of the liberal arts as they become embedded in new soil. Even as colleges and universities in the United States continue to suffer through financial crisis and a retreat from the liberal arts tradition, Kochhar-Lindgren notes that different Asian institutions are headed in a different direction. To be sure, many countries in Asia and elsewhere are coming to realize that modern knowledge societies require invention, collaboration, prototyping, failure, iteration, and innovation. Amid this economic transformation, Asian higher education is being forced to reconfigure itself to prepare students to assume fluid and adaptive positions in a rapidly changing global economy.

Daniel Araya emphasizes the value of liberal arts education as a means to augment human creativity and innovation in the context of rising "machine intelligence," in Chapter 13. He argues that the increasing pace of technological innovation now undermines simple conclusions about the future of work and learning. Just as the Industrial Revolution leveraged machines for factory production, so today the Computational Revolution is advancing computers to augment human intelligence. While examining the impact of computational technologies on postindustrial society, he ponders the value of a liberal arts education as a foundation to an era increasingly characterized by design, technology, and entrepreneurial disruption.

In Chapter 14, Warren Wilson College President Steven Solnick advocates two sources of experiential enhancement to the liberal arts available at most institutions but fully utilized by only a few: community engagement and on-campus work programs. Indeed, American liberal education has traditionally demonstrated a complicated—and often inconsistent—position on the goals of undergraduate education. A foundational argument for the liberal arts—and one that builds on the thinking of ancient Greece—has been its focus on critical thinking as a cornerstone of productive learning and preparation for engaged citizenship. Solnick notes that the liberal arts model in both its American and export variants has been defined by curricular breadth, self-directed inquiry, and a reliance on writing and debate. These are often juxtaposed against a more "vocational" approach of carefully specified learning plans and competence-based milestones. In Solnick's words, "The liberal arts are presented as learning to think, while vocational or professional education is associated with learning to do." This reductionist approach is unfortunate—and not simply because it undersells the value of critical thinking for vocational and professional success. It also overlooks the myriad ways in which experiential learning beyond the traditional lecture hall, seminar, or laboratory enhances the intellectual experience and builds the needed critical lens at the heart of liberal arts.

Christopher Nelson, long-time president of venerable St. John's College, discusses the promise of liberal education in the global era in Chapter 15. Since 1937, St. John's has had one purpose, one curriculum, and one vision of liberal education based on reading and discussing the Great Books of Western civilization. The college has a single academic program, which all students follow in its entirety, and challenges students to become purposeful and effective communicators, thoughtful and responsible citizens, and generous, collaborative learners. Can such a limited and rigid curriculum have relevance in the 21st century? Nelson extols the virtues of this simple pedagogical formula, one that epitomizes the liberal arts tradition and has made St. John's among the most productive sources of doctorates in the country.

Finally, the renowned Martha Nussbaum concludes this volume in Chapter 16 with her meditation on liberal education in an increasingly interdependent world. Nussbaum persuasively argues that an education based on inclusive global citizenship has the potential to transcend divisions created by distance, cultural difference, and mistrust. She trumpets key sentiments of the ancient liberal arts philosophy, and contends that cultivating compassionate imagination—putting oneself in another's shoes—is an urgent task of higher education.

## Conclusion

It is our goal that this collection may help to stimulate greater debate on the ways in which higher education can be improved, both within the United States and in countries around the world. Discourse is, after all, the essence of the liberal arts philosophy.

At a time when our species is better educated and more literate than ever in history, some 7 billion people around the world are becoming ever more interconnected. To be sure, we are now challenged to relate to one another as fellow citizens within a complex global community, one in which hard cartographical borders are withering in the face of increased trade, migration, communication, and capital flows. Yet, there remain significant obstacles to building community across the world's vast social and historical divides. In our global age, perhaps a resurgence of *artes liberales* can help narrow these gaps and foster productive, cooperative citizenship as the Greeks originally envisioned.

## References

Drucker, P. (1969). *The Age of Discontinuity: Guidelines to Our Changing Society*. New York: Harper & Row.

Bush, V. (1945). "Science: The Endless Frontier." *Transactions of the Kansas Academy of Science (1903–), 48*(3): 231–64.

Schumpeter, J. (1976 [1942]). *Capitalism, Socialism and Democracy*. New York: Harper & Row.

Zakaria, F. (2016). *In Defense of a Liberal Education*. New York: W. W. Norton & Company.

# PART I
# The American Tradition

# 1

# THE YALE REPORT OF 1828[1]

## Part 1: Liberal Education and Collegiate Life

*A Committee of the Corporation and the Academic Faculty*

What is the appropriate object of a college? If we have not greatly misapprehended the design of the patrons and guardians of this college, its object is to lay the foundation of a superior education, and this is to be done at a period of life when a substitute must be provided for *parental superintendence*. The groundwork of a thorough education must be broad, deep, and solid. For a partial or superficial education, the support may be of looser materials—and more hastily laid.

The two great points to be gained in intellectual culture are the *discipline* and the *furniture* of the mind, expanding its powers and storing it with knowledge. The former of these is, perhaps, the more important of the two. A commanding object, therefore, in a collegiate course should be to call into daily and vigorous exercise the faculties of the student. Those branches of study should be prescribed and those modes of instruction adopted that are best calculated to teach the art of fixing the attention; directing the train of thought; analyzing a subject proposed for investigation; following, with accurate discrimination, the course of argument; balancing nicely the evidence presented to the judgment; awakening, elevating, and controlling the imagination; arranging, with skill, the treasures that memory gathers; rousing and guiding the powers of genius.

All this is not to be effected by a light and hasty course of study, by reading a few books, hearing a few lectures, and spending some months at a literary institution. The habits of thinking are to be formed by long continued and close application. The mines of science must be penetrated far below the surface before they will disclose their treasures. If a dexterous performance of the manual operations in many of the mechanical arts requires an apprenticeship with diligent attention for years, much more does the training of the powers of the mind demand vigorous, steady, and systematic effort.

In laying the foundation of a thorough education, it is necessary that *all* the important mental faculties be brought into exercise. It is not sufficient that one or two be cultivated while others are neglected. A costly edifice ought not to be left to rest upon a single pillar. When certain mental endowments receive a much higher culture than others, there is a distortion in the intellectual character. The mind never attains its full perfection unless its various powers are so trained as to give them the fair proportions that nature designed. If the student exercises his reasoning powers only, he will be deficient in imagination and taste, in fervid and impressive eloquence. If he confines his attention to demonstrative evidence, he will be unfitted to decide correctly in cases of probability. If he relies principally on his memory, his powers of invention will be impaired by disuse.

In the course of instruction in this college, it has been an object to maintain such a proportion between the different branches of literature and science as to form in the student a proper *balance* of character. From the pure mathematics, he learns the art of demonstrative reasoning. In attending to the physical sciences, he becomes familiar with facts, the process of induction, and the varieties of probable evidence. In ancient literature, he finds some of the most finished models of taste. By reading English, he learns the powers of the language in which he is to speak and write. By logic and mental philosophy, he is taught the art of thinking; by rhetoric and oratory, the art of speaking. By frequent exercise on written composition, he acquires copiousness and accuracy of expression. By extemporaneous discussion, he becomes prompt, fluent, and animated. Eloquence and solid learning should go together. He who has accumulated the richest treasures of thought should possess the highest powers of oratory. To what purpose has a man become deeply learned if he has no faculty of communicating his knowledge? And of what use is a display of rhetorical elegance from one who knows little or nothing that is worth communicating? Our course, therefore, aims at a union of science with literature, of solid attainment with skill in the art of persuasion.

No one feature in a system of intellectual education is of greater moment than such an arrangement of duties and motives as will most effectually throw the student upon the *resources of his own mind*. Without this, the whole apparatus of libraries, instruments, specimens, lectures, and teachers will be insufficient to secure distinguished excellence. The scholar must form himself by his own exertions. The advantages furnished by a residence at a college can do little more than stimulate and aid his personal efforts. The *inventive* powers are especially to be called into vigorous exercise. However abundant may be the acquisitions of the student, if he has no talent at forming new combinations of thought, he will be dull and inefficient. The most sublime efforts of genius consist in the creations of the imagination, the discoveries of the intellect, the conquests by which the dominions of science are extended. But the culture of the inventive faculties is not the *only* object of a liberal education. The most gifted understanding cannot greatly enlarge the amount of science to which the wisdom of ages has contributed. If it were possible for a youth to have his faculties in the highest state of cultivation, without any of the knowledge that is derived from others, he would be but poorly fitted for the business of life. To the discipline of the mind, therefore, is to be added instruction. The analytic method must be combined with the synthetic. Analysis is most efficacious in directing the powers of invention but is far too slow in its progress to teach, within a moderate space of time, the sciences.

In our arrangements for the communication of knowledge and intellectual discipline, such branches are to be taught as will produce a proper symmetry and balance of character. We doubt whether the powers of the mind can be developed by studying languages alone, mathematics alone, or natural or political science alone. As the bodily frame is brought to its highest perfection not by one simple and uniform motion but by a variety of exercises, so the mental faculties are expanded, invigorated, and adapted to each other by familiarity with different departments of science.

College students are generally of an age that requires that a substitute be provided for *parental superintendence*. This consideration determines the *kind* of government that ought to be maintained in our colleges. Like the parent-child relationship, it should be founded on mutual affection and confidence. It should aim to effect its purpose principally by kind and persuasive influence, not wholly or chiefly by restraint and terror. Still, punishment may sometimes be necessary. The parental character of college government requires that the students should be so collected together as to constitute one family, that the intercourse between them and their instructors may be frequent and familiar. This renders it necessary that suitable *buildings* be provided for student residence.

----

Having now stated what we understand to be the proper *object* of an education at this college, we would ask permission to add a few observations on the *means* that are employed to attain this object.

In giving the course of instruction, it is intended that a due proportion be observed between *lectures* and *recitations*, that is, examinations in a textbook. The great advantage of lectures is that while they call forth the highest efforts of the lecturer and accelerate his advance to professional eminence, they give that light and spirit to the subject that awakens the interest and ardor of the student. Where instruments are to be explained, experiments performed, or specimens exhibited, they are the appropriate mode of communication. But we are far from believing that *all* the purposes of instruction can be best answered by lectures alone. They do not always bring upon the student a clear, pressing responsibility. He may repose upon his seat and yield a passive hearing to the lecturer without ever calling into exercise the active powers of his own mind. This defect we endeavor to remedy, in part, by frequent examinations on the subjects of the lectures. Still it is important that the student should have opportunities of retiring by himself and giving a more commanding direction to his thoughts than when listening to oral instruction. To secure his steady and earnest efforts is the ultimate object of the daily examinations or recitations. In these exercises, a textbook is commonly the guide.

Opportunity is given, however, to our classes for a full investigation and discussion of particular subjects in the written and extemporaneous *disputes*, which constitute an important part of our course of exercises. But the business of explaining and commenting is carried to an extreme whenever it supersedes the necessity of effort on the part of the learner. If we mistake not, some portion of the popularity of copious oral instruction is to be set to the account of the student's satisfaction in escaping from the demand for mental exertion. It is to secure the unceasing and strenuous exercise of the intellectual powers that the responsibility of the student is made so constant and particular.

For this purpose, our semi-annual *examinations* have been established. These, with the examination of the seniors in July, occupy from twelve to fourteen days in a year. Each class is divided into two portions, which are examined in separate rooms at the same time, seven or eight hours a day. A committee is present on the occasion, consisting of gentlemen of education and distinction from different parts of the state. The degree of correctness with which each student answers the questions put to him in the several branches is noted on the spot and entered into a record, permanently kept by the faculty. But to the instructors, the daily examinations in the recitation rooms are a more unerring test of scholarship than these public trials. The latter answer the purpose of satisfying the inquiries of strangers.

We deem it to be indispensable to a proper adjustment of our collegiate system that there should be in it both professors and tutors. There is wanted, on the one hand, the experience of those who have been long resident at the institution, and on the other, the fresh and minute information of those who, having more recently mingled with the students, have a distinct recollection of their peculiar feelings, prejudices, and habits of thinking. At the head of each great division of science, a professor must superintend the department, arrange the plan of instruction, regulate the mode of conducting it, and teach the more important and difficult parts of the subject. But students in a college who have just entered on the first elements of science are not principally occupied with the more abstruse and disputable points. Their attention ought not to be solely or mainly directed to the latest discoveries. They have first to learn the principles that have been in a course of investigation through the successive ages and have now become simplified and settled.

----

The collegiate course of study may be carefully distinguished from several *other* objects and plans with which it has been too often confused. The object is not to *finish* his education but to lay the foundation and to advance as far in rearing the superstructure as the short period of his residence here will admit. If he acquires here a thorough knowledge of the principles of science, he may then, in a great measure, educate himself. He has, at least, been taught *how* to learn. Wherever he goes, into whatever company he falls, he has those general views on every topic of interest that will enable him to understand, digest, and form a correct opinion on the statements and discussions that he hears. There are many things important to be known that are not taught in colleges because they can be learned anywhere.

The course of instruction that is given to undergraduates in college is not designed to include *professional* studies. Our object is not to teach that which is peculiar to any one of the professions but to lay the foundation that is common to them all. There are separate schools for medicine, law, and theology that are open for the reception of all who are prepared to enter upon the appropriate studies of their several professions.

But why should a student waste his time upon studies that have no immediate connection with his future profession? Will chemistry enable him to plead at the bar, conic sections qualify him for preaching, or astronomy aid him in the practice of physic? Why should not his attention be confined to the subject that is to occupy the labors of his life? The great object of a collegiate education, preparatory to the study of a profession, is to give that expansion and balance of the mental powers, those liberal and comprehensive views, and those fine proportions of character that are not to be found in him whose ideas are always confined to one particular channel.

When a man has entered upon the practice of his profession, the energies of his mind must be given, principally, to its appropriate duties. But if his thoughts never range on other subjects, if he never looks abroad on the ample domains of literature and science, there will be a narrowness in his habits of thinking—a peculiarity of character that will be sure to mark him as a man of limited views and attainments. On the other hand, he who is not only eminent in professional life but has also a mind richly stored with general knowledge has an elevation and dignity of character that gives him a commanding influence in society and a widely extended sphere of usefulness. His situation enables him to diffuse the light of science among all classes of the community. Is a man to have no other object than to obtain a *living* by professional pursuits? Has he not duties to perform to his family, his fellow citizens, and his country, duties that require various and extensive intellectual furniture?

Professional studies are deliberately excluded from the course of instruction at college to leave room for those literary and scientific acquisitions that, if not commenced there, will in most cases never be made. They will not grow up spontaneously, amid the bustle of business. We are not here speaking of those giant minds that, by their native energy, break through the obstructions of a defective education and cut their own path to distinction. These are honorable exceptions to the general law, not examples for common imitation. Franklins and Marshalls are not found in sufficient numbers to fill a college. And even Franklin would not have been what he was had there been no colleges in the country. When an elevated standard of education is maintained by the higher literary institutions, men of superior powers who have not had access to these are stimulated to aim at a similar elevation by their own efforts and by aid of the light that is thus shining around them.

Because our course of instruction is not intended to complete an education in theological, medical, or legal science, neither does it include all the minute details of *mercantile*, *mechanical*, or *agricultural* concerns. These can never be effectually learned except in the very circumstances in which they are to be practiced. The young merchant must be trained in the counting room, the mechanic in the workshop, the farmer in the field.

For what purpose, then, are young men who are destined to these occupations ever sent to a college?

They should not be sent with an expectation of *finishing* their education at the college but with a view of laying a thorough foundation in the principles of science, preparatory to the study of the practical arts. Since everything cannot be learned in four years, either theory or practice must be, in a measure at least, postponed to a future opportunity. But if the scientific theory of the arts is *ever* to be acquired, it is unquestionably first in order of time. The cornerstone must be laid before the superstructure is erected.

What is a young man fitted for when he takes his degree? Does he come forth from the college qualified for business? No—if he stops here. His education is begun but not completed. Is the college to be reproached for not accomplishing that which it has never undertaken to perform? Do we complain of the mason who has laid the foundation of a house that he has not finished the building, that the product of his labor is not habitable, and that, therefore, there is nothing practical in what he has done?

In education, as well as in morals, we often hear the suggestion that principles are of no consequence, provided the practice is right. Why waste on theories the time that is wanted for acquiring practical arts? The mariner can set his sails to the wind without understanding the laws of the decomposition of forces; the carpenter can square his framework without a knowledge of Euclid's Elements; the dyer can set his colors without being indoctrinated in the principles of chemistry. But the labors of such a one are confined to the narrow path marked out to him by others. He needs the constant superintendence of men of more enlarged and scientific information. If he ventures beyond his prescribed rule, he works at random with no established principles to guide him. By long continued practice, he may have attained a good degree of manual dexterity. But the arranging of plans of business, the new combinations of mechanical processes, the discoveries and improvements in the arts must generally come from minds more highly and systematically cultivated.

We are far from believing that theory *alone* should be taught in a college. It cannot be effectually taught except in connection with practical illustrations. These are necessary in exciting an interest in theoretical instructions and especially important in showing the application of principles. It is our aim therefore, while engaged in scientific investigations, to blend with them as far as possible practical illustrations and experiments.

But why should *all* the students in a college be required to tread in the *same steps?* Why should not each one be allowed to select those branches of study that are most to his taste, that are best adapted to his peculiar talents, and that are most nearly connected with his intended profession? To this we answer that our prescribed course contains those subjects only that ought to be understood by everyone who aims at a thorough education.

It is sometimes thought that a student ought not to be urged to the study of that for which he has *no taste* or *capacity.* But how is he to know whether he has a taste or capacity for a science before he has even entered upon its elementary truths? If he is really destitute of talent sufficient for these common departments of education, he is destined for some narrow sphere of action. But we are well persuaded that our students are not so deficient in intellectual powers as they sometimes profess to be, though they are easily made to believe that they have no capacity for the study of that which they are told is almost wholly useless.

When a class have become familiar with the common elements of the several sciences, the time is right for them to *branch off* into their favorite studies. They can then make their choice from actual trial. This is now done here, to some extent, in our junior year. The division might be commenced at an earlier period and extended farther, provided the qualifications for admission into the college were brought to a higher standard.

The object of the system of instruction at this college is not to give a *partial* education; nor, on the other hand, to give a *superficial* education; nor to *finish* the details of either a professional or practical education but to *commence* a *thorough* course and to carry it as far as the time of residence here will allow. It is intended to occupy to the best advantage the four years immediately preceding the study of a profession or of the operations that are peculiar to the higher mercantile, manufacturing, or agricultural establishments.

Because the instruction is only preparatory to a profession, the plan upon which it is conducted is not copied from professional schools. There are important differences arising from the different character of the two courses and the different age at which the student enters upon them. In the professional institution, it is proper that *subjects* should be studied rather than *textbooks.* At this period, the student is engaged not in learning the mere elements of the various sciences but in becoming thoroughly acquainted with one great department of knowledge, to the study of which several years are to be devoted. A much greater proportion of *lectures* is admissible in this stage of education. The deep interest excited by a long continued pursuit in the same field of inquiry supersedes the necessity of the minute responsibility that is required in elementary studies. The age of the student and the prospect of soon entering on professional practice will commonly be sufficient to secure his assiduous application without coercive influence of laws and penalties.

Our institution is not modelled exactly after the pattern of *European* universities. Difference of circumstances has rendered a different arrangement expedient.

It has been the policy of most monarchical governments to concentrate the advantages of a superior education in a few privileged places. But in this country, our republican habits and feelings will never allow a monopoly of literature in any one place. Nor would we complain of this arrangement as inexpedient, provided that starvation is not the consequence of a patronage so minutely divided. We anticipate no disastrous results from the multiplication of colleges as long as they are adequately endowed.

When the student has passed beyond the rugged and cheerless region of elementary learning into the open and enchanting field where the great masters of science are moving onward with enthusiastic emulation, then, instead of plodding over a page of Latin or Greek with his grammars, dictionaries, and commentaries, he reads those languages with facility and delight; when, after taking a general survey of the extensive and diversified territories of literature, he has selected those spots for cultivation that are best adapted to his talents and taste, he may then be safely left to pursue his course without the impulse of authoritative injunctions or the regulation of statutes and penalties. But we question whether a college of undergraduates, not provided with any substitute for parental control, would long be patronized in this country.

The first and great improvement that we wish to see made is an elevation in the standard of attainment for admission. Until this is implemented, we shall only expose ourselves to inevitable failure and ridicule by attempting a general imitation of foreign universities.

One of the pleas frequently urged in favor of a partial education is the alleged *want of time* for a more enlarged course. As we have already observed, a thorough education cannot be begun and finished in four years. But if three years immediately preceding the age of twenty-one be allowed for the study of a profession, there is abundant time previous to this for the attainment of all that is now required for admission into the college, in addition to the course prescribed for the undergraduates. Though the limit of age for admission is fixed by our laws at fourteen, how often have we been pressed to dispense with the rule on behalf of some youth who has completed his preparation at an earlier period and who, if compelled to wait till he has attained the requisite age, "is in danger of being ruined for want of employment?" May we not expect that this plea will be urged with still greater earnestness when the present improved methods of instruction in the elementary and preparatory schools are more and more accelerating the early progress of the pupil?

But suppose it should happen that the student, in consequence of commencing his studies at a later period, should be delayed a little longer before entering upon the duties of his profession; is this a sacrifice worthy to be compared with the immense difference between the value of a limited and a thorough education? Is a young man's pushing forward into business so indispensable to his future welfare that rather than suspend it for a single year, he must forego all the advantage of superior intellectual discipline and attainments?

We well know that the whole population of the country can never enjoy the benefit of a thorough course of education. A large portion must be content with the very limited instruction in our primary schools. Others may be able to add to this the privilege of a few months at an academy. Others still, with higher aims and more ample means, may afford to spend two or three years pursuing a partial course of study in some institution that furnishes instruction in any branch or branches selected by the pupil or his parents.

It is said that the public now demands that the doors should be thrown open to all; that education ought to be so modified and varied as to adapt it to the exigencies of the country and the prospects of different individuals; that the instruction given to those who are destined to be merchants, manufacturers, or agriculturalists should have a special reference to their respective professional pursuits.

The public are undoubtedly right in demanding that there should be appropriate courses of education accessible to all classes of youth. And we rejoice at the prospect of ample provision for this purpose in the improvement of our academies and the establishment of commercial high schools, gymnasia, lycea, agricultural seminaries, etc.

But does the public insist that every college shall become a high school, gymnasium, lyceum, and academy? The college has its appropriate object, and they have theirs. What advantage would be gained by attempting to blend them all in one? Why is a degree from a college more highly prized than a certificate from an academy if the former is not a voucher of a superior education? When the course of instruction in the one is reduced to the level of that in the other, to graduate either will be equally honorable. What is the characteristic difference between a college and an academy? Not that the former teaches more branches than the latter. There are many academies in the country whose scheme of studies, at least upon paper, is more various than that of the colleges. But while an academy teaches a little of everything, the college, by directing its efforts to one uniform course, aims at doing its work with greater precision and economy of time, just as the merchant who deals in a single class of commodities or a manufacturer who produces but one kind of fabrics executes his business more perfectly than he whose attention and skill are divided among a multitude of objects.

All the means that are now applied to the proper collegiate department are barely sufficient, or rather are insufficient, for the object in view. No portion of our resources, strength, or labor can be diverted to other purposes without impairing the education that we are attempting to give. A London university, commencing with a capital of several hundred thousand dollars and aiming to provide a system of instruction for the youth in a city whose population is more than a million, may well establish its higher and inferior courses, its scientific and practical departments, its professional, mercantile, and mechanical institutions. But shall a college, with an income of two or three thousand a year from funds, attempt to be at once a London university? Should we *ever* become such an institution, our present undergraduate course ought still to constitute one distinct branch of the complicated system of arrangements.

But by making the college more accessible to different descriptions of persons, might we not enlarge our *numbers* and in that way increase our income? This might be the operation of the measure for a very short time, assuming a degree from the college retains its present value in public estimation—a value depending entirely upon the character of the education that we give. But the moment it is understood that the institution has descended to an inferior standard of attainment, its reputation will sink to a corresponding level. There is no magical influence in an act of incorporation to give celebrity to a literary institution that does not command respect for itself by the elevated rank of its education. When the college has lost its hold on the public confidence by depressing its standard of merit, by substituting a partial for a thorough education, we can expect that it will be deserted by that class of persons who have hitherto been drawn here by high expectations and purposes. Even if we should *not* immediately suffer in point of *numbers*, we shall exchange the best portion of our students for others of inferior aims and attainments.

As long as we can maintain an elevated character, we need be under no apprehension with respect to numbers. Without character, it will be in vain to think of retaining them. It is a hazardous experiment to act upon the plan of gaining numbers first and character afterward.

The call is frequently made upon us to admit students into the college with *defective* preparation. Parents are little aware to what embarrassments and injury they are subjecting their sons by urging them forward to a situation for which they are not properly qualified. Of those who are barely admitted, one and another is, from time to time, dropped off from the class. Here and there one, after making his way with much perplexity and mortification through the four years, just obtains a degree at last that is nearly all the benefit that he derives from his residence here. Whereas, if he had come to us well prepared, he might have held a respectable rank in his class and acquired a substantial education.

Another serious difficulty with which we have to contend is the impression made on the minds of a portion of our students that the study of anything for which they have not an instinctive relish, or which requires vigorous and continued effort, or which is not immediately connected with their intended professional pursuits is of no practical utility. They of course remain ignorant of that which they think not worth the learning. We are concerned to find that not only students but their parents also seem frequently more solicitous for the *name* of an education than the substance.

It is far from being our intention to dictate to *other* colleges a system to be adopted by them. There may be good and sufficient reasons why some of them should introduce a partial course of instruction. We are not sure that the demand for thorough education is, at present, sufficient to fill all the colleges in the United States with students who will be satisfied with nothing short of high and solid attainments. But it is to be hoped that, at no very distant period, they will be able to rise to this elevated ground and leave the business of second-rate education to the inferior seminaries.

The competition of colleges may advance the interests of literature if it is a competition for *excellence* rather than for numbers, if each aims to surpass the others not in an imposing display but in the substantial value of its education. When the rivalry becomes a mere scramble for numbers, a dexterous arrangement of measures in beating up for recruits, the standard of attainment will sink lower and lower till the colleges are brought to a level with common academies. Does it become the patrons and guardians of sound learning to yield to this depressing and deteriorating influence? Our country has ample resources for furnishing to great numbers the means of a thorough education. At the same time, peculiar temptations are here presented to our youth to induce them to rest satisfied with a partial and superficial course of study. The field of enterprise is so wide, the demand for even ordinary learning is so urgent, and the occupations that yield a competent living are so numerous and accessible that a young man of a very limited stock of knowledge, if he have a good share of self-confidence and a driving, bustling spirit, can push himself forward into notice and employment. He may even mount the steps that lead to office and popular applause. If he fails to enlighten his countrymen by his intellectual superiority, he may at least attract their gaze by the tinsel of his literary ornaments. This is the allure of a hurried and superficial education. We have abundant supplies of this Lombardy-poplar growth—slender, frail, and blighted. We should like to see more of the stately elm, striking deep its roots, lifting its head slowly to the skies, spreading wide its grateful shade, and growing more venerable with years.

Our duty to our country demands of us an effort to provide the means of a thorough education. There is perhaps no nation whose interests would be more deeply affected by a substitution of superficial for solid learning. The universal diffusion of the common branches of knowledge renders it necessary that those who aspire to literary eminence would ascend to very elevated ground.

Our republican form of government renders it highly important that great numbers should enjoy the advantage of a thorough education. *Merchants, manufacturers*, and *farmers*, as well as professional gentlemen, take their places in our public councils. A thorough education ought therefore to be extended to all these classes. It is not sufficient that they be men of sound judgment who can decide correctly and give a silent vote on great national questions. Their influence upon the minds of others is needed—an influence to be produced by extent of knowledge and the force of eloquence. Ought the speaking in our deliberative assemblies to be confined to a single profession? If it is knowledge that gives us the command of physical agents and instruments, much more is it that which enables us to control the combinations of moral and political machinery.

The object of the undergraduate course is not to finish a preparation for business but to impart that various and general knowledge that will improve, elevate, and adorn any occupation. Can merchants, manufacturers, and agriculturists derive no benefit from high intellectual culture? They are the very classes that have the best opportunities for reducing the principles of science to their practical applications. The large estates that the tide of prosperity in our country is so rapidly accumulating will fall mostly into their hands. Is it not desirable that they should be men of superior education, of large and liberal views, of those solid and elegant attainments that will raise them to a higher distinction than the mere possession of property?

The active, enterprising character of our population renders it highly important that this bustle and energy should be directed by sound intelligence, the result of deep thought and early discipline. Where a free government gives full liberty to the human intellect to expand and operate, education should be proportionately liberal and ample. When even our mountains, rivers, and lakes are on a scale that suggests we are destined to be a great and mighty nation, shall our literature be feeble, scanty, and superficial?

## Note

1 This famous document was provoked by a September 1827 resolution by Yale's President Jeremiah Day to organize a faculty committee to consider altering the college's curriculum and removing "dead languages"—specifically ancient Greek and Latin. Nearly one year later, the faculty responded with a report in two parts. Part 1 outlined and argued the overall philosophy of Yale's curriculum, and Part 2 defended ancient Greek and Latin as the foundations of liberal education. The version in this volume has been edited from Part 1.

# 2

# THE DECLENSION NARRATIVE, THE LIBERAL ARTS COLLEGE, AND THE UNIVERSITY[1]

*Bruce A. Kimball*

Among the Jeremiads echoing through higher education in recent decades, one of the most often heard is the declension narrative of the liberal arts college. According to the declension narrative in its strongest form, the university and the liberal arts college represent two distinct and competing educational and institutional ideologies. Furthermore, the university—especially the public university—has grown stronger, while the liberal arts college, particularly the private liberal arts college, has weakened over the past 125 years. In fact, the university has overwhelmed the beleaguered liberal arts college, which has inexorably declined toward extinction, except for a small and diminishing number of well-endowed outliers.

Some of the most prominent documents in the declension literature include the following. In 1884 a leading professor at Columbia University, John W. Burgess, published a treatise in which he wrote, "I am unable to divine what is to be ultimately the position of Colleges, which cannot become Universities and which will not be Gymnasia. I cannot see what reason they will have to exist. It will be largely a waste of capital to maintain them, and largely a waste of time to attend them. It is so now."[2] In 1900 William Rainey Harper, the founding and reforming president of the University of Chicago, announced that nearly all liberal arts colleges would fail, unless they evolved into universities or devolved into two-year junior colleges.[3] Echoing Harper in 1902, Nicholas Murray Butler, the new president of Columbia University, argued that the four-year B.A. college course was no longer viable at Columbia or elsewhere.[4] In the following year, President David Starr Jordan of Stanford University published an essay famously stating: "The college is a small university, antiquated, belated, arrested, starved, as the case may be.... As time goes on, the college will disappear in fact, if not in name."[5]

In 1924 those university prophets were invoked by Leon Richardson in *A Study of the Liberal College*, and a process of documentary sedimentation thus commenced.[6] In 1962 Richardson's study was referenced by another major document in the declension literature, the landmark history of the American college and university authored by Frederick Rudolph. In a closing chapter, Rudolph cited all the foregoing sources, while quoting the provocative words of Jordan.[7] Rudolph's book rapidly became the standard history of American higher education, and his references to the university advocates were subsequently adduced to evidence the 125-year declension. For example, in a collection of essays marking the 75th anniversary of the Association of American Colleges in 1988, the president, historian Mark Curtis, invoked Rudolph's account, observing that "from 1890 to 1910 … the traditional college appeared to be losing out to both the new private universities and to public tax-supported institutions like land-grant colleges and state universities."[8] In 1993 Curtis's account was cited in a collection of essays on the future of American higher education edited by Arthur Levine, president of the Woodrow Wilson Fellowship Foundation.[9]

In the following year, economist David Breneman, former president of Kalamazoo College, published his acclaimed *Liberal Arts Colleges: Thriving, Surviving, or Endangered?*, and cited to Rudolph on "The Harper-Butler-Jordan Forecasts of Demise." Breneman calculated that there remained only about 206 liberal arts colleges that awarded at least 40 percent of their degrees in the liberal arts, as opposed to professional fields.[10] His book served to place the liberal arts college on the list of endangered species, and the authority and prominence of Rudolph and Breneman, referencing the earlier works, subsequently contributed to the proliferation of the declension narrative.

In 1999 economists Michael McPherson, now president of the Spencer Foundation, and Morton Schapiro, now president of Northwestern University, relied on Breneman in a noted essay published by the American Academy of Arts and Sciences in a collection on the liberal arts college. McPherson and Shapiro concluded that only about 100,000 students attend colleges where most students major in the liberal arts.[11] In 2005, at a conference on the liberal arts college sponsored by the American Council of Learned Societies, the distinguished historian and president emeritus of Williams College, Francis Oakley, noted that a century-long "narrative of decline" had emerged in the literature, relying on Breneman, Rudolph, Burgess, Harper, and Jordan. While cautioning that "the declension narrative may … serve to mislead," Oakley observed, "So far as numbers go, the downward trajectory [of liberal arts colleges] would indeed appear to be unquestionable."[12] In 2011 Victor Ferrall, president emeritus of Beloit College, published a major study with Harvard University Press that drew on Breneman extensively. Ferrall concluded that private liberal arts colleges are "at the brink" of closing or capitulating to professional studies, save for the fifty or so that are richly endowed.[13] Finally, in 2012, a study published by the Association of American

Colleges and Universities replicated Breneman's study, and concluded that out of Breneman's 206, merely 130 "true liberal arts colleges" remain today.[14]

Culminating in this dismal conclusion, the declension narrative now constitutes a premise in virtually any discussion of the relations between the liberal arts college and the research university. Given this influence, the documents, the data, and the reasoning of the declension narrative deserve careful scrutiny, which yields some surprising conclusions.

# I

The 1884 view of Burgess that colleges are "largely a waste of capital" and "a waste of time" certainly reflected his own academic background. After graduating from Amherst College in 1867, he studied for several years at German universities and embraced their rigorous methods of research and scholarship. Upon his return to the United States, Burgess tried unsuccessfully to persuade Amherst to adopt those methods, and then moved in 1876 to Columbia College in New York City, where he subsequently championed the German methods and founded the first academic journal and the first PhD program in Political Science.[15] Burgess thus pioneered the research university, which was still new territory in the United States.

At his inauguration in 1869, Harvard president Charles W. Eliot declared that no true university yet existed in the United States.[16] Soon after its opening in 1876 as an all-graduate institution, Johns Hopkins gained recognition as the first American university, and by 1884 only Cornell, Harvard, Michigan, and, perhaps, Wisconsin had committed to follow its lead. Columbia was making strides, but was still dominated by a collegiate ethos, as were Yale and Princeton. Thus, only a handful of true universities existed in the country, and the liberal arts college remained the institutional norm in American higher education, notwithstanding the founding of state and land-grant universities.[17] Recognizing this, Burgess stated that Boston was the only city in the nation with the means and disposition to support a university and titled his treatise prospectively *The American University: When Shall It Be? Where Shall It Be? What Shall It Be?*[18] Consequently, Burgess's assessment is not so much a self-assured proclamation, as a zealous prophecy tinged, with some disappointment that his alma mater had not responded to his entreaties.

The situation had changed dramatically by 1900, when fifteen research universities formed the Association of American Universities. Among them was the University of Chicago, which Harper had built into a research university with the financial support of John D. Rockefeller. In his address "The Situation of the Small College" delivered in July 1900 to the National Education Association, Harper identified several threats to the liberal arts college: the development of public high schools, which elevated academic standards from below; the emergence of many fields of specialized study, which small colleges could not sustain; the lack of financial resources to compete with universities in paying salaries for faculty or providing libraries or laboratories; and the low tuition and other subsidies of the state university. Due to these factors, Harper predicted that only about a quarter of liberal arts colleges would survive; the rest would become academies or two-year junior colleges.[19]

In 1903 President Jordan of Stanford held out even less hope in a published essay. The most often quoted lines bear repeating: "the college is a temporary feature of American educational history. The college is a small university, antiquated, belated, arrested, starved, as the case may be, but with university aspirations to be realized in such degree as it can.... As time goes on, the college will disappear in fact, if not in name. The best and richest colleges will become universities, following the example of Harvard, Yale, and Princeton. The others will return to their places as academies."[20]

Jordan's words certainly suggest that the research university was driving the liberal arts college to extinction, and both Harper and Jordan did subscribe to a kind of institutional Darwinism. As Harper wrote, "The laws of institutional life are very similar to those of individual life, and in the development of institutions we may confidently believe in "the survival of the fittest....The institution which has survived the trials and tribulations of early years, and ... justified its existence, ... deserves to live; ... In this struggle for existence, ... some of the colleges ... will be compelled to limit their activity to the ... preparatory, field."[21] According to Harper and Jordan, changes in the academic climate during the previous twenty-five years had made the liberal arts college unfit, while, for the university "great things are to be expected ... in the next twenty-five years."[22]

Nevertheless, some defensiveness appeared between the lines of these bold statements. Jordan titled his address "An Apology for the University," and began with the words: "Now and then in these days some successful businessman raises his eyes from his counter to question the American university's right to exist." [23] Moreover, Jordan first delivered his "Apology" at the Stanford commencement of 1898, and these words intimate his difficult relations with Jane Stanford, who became the university's patron after her husband, the railroad baron, died in 1893. Jane Stanford tightly controlled Jordan's spending and often treated the university as a low-grade technical institute.[24] Jordan's "Apology" therefore presents a justification for university patronage, and deflects criticism that higher education is irrelevant, arcane, or elitist toward the convenient target of the traditional college. Thus, Jordan says that critics of the university actually have in mind "the starveling colleges" of the past, when "college education was not related to life" and "had nothing to with action," since "the old-time ... college education was ... valued for the feeling of superiority which it engendered."[25]

Meanwhile, at the University of Chicago, Harper also had difficulties with his patron, who had a more technical and utilitarian vision of the university than did Harper. More significantly, Rockefeller grew disgusted at Harper's imprudent deficit spending to develop the university, and in 1898 decided that he would no longer meet with Harper, who was crushed by losing the cherished privilege of direct access to Rockefeller.[26] By 1900 both Jordan and Harper needed to assure their skeptical or estranged patrons that the future lay with the university. To bolster this assurance, these two presidents invoked Darwinian "laws of institutional life" and the invidious comparison with the liberal arts college.

Likewise, Nicholas Murray Butler at Columbia University, in his first annual report in 1902, projected that, in the future, the liberal arts college could serve best by providing two years of general education. Then with some bravado, Butler declared that a plan should be drawn up for the citizens of New York to give the "urgently needed" sum of ten million dollars to Columbia University.[27] This amount was larger than all but two of the university endowments of the day, and neither the money or the plan materialized. Consequently, the pronouncements of these early university advocates are not measured assessments, and their confident trumpeting almost drowns out the prophetic and defensive undertones.

The equivocal message of the early declension literature came fully to light in Richardson's 1924 study, which reported the results of a national survey undertaken at the request of the president of Dartmouth College. Richardson cited Butler and Jordan and then made a surprising assessment:

> Nearly a generation has gone by since these confident predictions were made, and there is little indication that that their verification is approaching. In fact, there has never been a time when the college, either as a branch of the university or as an independent institution, has seemed more alive, more virile, more confident of its position, than today. There has never been a time when its recognition as the heart of the American system of higher education has been more general.[28]

Consequently, this central text of the declension literature actually negates the narrative in the mid-1920s.

Richardson's view is corroborated by the presidency of Abbott Lawrence Lowell, who succeeded Eliot at Harvard in 1909. Lowell actively sought during the 1910s and 1920s to strengthen collegiate culture at Harvard, which had deteriorated under the university-builder Eliot. Lowell's concern exemplifies the broad reaction against the research university movement that began in about 1910 and continued in subsequent decades.[29] This reaction strengthened both the "liberal culture" and the liberal arts colleges that leaders of the research universities had subordinated in previous decades.

The next landmark document in the declension literature confirms this interpretation. In 1962 Rudolph invoked Burgess, Butler, Harper, and Jordan in a chapter entitled "Counterrevolution," in which he wrote: "Collegiate ideals were, therefore, never entirely eclipsed by the university movement, and by the 1920s the temper of American higher education was really counterrevolutionary."[30]

Rudolph therefore cited the university prophets by way of rebutting them. "The tug of the collegiate way was too strong" on higher education, he concluded.[31]

Certain texts in the declension literature subsequently recognized these qualifications on the university advocates. Breneman astutely held "the Harper-Butler-Jordan forecasts of demise to be extreme," for example. But he then concluded that "private colleges have been … increasingly marginalized during this century as public universities and community colleges have grown dramatically in size and number."[32] Hence, Breneman discounted the inception of declension and then affirmed the century-long decline. Such equivocation typifies the declension literature, which often qualifies the waning of colleges even while affirming that their decline has been unchecked and inexorable or "downhill all the way."[33]

This equivocation stems partly from a misleading reliance on proportional arguments. For example, several distinguished authorities have cited the following data to show the decline of colleges: between 1955 and 1970 the percentage of liberal arts colleges among institutions of higher education dropped from 40 percent to 24 percent, and the enrollment of liberal arts colleges dropped from 26 percent to 8 percent of students in higher education. Hence, liberal arts colleges became "a much diminished part of the educational landscape" in the words of Breneman and others.[34]

These percentages actually indicate that the *share* or *fraction* of liberal arts colleges and their enrollment decreased within higher education. Yet, during the period from 1950 to 1970 federal financial aid for students grew enormously due to the G.I. Bill following World War II, the National Defense Education Act of 1958, and the Higher Education Act of 1965. Meanwhile, the research universities received vast new financial resources through federal funding for research, led by the National Science Foundation, which was established soon after World War II. As a result, between 1950 and 1970 the undergraduate enrollment in the nation increased nearly four times from 2.3 million to 8.6 million, while the number of colleges and universities rose from about 1,800 to about 2,800.[35]

A decreasing proportion during a period of massive expansion in absolute numbers does not demonstrate, of course, that the absolute number of liberal arts colleges or their students declined between 1945 and 1970. In fact, it has been suggested that many liberal arts colleges actually increased their enrollment of liberal arts majors between 1956 and 1970.[36] Whether or not that is true, there appears to be no authority in the declension literature maintaining that the absolute number of liberal arts colleges or their enrollment declined between 1945 and 1970. Nevertheless, the lamentation that liberal arts colleges were "much diminished" persisted subsequently in the declension literature.[37]

Apart from equivocation, the critical point here is that the serious decline in the number of liberal arts colleges begins only after 1970. Indeed, Breneman focused his research on the years from 1972 to 1988. According to his analysis of the degrees awarded by the 540 Liberal Arts Colleges so designated by the Carnegie Foundation for the Advancement of Teaching, these colleges were shifting rapidly toward offering vocational education in order to recruit students and survive financially. Breneman concluded that the number of liberal arts colleges awarding at least 40 percent of their degrees in the liberal arts dropped precipitously from 540 to 206 between 1972 and 1988. The other 334 closed, expanded into comprehensive institutions, or converted into "professional colleges" and lost their standing as "liberal arts colleges" in Breneman's terms.[38]

This finding attracted much attention and stoked the declension narrative, as scholars subsequently maintained that "the liberal arts colleges continue to struggle on several fronts" during the 1990s and the first decade of the 2000s.[39] But no major study evidenced the trend with comprehensive data until 2011, when another major quantitative study in the declension narrative published. Ferrall, an enthusiastic defender of the private liberal arts college, examined the 225 small, private liberal arts colleges identified by *U.S. News & World Report*. In the previous two decades between 1987 and 2008, Ferrall found a marked trend toward granting degrees in vocational subjects.[40] He concluded:

> all liberal arts colleges … are threatened with sliding over the brink…. Impoverished colleges … are … being forced to close their doors, sell out to for-profits, or completely abandon liberal arts. Wealthy … colleges face becoming mere credential generators—isolated marginalized remnants of economic privilege….The gravest threat may be to the middle group, … which … suffer the most in the competition with tax-supported, low-tuition, public universities.[41]

Nevertheless, the endpoint of Ferrall's study was the academic year 2007–2008, and if his data are recalculated in terms of Breneman's standards twenty years earlier, a surprising result appears.

First, consider the threshold of granting at least 40 percent of degrees in the liberal arts. Breneman found 206 such colleges in 1988; Ferrall found 209 such colleges in 2008. Next, consider the higher standard of granting at least 75 percent degrees in the liberal arts. Breneman found 90 such colleges in 1988; Ferrall found 91 such colleges in 2008.[42] Even granting the variability in these kinds of data, it is remarkable that these two independent studies arrive at nearly identical numbers for liberal arts colleges in 1988 and 2008.

The issue becomes even more intriguing in light of the 2012 study, published by the AACU. This study extended the declension narrative by updating Breneman's study while replicating his "methodology for classifying liberal arts colleges." The researchers concluded that only 130 liberal arts colleges remain of the 206 that Breneman identified, a finding that differs dramatically from the 209 liberal arts colleges identified one year earlier by Ferrall.[43] This difference cannot be explained by the notorious problem of defining the liberal arts. Breneman in 1988, Ferrall in 2011, and the 2012 AACU study all employed closely similar and fairly conservative definitions of liberal arts majors, based on traditional disciplinary fields. Instead, much of the difference may be explained by the Great Recession, beginning with the stock market crash of 2008.

Ferrall's study was based on data from the 2007–2008 academic year, just before the onset of the recession.[44] The 2012 study was based on data from the 2008–2009 academic year, right after the stock market crash.[45] The best explanation for the precipitous drop in liberal arts majors between 2007–2008 and 2008–2009 may be the recession, which, Ferrall predicted, "will accelerate" the movement of "liberal arts colleges ... toward vocational courses and majors."[46] This explanation also consists with the finding above that liberal arts colleges and majors held fairly steady in the two decades between 1988 and 2008. In sum, these points mean that the understanding of declension must be thoroughly revised.[47]

## II

The number of liberal arts colleges has dropped over time, but not as presented in the narrative of "downhill all the way" during "this past century"[48] due to inability to compete with the research university or professional studies in the fight for institutional survival. Instead, it appears that the declension has occurred relatively recently and in discontinuous precipitous episodes during periods of economic stress or upheaval.

Near the end of the nineteenth century, the early advocates of the research universities announced the demise of liberal arts colleges, but the validity of their assessment was undermined by their prophetic zeal and defensive concerns for patronage. In the 1910s and 1920s a strong reaction of "liberal culture" pushed back against the research universities. At that time, many liberal arts colleges still perceived themselves as "the heart of the American system of higher education," in the words of Richardson. During the 1930s and 1940s, the Depression, World War II, and the return of the G.I.s likely drew liberal arts students and colleges toward vocational fields. Thus, one study in the declension literature found that by 1956, some 164 of the 540 liberal arts colleges that Breneman later examined had already lost that status, according to his definition.[49]

In the 1970s and 1980s, liberal arts colleges again faced economic stress and upheaval. During the mid-1970s, there was double-digit inflation and high unemployment, and in the recovery between 1979 and 1986, college graduates earned a historically high wage premium over high school graduates. As a result, students went to college to acquire job skills throughout the period that Breneman studied from 1972 to 1988. In addition, during the 1970s and 1980s, the vast number of new students entering higher education were "non-traditional"—older, working, married, part-time, and working-class.[50] These two factors explain why, between 1972 and 1988, the proportion of new college students seeking primarily to become "very well-off financially" rose from about 40 percent to 74 percent, and those seeking primarily "a meaningful philosophy of life" moved inversely from about 74 percent to 46 percent.[51] Due to the economic stress and upheaval, as well as the massive influx of non-traditional students, both the absolute number and the proportion of liberal arts colleges in higher education decreased.

Nevertheless, Breneman's findings about this extraordinary period were subsequently assimilated into the declension narrative of liberal arts colleges as evidence of a steady steep decline. Meanwhile, during the prosperous 1990s and early 2000s, no study apparently presented comprehensive data indicating a decrease in the number of liberal arts colleges. In fact, it has been shown that "a modest but continuing increase in the percentage of degrees in the liberal arts" began to occur in the late 1980s.[52] Then, an economic shock occurred in 2008-2009 when the Great Recession began, and another decline ensued.

If all this is roughly accurate, then the so-called declension of the liberal arts college has not been a Darwinian process of extinction. It has not been a continuous inexorable decline whereby each year ten or twenty liberal arts colleges go "over the brink," unable to conform to or compete with university mores or professional studies, which draw students from the liberal arts. Rather, the declension has occurred more recently than is commonly supposed, and in discrete precipitous episodes during periods of economic stress or upheaval. Between such episodes, the liberal arts colleges held their own. After such episodes—and this is a critical point—the lost colleges never recovered. So the absolute number kept falling.

Another critical point is that the declension narrative has obscured the actual pattern and process of decrease. On the one hand, the narrative obscures by presuming a steady inexorable decline over 125 years. On the other hand, the narrative obscures by implicitly equating liberal arts education and the liberal arts college. This latter point requires further explanation.

The declension literature generally assumes that liberal arts education occurs only or best in a liberal arts college, especially a private liberal arts college. As a corollary, the narrative also assumes that liberal arts students are enrolled only at liberal arts colleges, not elsewhere. These two assumptions are often denied or qualified, out of desire not to appear invidious.[53] Nevertheless, most laments about the decline of liberal arts colleges implicitly shift into laments about the decline of liberal arts education in general.

For example, Ferrall studied the private liberal arts college, but he titled his book *Liberal Arts at the Brink*, and he meant it.[54] Similarly, the economist presidents McPherson and Schapiro state that the "fundamental problem" of liberal arts colleges "is the lack of a customer base that is willing and able to cover the costs." But, a few lines later, they conclude that the "underlying problem [is] that many [students] are less interested … than they used to be."[55] Through such language, the declension problem subtly shifts from students' unwillingness to pay for liberal arts colleges, to students losing interest in the liberal arts. If students choose not to attend a liberal arts college, they lack interest in the liberal arts. Furthermore, the decreasing enrollment in liberal arts colleges means that the number of liberal arts students is decreasing, and the decline of liberal arts colleges means the decline of liberal arts education.

This implicit equating of liberal arts education with the liberal arts college in the declension narrative obscures the actual pattern of decline in two paradoxical ways. On the one hand, the declension narrative inflates the potential enrollment of liberal arts colleges; on the other hand, it undercounts the actual population of liberal arts students. Taken together, these two points serve to magnify the crisis.

Inflating the potential enrollment of liberal arts colleges appears in the lament, discussed above, that these colleges have become "a much diminished part" of higher education.[56] This lament about diminishing proportion assumes that liberal arts students—and therefore the enrollment in liberal arts colleges—should maintain their same proportion of the total enrollment in higher education. Yet, between 1939 and 2009 the fraction of the United States population attending higher education grew almost six times, from 1.1 percent to 6.4 percent.[57] Consequently, the lament about proportional decline assumes that the fraction of the total population enrolling in liberal arts colleges should have increased by nearly six-fold between 1939 and 2009. Nowhere is this assumption justified or even identified. The lamenters take it for granted that everyone should be liberally educated, as did University of Chicago President Robert M. Hutchins in 1936, asking "why should he not be?"[58]

But historical data suggest otherwise.[59] During the first half of the 1800s students in higher education in the United States constituted between 0.1 and 0.2 percent of the total population, and nearly all were enrolled in liberal art colleges. By 1899 about 0.3 percent of all Americans were enrolled in higher education. This rise in the percentage might suggest an increasing proportion in liberal arts colleges, given the proliferation of Catholic colleges, women's colleges, and black colleges. Indeed, in the early 1800s virtually all of the students in higher education were white males, whereas by 1910 women constituted nearly 40 percent of those enrolled in higher education, and some 25 "negro colleges" were operating. But these new populations in higher education did not enroll in liberal arts colleges at a greater rate than the white males. In fact, the fraction of women enrolling in female colleges peaked in 1880 at 28 percent, and thereafter women increasingly enrolled in co-educational institutions, reaching 90 percent in 1920.[60] The overall increase to 0.3 percent of the population was not large, and most of the additional students between 1860 and 1899 enrolled in the new research universities, state universities, land-grant institutions, and professional schools. So the percentage of liberal arts college students had not changed greatly.

By 1939 higher education enrolled about 1.1 percent of the total population, a fraction three or four times larger than forty years earlier. But the period from 1900 to 1939 had seen the emergence of scores of two-year colleges, the elevation of hundreds of normal schools to teachers colleges, the immense growth of technical institutions and degree-granting professional schools, and the expansion of graduate education and state universities, all of which account for most of the increase to 1.1 percent. Consequently, the proportion of liberal arts college students among the total population was still a few tenths of one percent in

1939. In 2008, almost seventy years later, Ferrall's data indicate that the 225 liberal arts colleges enrolled about 349,000 students, which was still between 0.1 and 0.2 percent of the total population of the United States.[61] The number of liberal arts colleges had decreased, but many of the remaining colleges had increased their enrollment significantly, particularly as single-sex colleges adopted co-education.

Hence, these rough figures suggest that the percentage of the population enrolling in liberal arts colleges has remained remarkably stable over the last two centuries at a few tenths of one percent of the total population and certainly within the same order of magnitude. Apparently, then, in the history of the United States, liberal arts colleges have consistently served about two percent of the "talented tenth" of the entire population, far fewer of the potential leaders in all fields than liberal arts advocates wished to reach.[62] Given this, proportional laments that "the share of B.A. degrees awarded in the liberal arts has declined" over "the past century" rest on the assumption that a much larger proportion of the total population should be engaged in liberal arts education and enrolled in liberal arts colleges, than has ever been the case historically.[63] In this way, laments about proportional decline overestimate the potential population of liberal arts students.

Paradoxically, the declension narrative also undercounts the actual population of liberal arts students. For example, Farrell maintains that about one-quarter of the 349,000 students in the liberal arts colleges were enrolled in vocational majors, dropping the number of liberal arts students to about 261,000.[64] This latter figure would bring the total of liberal arts students, so defined, below 0.1 percent of the population and below their historical norm in the population. Whether students at liberal arts colleges in the past, even in the nineteenth century, were predominantly enrolled in the liberal arts course has, in fact, been challenged.[65] But the larger difficulty is that this asserted drop in liberal arts students presumes that students outside of liberal arts colleges are not enrolled in the liberal arts.

Granted, some justification exists for this view. Many would argue that the "college of arts and sciences" at a research university does not provide the "vibrant community of learning" that a liberal arts college does and that liberal arts education requires.[66] Certainly, a university faculty does not usually constitute a community of learning in the way that a liberal arts college faculty usually does, because most university faculty identify more strongly with their discipline than their institution, as compared to faculty at a liberal arts college.[67] Insofar as a liberal arts education depends on a vibrant community of learning and insofar as such a community at an institution depends on the faculty being a community of learning, there is justification for distinguishing the college of arts and sciences at a university from liberal arts education, while there may also be other grounds for this distinction, such as class size and the amount of student-faculty contact.

Furthermore, liberal arts enrollment has evaporated at "the second- and third-tier public institutions that educate the overwhelming bulk of American undergraduates."[68] In order to address the strongest form of the declension narrative for purposes of argument, the general student body of these institutions may therefore be excluded, as well as the college of arts and sciences at research universities. Where else could liberal arts students possibly enroll apart from liberal arts colleges? They enroll, I suggest, in the some 400 honors programs or colleges that have sprung up at universities throughout the country during the last 40 years.

## III

Honors programs strive to create the academic experience of a small liberal arts college within a large university. They generally receive extensive supplementary resources supporting special courses, advising, dormitories, and requirements, all of which aim to build a community of learning devoted to liberal arts education. They usually have a great deal of scholarship money to recruit students. In the past four decades, the number of honors programs or colleges at universities has quietly surpassed the number of liberal arts colleges in the country. Indeed, their numbers have moved inversely. While the number of liberal arts colleges in the country has fallen from about 500 to about 200, the number of honors programs at universities has grown from about 100 to about 400. Most of these have arisen at second or third-tier institutions or state universities.[69]

These are the most significant alternatives to liberal arts colleges for enrollment, although the declension literature scarcely mentions them. Ferrall devotes a good deal of attention to the "threat" posed by publically subsidized universities to private liberal arts colleges, but he nowhere mentions honors programs.[70] They are overlooked because the declension literature assumes that decreasing enrollment in liberal arts colleges means a decreasing number of liberal arts students overall. In this fashion, the declension literature undercounts the actual number of liberal arts students.

In fact, the enrollment of liberal arts students has evidently not been dropping over the last four decades, but *shifting* from liberal arts colleges to their counterpart in universities—the honors programs and colleges. This shift means that the percentage of students enrolled at liberal arts colleges or their counterparts has held to the historical norm of a few tenths of one percent of the population. But that consistent percentage has divided into two hemispheres, as liberal arts colleges have suffered economic reverses for various reasons and a few hundred honors programs at universities have supplanted a few hundred liberal arts colleges. As a result, liberal arts education is increasingly distributed into a sector of well-endowed liberal arts colleges and a sector of highly subsidized honors programs at universities. The shift also helps to explain why liberal arts colleges do not recover after one of the episodic periods of decline. The honors programs absorb the lost enrollment of the colleges.

Given this, what can be concluded about the declension narrative and the liberal arts college? Ironically, it would appear that the university prophets were right, but for the wrong reason. Yes, the universities have displaced many liberal arts colleges. But the reason is not that it has been "largely a waste of capital to maintain [the colleges], and largely a waste of time to attend them," as Burgess wrote. The reason is not that the colleges do not "deserve to live" according to "the laws of institutional life," as Harper maintained. Nor is the reason that "the college is a small university, antiquated, belated, arrested, starved," as Jordan stated.

In fact, the university has triumphed, if it has, by assimilating the liberal arts college. True, the university at large has not adopted "the vision of a real community of learning, whose members shape its curriculum in their very own way and yet think it through carefully so as to be able to give an account of its result."[71] But the university has replicated and intensively subsidized the liberal arts college in the form of honors programs and colleges. In this fashion, the university has enshrined the liberal arts college as the most valued form of undergraduate education, and the declension narrative has proved correct, ironically, because "the tug of the collegiate way was too strong," as Rudolph wrote insightfully.

This development seems to ensure that liberal arts enrollment in the United States will continue in the range of one to two percent of the "talented tenth" in the population. But whether this shift to honors programs in universities is to the benefit or the detriment of liberal arts education deserves careful consideration.

The university is dedicated fundamentally to the advance of knowledge and specialized research and relies on technical rationality and Cartesian reasoning, known historically in Greek as *episteme* and in German as *wissenschaft*. Hence, the university embraces the marketplace of ideas and often considers the goal of undergraduate education to be the development of critical reasoning and command of research method. Even though the faculty of liberal arts colleges have increasingly embraced these views due to their graduate training, the college, more than the university, has valued general education, aiming at the formation of character and citizenship, the inculcation of intrinsic values, and the development of judgment and wisdom, known historically in Greek as *paideia* and in German as *bildung*.[72]

As wrote John Henry Newman, one of the foremost commentators on this relationship:

> A University embodies the principle of progress, and a College that of stability; the one is the sail, and the other the ballast; each is insufficient in itself for the pursuit, extension, and inculcation of knowledge; each is useful to the other....The University is for theology, law, and medicine, for natural history, for physical science, and for sciences generally and their promulgation; the College is for the formation of character, intellectual and moral, for the cultivation of the mind, for the improvement of the individual, for the study of literature, for the classics, for those rudimental sciences which strengthen and sharpen and intellect....But such a union, such salutary balance and mutual complement of opposite advantages, is of difficult and rare attainment.[73]

Indeed, to the extent that an honors program or college replicates the culture, community, and goals of a liberal arts college, it is open to question whether "the difficult and rare attainment" can be sustained within the university. The collegiate liberal arts education in an honors program exists within an alien, even antagonistic, environment at the university, which may weaken it over time. In addition, shifts in university leaders' priorities always threaten the strength of the honors program or college, since its collegiate liberal arts education does not directly serve the university's highest purpose of specialized research.

This threat may be less grave at a second or third-tier university, where the pursuit of research may be attenuated and where the high status of an honors program serves the institutional interests of the university. But interest in vocational or technical education often becomes stronger at a comprehensive university, posing another challenge to the collegiate liberal arts education lodged in an honors program or college. Furthermore, a comprehensive university, as well as the research university to a lesser extent, embraces the relativistic conception of the multiversity.[74] The comprehensive university adds programs that serve constituencies and closes them when the market for them disappears. Not only does this instrumental and marketplace approach threaten a well-supported honors program when leaders' priorities or politics change, but that approach again presents an alien, even antagonistic, environment for the collegiate liberal arts education of an honors program or college.

These considerations suggest that the declension of liberal arts colleges poses a serious threat to the collegiate understanding of liberal arts education, even if the enrollment shift apparently ensures that liberal arts enrollment in the United States continues at a few tenths of one percent of the population, as has been the case since the founding of the Republic.

## Notes

1 This essay was delivered as an address to the Conference on The Research University and the Liberal Arts, sponsored by the Institute for Scholarship in the Liberal Arts, University of Notre Dame (June 2013) and the Association for Core Texts and Courses.
2 John W. Burgess, *The American University: When Shall It Be? Where Shall It Be? What Shall It Be?* (Boston: Ginn, Heath, 1884), 5.
3 William R. Harper, "The Situation of the Small College," in *The Trend in Higher Education in America* (Chicago: University of Chicago Press, 1905), 349–89.
4 Nicholas Murray Butler, *Annual Report of the President of Columbia University 1901–1902* (New York: Columbia University, 1902), 37–43.
5 David Starr Jordan, "An Apology for the American University," 53–4, in *The Voice of the Scholar with Other Addresses* (San Francisco: Paul Elder, 1903).
6 Leon B. Richardson, *A Study of the Liberal College* (Hanover, NH: Dartmouth College, 1924), 15.

7 Frederick Rudolph, *The American College and University: A History* (New York: A. A. Knopf, 1962), 443–4.

8 Mark H. Curtis, "Crisis and Opportunity: The Founding of AAC," 5–6, in *Enhancing, Promoting, Extending Liberal Education: AAC at Seventy-Five* (Washington, D.C.: Association of American Colleges, 1988).

9 David Breneman, "Liberal Arts Colleges. What Price Survival?" in Arthur Levine, ed., *Higher Learning in America, 1980–2000,* rev. ed. (Baltimore, MD: Johns Hopkins University Press, 1993), 87.

10 David W. Breneman, *Liberal Arts Colleges: Thriving, Surviving, or Endangered?* (Washington, D.C.: Brookings Institution, 1994), 20–1. Breneman actually identified 212 liberal arts college, but included six colleges that granted less than 40 percent of their degrees in the liberal arts. The figure 206 is used here to maintain consistency with Breneman's own standard. Breneman, *Liberal Arts,* 2, 11–4, 139–40. See David W. Breneman, "Are We Losing Our Liberal Arts Colleges?" *AAHE Bulletin* 43.1 (1990): 3–6.

11 Michael S. McPherson and Morton O. Schapiro, "The Future Economic Challenges of the Liberal Arts Colleges," *Distinctively American: The Residential Liberal Arts College, Daedalus* 128.1 (Winter 1999): 49–50.

12 Francis Oakley, "Prologue: The Liberal Arts College: Identity, Variety, Destiny," 5–6, *Liberal Arts Colleges in American Higher Education: Challenges and Opportunities* (New York: ACLS, 2005).

13 Victor E. Ferrall, Jr., *Liberal Arts at the Brink* (Cambridge, MA: Harvard University Press, 2011).

14 Vicki L. Baker, Roger G. Baldwin, and Sumedha Makker, "Where Are They Now? Revisiting Breneman's Study of Liberal Arts Colleges," *Liberal Education* 98.3 (Summer 2012). Retrieved from www.aacu.org/liberaleducation/le-su12/baker_baldwin_makker .cfm (accessed May 2013).

15 Robert A. McCaughey, *Stand, Columbia: A History of Columbia University in the City of New York, 1754–2004* (New York: Columbia University Press, 2003), 160–3, 246.

16 Charles W. Eliot, *A Turning Point in Higher Education: The Inaugural Address of Charles William Eliot as President of Harvard College, October 19, 1869* (Cambridge, MA: Harvard University Press, 1969).

17 Laurence R. Veysey, *The Emergence of the American University* (Chicago: University of Chicago Press, 1965).

18 Burgess, *American University,* 9.

19 Harper, "The Situation," 378.

20 Jordan, "An Apology," 53–4.

21 Harper, "The Situation," 375, 377. See David S. Jordan, *The Blood of the Nation: A Study of the Decay of Races through the Survival of the Unfit* (Boston: American Unitarian Association, 1902).

22 Harper, "The Situation," 369. See Jordan, "An Apology," 47.

23 Jordan, "An Apology," 44.

24 Orrin L. Elliott, *Stanford University: The First Twenty-Five Years* (Stanford, CA: Stanford University Press, 1937). See David Starr Jordan, "An Apology for the American University," 217, 213–25. National Education Association, *Journal of the Addresses and Proceedings of the Thirty-Eighth Annual Meeting held at Los Angeles, California, July 11–14, 1899,* vol. 38 (Chicago: University of Chicago Press, 1899).

25 Jordan, "An Apology," 46, 48–9.

26 Richard J. Storr, *Harper's University: The Beginnings; a History of the University of Chicago* (Chicago: University of Chicago Press, 1966), 260; Ron Chernow, *Titan: The Life of John D. Rockefeller, Sr.* (New York: Random House, 1998), 318, 329.

27 Butler, *Annual Report*, 15, 37–43.

28 Richardson, *A Study*, 15.

29 Hugh Hawkins, *Between Harvard and America; the Educational Leadership of Charles W. Eliot* (New York: Oxford University Press, 1972), 263–90; Henry A. Yeomans, *Abbott Lawrence Lowell 1856–1943* (Cambridge: Harvard University Press, 1948), 253.

30 Rudolph, *The American*, 449.

31 Rudolph, *The American*, 443, 447.

32 Breneman, "Liberal Arts," 88; Breneman, *Liberal Arts*, 21. See Hugh Hawkins, "The Making of the Liberal Arts College Identity," *Distinctively American: The Residential Liberal Arts College, Daedalus* 128 (1): 8–12; Curtis, "Crisis," 5.

33 Quotation is from Oakley, "Prologue," 2. See Curtis, "Crisis," 5.

34 Breneman, *Liberal Arts*, 21. See Hawkins, "The Making," 15–6; Oakley, "Prologue," 5.

35 Richard M. Freeland, *Academia's Golden Age: Universities in Massachusetts 1945–1975* (New York: Oxford University Press, 1992), 70–120; Breneman, *Liberal Arts*, 21; McPherson and Schapiro, "The Future," 48.

36 Joan Gilbert, "The Liberal Arts College—Is It Really an Endangered Species?" *Change* 27.5 (Sept.–Oct. 1995): 41–2.

37 Breneman, *Liberal Arts*, 2; Hawkins, "The Making," 15–6; Oakley, "Prologue," 5.

38 Breneman, *Liberal Arts*, 139–40.

39 McPherson and Schapiro, "The Future," 48. Oakley, "Prologue," 5, 1–14.

40 Ferrall, *Liberal Arts*, argues that in the two decades after 1987, "the percentage of graduates of the 225 liberal arts colleges … who majored in vocational disciplines increased from 10.6 percent to 27.8 percent" (p. 155). But this conclusion raises a significant definitional issue. For example, over this period, Amherst College supposedly went from 0.0 to 4.8 percent vocational majors, while Bowdoin went from 0.0 to 6.2 percent. Among the list of majors at Amherst, the only vocational possibilities seem to be: Computer Science, Theater and Dance, Film and Media Studies, and Legal Studies as a Liberal Discipline. At Bowdoin, only Computer Science, Government and Legal Studies, and Educational Studies seem to be candidates. One doubts that the Amherst or Bowdoin faculty would agree with Farrell, who does not identify the vocational fields, apart from legal studies (p. 9).

41 Ferrall, *Liberal Arts*, 157, 75–8. There are 265 such colleges, but Ferrall studied 225, omitting those that are public and unranked.

42 Breneman, *Liberal Arts*, 2, 139–40; Ferrall, *Liberal Arts*, 184–95.

43 Baker, Baldwin, and Makker, "Where Are They Now?"

44 Ferrall, *Liberal Arts*, 184–95.

45 Baker, Baldwin, and Makker, "Where Are They Now?"

46 Ferrall, *Liberal Arts*, 59.

47 Francis Oakley has pursued "forms of significance other than the statistical" in suggesting, "the drop in numbers notwithstanding, that the declension narrative may still serve to mislead. Certainly, … it is far from catching or disclosing the full story, which coveys … some real grounds for encouragement." "Prologue," 6. The following argument challenges the inferences of the declension narrative that are drawn from the statistical drop in numbers.

48 Gilbert, "The Liberal Arts," 36–7.

49 Gilbert, "The Liberal Arts," 41–2.

50 Breneman, *Liberal Arts*, 30–1; T. D. Snyder, ed., *120 Years of American Education: A Statistical Portrait* (Washington, D.C.: National Center for Educational Statistics, 1993); Susan B. Carter, Scott Sigmund Gartner, Michael R. Haines, Alan L. Olmstead, Richard Sutch, Gavin Wright, eds., *Historical Statistics of the United States, Millennial Edition On Line* (Cambridge, UK: Cambridge University Press, 2006), "Table Bc523-536: Enrollment in Institutions of Higher Education, by Sex, Enrollment Status, and Type of Institution: 1869–1995," Retrieved from http://hsus.cambridge.org/HSUSWeb/HSUSEntryServlet (accessed May 2013); National Center for Education Statistics, *Higher Education General Information Survey* [HEGIS] (2008). (Washington D.C.: U.S. Department of Education, 2009), "Fall Enrollment in Colleges and Universities" surveys, 1966 through 1985; and 1986 through 2007 Integrated Postsecondary Education Data System, "Fall Enrollment Survey" (IPEDS-EF:86–99), and Spring 2001 through Spring 2008, Retrieved from http://nces.ed.gov/ipeds/glossary/?charindex=H (accessed May 2013).

51 Breneman, *Liberal Arts*, 141.

52 Gilbert, "The Liberal Arts," 37–8.

53 Breneman, *Liberal Arts*, 11n30. The belief is sometimes qualified by saying that liberal arts colleges are indispensable because they preserve the "understanding of what liberal arts teaching really is." McPherson and Schapiro, "The Future," 69.

54 Ferrall, *Liberal Arts*, 20–1, 154. The decline of liberal arts colleges is often cited to demonstrate the general decline of students in the liberal arts. See Frank Donoghue, *The Last Professors: The Corporate University and the Fate of the Humanities* (New York: Fordham University Press, 2008), xvii–xviii, 1, 3, 125; Louis Menand, *The Marketplace of Ideas: Reform and Resistance in the American University* (New York: W. W. Norton, 2010), 145; Ellen Schrecker, *The Lost Soul of Higher Education: Corporatization, the Assault on Academic Freedom, and the End of the American University* (New York: Free Press, 2010), 187–91.

55 McPherson and Schapiro, "The Future," 56.

56 Breneman, *Liberal Arts*, 21. See Gilbert, "The Liberal Arts," 36–8; Hawkins, "Making," 15–6; Oakley, "Prologue," 5.

57 Snyder, ed., *120 Years*; Carter, et al., *Historical Statistics*; HEGIS, 2008; National Center for Education Statistics, *Digest of Education Statistics, 2008* (Washington D.C.: U.S. Department of Education, 2009), ch. 3. Retrieved from http://nces.ed.gov/pubsearch/pubsinfo.asp?pubid=2009020 (accessed May 2013).

58 Robert M. Hutchins, *The Higher Learning in America* (Chicago: University of Chicago Press, 1936), 80.

59 On the following, see Robert L. Church and Michael W. Sedlak, *Education in the United States: An Interpretive History* (New York: The Free Press, 1976), 41–60; U.S. Secretary of the Interior, Statistics of the United States … The Final Exhibit of the Eighth [1860] Census (Washington, D.C.: G.P.O., 1866), x, xiv; Snyder, ed., *120 Years*; Carter, et al., *Historical Statistics*; HEGIS, 2008; *Digest of Education Statistics, 2008*.

60 W. E. B. DuBois and Augustus G. Dill, *The College-Bred Negro American* (Atlanta, GA: Atlanta University Press, 1910); Mabel L. Robinson, *The Curriculum of the Woman's College*, Bulletin, 1918, No. 6, U.S. Bureau of Education (Washington, DC: GPO, 1918); Lynn D. Gordon, *Gender and Higher Education in the Progressive Era* (New Haven, CT: Yale University Press, 1990).

61 Ferrall, *Liberal Arts*, 2.

62 See W. E. B. Du Bois, "The Talented Tenth," in *The Negro Problem: A Series of Articles by Representative American Negroes of To-Day* (New York: James Pott, 1903), 33–63.

63 Gilbert, "The Liberal Arts," 36–7.

64 Ferrall, *Liberal Arts*, 2, 195.

65 See Roger L. Geiger, "The era of multipurpose colleges in American higher education, 1850–1890," 127–52, in *The American College in the Nineteenth Century* (Nashville, TN: Vanderbilt University Press, 2000).

66 Mark Roche, *Why Choose the Liberal Arts?* (South Bend, IN: University of Notre Dame Press, 2010), 47, 1–14. See the excellent analysis in Francis Oakley, *Community of Learning: The American College and the Liberal Arts Tradition* (New York: Oxford University Press, 1992).

67 See Christopher Jencks and David Riesman, *The Academic Revolution*, 2nd ed. (New York: Doubleday, 1969), 20–7.

68 Schrecker, *The Lost Soul*, 115.

69 National Collegiate Honors Council (2011) "About NCHC." (2011). Retrieved from www.nchchonors.org/aboutnchc.shtml (accessed July 2011); and "Members" (2013), retrieved from http://nchchonors.org/members-area/member-institutions-4/ (accessed May 2013).

70 Victor E. Ferrall, Jr., *Liberal Arts at the Brink* (Cambridge, MA: Harvard University Press, 2011).

71 Eva T. H. Brann, "Do Colleges Have Something to Offer Universities concerning Liberal Education," 4, Conference on the Liberal Arts College and the Research University, University of Notre Dame, June 9–11, 2013. Retrieved from www.coretexts.org/conferences/research-university-and-liberal-arts-college-conference-june-9-11-2013/.

72 Roosevelt Montás, "By Order of the God: The College, the Research University, and the Humanist Vocation," Wilfrid McCray, "From Core to Periphery and Back Again," Bainard Cowan, "Liberal Education in the College," Conference on the Liberal Arts College and the Research University, University of Notre Dame, June 9–11, 2013. Retrieved from www.coretexts.org/conferences/research-university-and-liberal-arts-college-conference-june-9-11-2013/.

73 John Henry Newman, "Rise and Progress of Universities," in *Historical Sketches* (London: Longman, Green, 1909), v. 3, p. 229.

74 Clark Kerr, *The Uses of the University* (Cambridge, MA: Harvard University Press, 1963).

# 3

# AMENDING THE LIBERAL ARTS

## An Analysis of Learning Outcomes for Professional Majors

*Graham N. S. Miller, Cindy A. Kilgo, Mark Archibald, and Ernest T. Pascarella*

Liberal arts colleges' adoption of professional major programs, such as business and engineering, have become a popular tool to improve a campus's financial stability (Kraatz & Zajac, 1996). Some research and commentary, however, has expressed dissatisfaction at this trend, highlighting decreasing enrollments in the humanities (American Academy of Sciences, 2016) and raising alarms about the encroachment of vocational programs into the liberal arts curriculum (Ferrall, 2011). Do professional majors at traditional liberal arts colleges represent a threat to the liberal arts? Specifically, do liberal arts colleges undermine educational goals if they adopt professional majors? In this study, we examined how academic major (traditional liberal arts major versus professional major) at a liberal arts college influences students' growth on eight educational learning outcomes.

To conduct this study, we first examined recent history around small American liberal arts colleges and the environmental conditions that have led them to adopt professional programs. These programs have been an effective strategy for increasing student enrollments and organizational revenues during uncertain economic times (Kraatz & Zajac, 1996). Adverse economic conditions have persisted, and colleges continue to introduce professional majors into their curricula. Some institutions have even eliminated liberal arts disciplines from their curriculum altogether (Hartocollis, 2016). While program elimination is certainly a worrisome trend, integrating professional majors into traditional liberal arts settings may be less so. We present evidence demonstrating that students enrolled in traditional liberal arts majors (e.g., English, history, natural and physical sciences), on balance do not experience greater educational gains than students enrolled in professional majors (e.g., business, engineering, nursing). Rather, our research indicates that students majoring in a professional field have similar growth on learning outcomes as their peers in liberal arts majors. These results suggest variables other than a student's discipline of study lead to growth in learning.

## Background

For over 30 years, scholars, pundits, and media outlets predicted that many small colleges would close. Astin and Lee (1972), for example, asserted that many small, liberal arts colleges would be forced to close their doors. These colleges faced new competition in the form of low-cost public institutions. This prediction, however, was never fulfilled, as colleges pivoted their curriculum to meet student demands. Rather than closing, colleges offered new, professional majors, ultimately attracting improved enrollments and bolstering their bottom lines (Kraatz & Zajac, 1996).

Recently, ominous predictions have been renewed both for small, liberal arts colleges as well as for the liberal arts in general. Moody's recently predicted that closures of small colleges will triple in the near future, predicting 15 in 2017 (Woodhouse, 2015). The *New York Times* additionally highlighted the financial troubles faced by small colleges, saying that many may close or drastically reorient their mission (Hartcollis, 2016). While many colleges have avoided closure, they have often done so by increasing undergraduate enrollments, expanding curriculum, and introducing graduate programs. The proof is in the numbers. In 2000, Carnegie classified 219 institutions as liberal arts colleges (Indiana University Center for Post-secondary Research, n.d.). By 2010, only 181 colleges were identified as liberal arts colleges, and in the most recent set of classifications in 2015, only 171 colleges were listed as liberal arts colleges. Meanwhile, the number of comprehensive masters' colleges and universities has grown. This shifting balance demonstrates that colleges are finding that remaining a strictly liberal arts college is increasingly untenable. As a consequence, colleges have turned toward an expanded curriculum, both in undergraduate and in graduate studies, in order to buffer themselves against financial pressures.

Apart from the threats to liberal arts institutions, scholars have additionally highlighted the uncertain future facing liberal arts disciplines. The Yale faculty first raised alarms about change in the liberal arts in the famous *Yale Report of 1828*, warning that new disciplines of study were infiltrating the college curriculum and undermining educational goals. In this report, the faculty questioned inclusion of new disciplines within the framework of the traditional liberal arts. Though the faculty acknowledged room for change across higher education institutions and admitted that Yale had already expanded its curriculum to include the natural sciences, faculty members maintained that change should occur slowly (Pak, 2008). Several recent articles and books have raised similar concerns. Ferrall (2011; 2015), for example, warns that enrollment in liberal arts majors is being replaced by enrollments in professional majors. Another recent study documented declining the number of humanities degrees awarded (American Academy of Arts and Sciences, 2016). Ferrall was additionally concerned with organizational practices and argued that, as colleges and universities saw the potential revenues that accompanied professional majors, they have shifted to meet student demands. Similarly, some recent news coverage has centered on colleges and universities that have closed programs central to the liberal arts, such as philosophy (e.g., Flaherty, 2015;

Seltzer, 2016). Delucchi (1997) raised similar concerns, finding that while many post-secondary institutions advertised liberal arts as a central tenet, few actually live up to that claim.

The research cited above raises important concerns about the status and viability of the liberal arts in American higher education. Our goal in this study was to ask whether liberal arts colleges effectively support learning outcomes for students enrolled in professional major programs. In subsequent sections, we define a liberal arts mission in order to identify divergent change from that mission. We then analyzed data on student learning outcomes in order to determine how divergent change, in the form of professional majors, influenced students' development during their college experience.

## The Liberal Arts Mission

In a well-cited book, Breneman (1994) defines the boundaries of liberal arts colleges. Ultimately, he determined that a liberal arts college should award at least 60 percent of undergraduate degrees in a liberal arts discipline. In the most recent set of basic Carnegie Classifications in 2015, baccalaureate colleges that awarded 50 percent of degrees in the liberal arts were defined as "arts and sciences" colleges (The Indiana University Center for Post-secondary Research, n.d.). Majors considered "arts and sciences" typically included natural, physical, and social sciences, as well as humanities and fine arts. Major disciplines, as defined by both Breneman and the Carnegie Classifications, help to constitute a liberal arts college's mission.

Several other organizational features additionally characterize a liberal arts institution, however. Breneman (1990) points to the small, residential college campus, with a low faculty to student ratio. This small, intimate educational setting facilitates small class size and therefore greater interaction with faculty. Liberal arts colleges additionally focus greater effort on teaching, rather than on research, allowing faculty members more time and greater rewards for improving teaching practices. Indeed, one recent study found that students were more likely to encounter deep-learning teaching practices, leading to improved educational outcomes among students (Pascarella, Wang, Trolian, & Blaich, 2013).

King, Kendall Brown, Lindsay, and VanHecke (2007) laid out a set of learning outcomes associated with a liberal arts education. These learning outcomes, including critical thinking, moral development, and several others, intend to prepare students for a life of meaning, with a broad set of conceptual skills that are adaptable to shifting contexts. The learning outcomes relate closely to what the Yale faculty called in their 1828 report, "the discipline of the mind" (Committee of the Corporation and the Academic Faculty). These skills prepare students to learn throughout their lives, rather than providing only information and material to fill their minds. These features cited in the literature comprise the central tenets of a liberal arts education: liberal arts disciplines, learning environment, and learning outcomes.

## Divergent Change

Jaquette (2013) conceptualized the liberal arts college framework that defined a liberal arts college as an organizational template. This template constrains activities at a liberal arts college, and indeed, activities outside of those defined within the template undermine the institution's adherence to the liberal arts mission. Thus, any change that deviates from this template represents divergent change. Liberal arts colleges offering professional majors or expanded graduate programs are therefore engaged in activities outside of the liberal arts template. Ultimately, if a liberal arts college departs too greatly from its template, its identity claims become untenable. At this point, Jaquette argues, colleges adopt the "university" moniker in order to align their name with organizational activities.

The current study does not examine those colleges that become universities, but research on organizational change as well as Jaquette's (2013) work is helpful for answering why colleges engage in expanded organizational activities. Kraatz and Zajac (1996), for example, examined how expanded organizational activities at liberal arts colleges influenced organizational outcomes. Predicting that introducing professional majors would undermine colleges' legitimacy, the authors, in fact, found evidence suggesting the opposite: colleges that introduced professional majors enjoyed larger enrollments and improved financial positions. In a later study, Kraatz and Zajac (2001) found that engaging in divergent organizational change was an effective strategy only for colleges that had relatively limited financial resources. Simply put, research found that colleges pursued change in order to secure their financial positions.

Jaquette (2013) made a similar argument, though he additionally incorporated organizational status as a motivating factor. Colleges changed not only to meet student demands and to reap financial rewards associated with change, but to opt into a less hierarchical organizational category. While elite liberal arts colleges define an ideal organizational type, colleges that become comprehensive universities face a much less vertically stratified playing field. As a consequence, colleges that become comprehensive universities may enjoy not only greater financial stability, but no longer face comparisons to elite colleges. In this study, we ask, however, what happens at colleges that do not become universities? Specifically, we seek to understand whether students enrolling in professional majors at liberal arts colleges face a penalty in their improvement in liberal arts learning outcomes over time.

We focused our study specifically on outcomes because of continued insistence that liberal arts education is characterized by its educational goals. The American Association of Colleges and Universities (AAC&U) stated that "A truly liberal education is one that prepares us to live responsible, productive, and creative lives in a dramatically changing world" (1998, para. 1). The organization's *Statement on Liberal Learning* proposed that a liberal education is one "that fosters a well-grounded intellectual resilience, a disposition toward lifelong learning, and an acceptance of responsibility for the ethical consequences of our ideas and actions" (AAC&U, 1998, para. 1). This broad statement provided enough flexibility that seemingly any college or university can rightfully claim to provide a "liberal education." We therefore seek to determine whether a student's major, liberal arts or professional, in college affects attainment of liberal arts learning outcomes.

## The Study

Our research question is: does a student's major influence student improvement across eight liberal learning outcomes? If academic major is an essential ingredient to improvement in student outcomes, then majoring in a professional field might influence gains in liberal learning outcomes because these students would not have the same exposure to the liberal arts curriculum. We therefore hypothesize that academic major will influence students' growth in liberal learning outcomes.

To answer our question, we relied on Astin's (1993) I-E-O framework. This framework proposed that students enter college with preexisting characteristics, or *inputs*, such as race, academic achievement, and family background. Students then experience their college *environment*, the framework's "E," which can include exposure to certain teaching methods or engagement in extracurricular activities, or in this study, a student's major discipline of study. Students ultimately graduate with *outcomes* based on their interaction with the environment. The I-E-O model helps to explain why experiences at a liberal arts college might contribute to improvement in liberal learning outcomes. This framework has been used multiple times and has been applied to many different subpopulations of students.

## Methods

The current study draws on data from the Wabash National Study of Liberal Arts Education (WNS), a national, longitudinal, pretest/posttest design study that examines the effects of liberal arts college experiences on a variety of liberal arts student learning outcomes. The WNS institutional sample includes three cohorts (2006–2010, 2007–2011, and 2008–2012) of students from institutions varying in selectivity, size, geographic region, and control. Liberal arts colleges were purposefully oversampled for the purposes of WNS. The current study's institutional sample consisted of 28 four-year liberal arts colleges that participated in any of the three institutional cohorts.

Student-level data collection occurred at three intervals for each cohort. Initial data collection occurred in the fall semester of the students' first year of college (fall 2006, 2007, 2008). During initial data collection, student demographic information and precollege characteristics and experiences were collected, along with precollege levels of a variety of both cognitive and affective liberal arts student-learning outcomes. At the end of the students' first year of college (spring 2007, 2008, 2009), the first follow-up data collection occurred. During this first follow-up data collection, college experiences were collected from the first year, as well as end-of-first-year levels of the same liberal arts student learning outcomes collected during the first data collection. The final data collection occurred during the spring semester of students' fourth year of college (spring 2010, 2011, 2012). The final follow-up data collection collected college experiences over four years of college, as well as the end-of-fourth-year levels of the same liberal arts student-learning outcomes collected during the first two intervals of data collection. During both follow-up data collection intervals, students completed both the WNS Student Experiences Survey (WSES) and the National Survey of Student Engagement (NSSE). Students who participated in the 2006 WNS cohort were given $50 for each data collection interval, while students who participated in the 2007 or 2008 were not compensated for participating in the WNS. All data collection for the WNS was conducted by American College Testing Program (ACT).

## Dependent Measures

We included the following outcomes in our study: critical thinking, moral reasoning, inclination to inquire and lifelong learning, intercultural effectiveness (two separate measures), psychological well-being, and leadership. These seven dependent measures effectively capture the goals of a liberal arts education advanced both by Breneman (1994) and the AAC&U (1998). Students completed each of these outcome measures at all three data intervals, with the exception of students completing either the measure for critical thinking or for moral reasoning. This decision was made because of time required to complete these measures and is the reason for the corresponding lower sample sizes for the models corresponding to these two outcome measures. All of our dependent measures are from the second follow-up data collection, at the end of students' fourth year of college.

**Critical thinking.** The Collegiate Assessment of Academic Proficiency (CAAP) was the measure for critical thinking. The CAAP was developed by the ACT and measures the ability of students to interpret, analyze, assess, and extend arguments. The CAAP is a 32-item scale that has internal reliability consistencies ranging from 0.81 to 0.82 (ACT, 1991).

**Moral reasoning.** The N2 score of the Defining Issues Test-2 (DIT-2) was the measure for moral reasoning. The DIT-2 was developed to measure students' level of moral reasoning by responses to social dilemmas. The DIT-2 has internal reliability consistencies ranging from 0.74 to 0.77 (Rest, Narvaez, Thoma, & Bebeau, 1999).

**Inclination to inquire and lifelong learning.** We used two measures to capture inclination to inquire and lifelong learning: the Positive Attitude toward Literacy (PATL) scale and the Need for Cognition Scale (NCS). The PATL was developed to measure levels of enjoyment and pleasure in a variety of literacy-related activities, such as reading and writing poetry. The PATL is a six-item scale that has an internal consistency reliability of 0.71. The NCS measures students' "tendency to engage in and enjoy effortful cognitive activity" (Cacioppo, Petty, Feinstein, & Jarvis, 1996, p. 197). The internal consistency reliabilities for the NCS range from 0.83 to 0.91 (Cacioppo et al., 1996).

**Intercultural effectiveness.** We used two measures to capture intercultural effectiveness: the Openness to Diversity/Challenge Scale (ODC) and the Miville-Guzman Universality-Diversity Scale (M-GUDS). The ODC was developed to measure levels of enjoyment in students' interactions with diverse peers and challenge faced regarding diverse perspectives and views (Pascarella, Edison, Nora, Hagedorn, & Terenzini, 1996). The ODC is a seven-item scale that has an internal consistency reliability that ranges from 0.83 to 0.87. The M-GUDS measures "an awareness and potential acceptance of both similarities and differences in others that is characterized by interrelated cognitive, behavioral, and affective components" (Fuertes, Miville, Mohr, Sedlacek, & Gretchen, 2000, p. 158). This awareness is Universality-Diversity orientation (UDO). The M-GUDS is a 15-item scale with an internal consistency reliability of 0.85.

**Psychological well-being.** The overall mean score for the Ryff Scales of Psychological Well-Being (RYFF) was used to measure various levels of psychological well-being. The RYFF is a 54-item scale that has an internal consistency reliability of 0.88.

**Leadership.** The overall mean score for the Socially Responsible Leadership Scale (SRLS) was the measure used to capture leadership. The SRLS measures eight areas of the Social Change Model (see Astin, A., Astin, H., Boatsman, Bonous-Hammarth, Chambers, Goldberg, 1996; Dugan, 2006). The SRLS is a 68-item scale with an internal consistency reliability of 0.92.

### Independent Measures

Our independent variable of interest was academic major. We dichotomized the variable for major into professional majors and traditional liberal arts majors. We coded the variable (1 = professional majors: business, education, engineering, and professional, and 0 = arts and humanities, biological sciences, physical sciences, social sciences, and other). (Note: We ran the analyses with "other" included and with "other" not included. There were no statistically significant differences between the two samples. We therefore decided to leave the 161 students who reported "other" major within the sample.) Precollege covariates included: race (three dichotomized variables—Black, Asian, and Hispanic [with White serving as the omitted category for all three variables]), gender (male versus female), ACT Composite Score or SAT equivalent (coded as a continuous measure), first generation college status (dichotomized first generation college status versus continuing generation college status, with first-generation status being defined as having neither parent complete a four-year college degree), high school GPA (coded as a continuous variable), precollege educational aspirations (coded as a continuous variable), and precollege academic motivation (eight-item continuous measure ranging from 1 = low academic motivation to 5 = high academic motivation, $\alpha = 0.74$).

Our model additionally included a dummy variable to measure students' college aspirations. This variable measured whether a student intended to enroll in a professional major or liberal arts major. It is of course important to control for a student's propensity to select into a specific environment (Astin & Sax, 1998). We are consequently able to estimate the effects of a student's major selection while controlling for characteristics that may have led a student toward her major. We elected not to use propensity score matching because of the assumption within propensity-score matching that covariates are causally related to the experience (in our study, a student's academic major) (Reynolds & DesJardins, 2009). Further, there is evidence that regression analyses—as conducted in the current study— parallel the findings from propensity-score matching analyses (Foster, Wiley-Exley, & Bickman, 2009; Pascarella et al., 2013; Shah, Laupacis, Hux, & Austin, 2005; Zanutto, 2006). Together, these variables represent a student's *inputs*.

We included a variable for institutional selectivity, which was created using the college's mean ACT Composite Score. We also included variables indicating in which cohort the institutions participated and if institutions participated in more than one cohort of the WNS. We additionally included four college-level covariates in our models: membership in an academic honors program (dichotomized membership versus no membership), co-curricular involvement (coded as a continuous variable, defined by hours spent per week on co-curricular activities), fourth-year level on the professional/career success scale (five-item continuous measure illustrating students' desire to accomplish career or professional success, $\alpha = 0.74$), and meaningful interactions with diverse peers (three-item continuous measure capturing the level of positive interactions with diverse peers students have had over their four years of college, $\alpha = 0.83$). These items represent the student's *environment* in the I-E-O framework.

We additionally included a final control variable for completion of the first follow-up or second data collection interval. We included this dichotomous control to account for the number of times students' completed the liberal arts learning outcomes. For example, based on the variables we included in our models, students could have participated in the first data collection and the final data collection, but not the second data collection. This variable allowed us to control for whether students participated three times or two times. Approximately 33 percent of our sample participated in the first and third data collection intervals, but did not participate in the second data collection interval.

## Analyses

We computed series of ordinary least squares (OLS) regressions for each of the eight dependent measures. All continuous measures were standardized. The student-level data sample for the current study varied from 1,202 to 2,617 total students after we completed listwise deletion for each of the outcome measures. In order to check for issues of multicollinearity within our regression models, we conducted two post-estimation tests. We computed a correlation matrix between the independent variable of interest and the covariates. The correlation matrix is illustrated in Table 3.1.

**TABLE 3.1** Correlation Matrix of All Independent Variables

| | 1 | 2 | 3 | 4 | 5 | 6 | 7 | 8 | 9 | 10 | 11 | 12 | 13 | 14 | 15 | 16 |
|---|---|---|---|---|---|---|---|---|---|---|---|---|---|---|---|---|
| 1. Black | 1.00 | | | | | | | | | | | | | | | |
| 2. Asian | -0.04 | 1.00 | | | | | | | | | | | | | | |
| 3. Hispanic | -0.04 | -0.05 | 1.00 | | | | | | | | | | | | | |
| 4. Male | -0.03 | -0.01 | -0.03 | 1.00 | | | | | | | | | | | | |
| 5. ACT Composite Score | -0.21 | 0.05 | -0.15 | 0.03 | 1.00 | | | | | | | | | | | |
| 6. First Generation Status | 0.08 | 0.04 | 0.15 | -0.03 | -0.30 | 1.00 | | | | | | | | | | |
| 7. High School GPA | -0.09 | -0.01 | -0.05 | -0.05 | 0.34 | -0.06 | 1.00 | | | | | | | | | |
| 8. Precollege Educational Aspirations | 0.05 | 0.05 | 0.03 | 0.06 | 0.16 | -0.05 | 0.18 | 1.00 | | | | | | | | |
| 9. Precollege Academic Motivation | 0.06 | 0.03 | 0.05 | -0.12 | 0.06 | 0.04 | 0.18 | 0.25 | 1.00 | | | | | | | |
| 10. Institutional Selectivity | 0.00 | -0.01 | -0.03 | 0.10 | -0.20 | 0.09 | -0.02 | -0.07 | -0.03 | 1.00 | | | | | | |
| 11. Academic Honors Program | -0.11 | 0.08 | -0.04 | 0.01 | 0.62 | -0.26 | 0.27 | 0.16 | 0.06 | -0.25 | 1.00 | | | | | |
| 12. Co-Curricular Involvement | 0.00 | 0.00 | 0.01 | -0.11 | -0.03 | 0.01 | 0.08 | 0.03 | 0.10 | 0.03 | -0.18 | 1.00 | | | | |
| 13. Professional/Career Success Scale | -0.02 | -0.03 | -0.06 | 0.15 | -0.01 | -0.06 | 0.03 | 0.03 | -0.01 | 0.06 | 0.03 | 0.01 | 1.00 | | | |
| 14. Meaningful Interactions with Diverse Peers | 0.10 | 0.07 | 0.04 | 0.14 | -0.25 | 0.08 | -0.13 | 0.07 | 0.07 | 0.15 | -0.16 | 0.04 | 0.10 | 1.00 | | |
| 15. Professional Major | 0.09 | 0.10 | 0.13 | 0.01 | -0.05 | 0.00 | -0.04 | 0.09 | 0.12 | -0.08 | 0.07 | -0.01 | 0.08 | 0.10 | 1.00 | |
| 16. Propensity to Enroll in a Pre-Professional Discipline | -0.02 | -0.04 | -0.03 | -0.06 | -0.21 | 0.08 | -0.05 | -0.19 | -0.06 | 0.33 | -0.24 | 0.05 | -0.02 | 0.04 | -0.13 | 1.00 |

Table 3.1 demonstrates that none of the variables should lead to any issues of multicollinearity. ACT Composite Score and Institutional Selectivity had the highest correlation ($r = 0.62$), but because institutional selectivity was created using average ACT scores at each institution, this was expected. We additionally computed variance inflation factors (VIFs) for each model. The VIFs ranged from 1.20 to 2.15. None of the VIFs reached Allison's (1999) conservative threshold of 2.5 nor did any come close to the less conservative threshold of 10.0 (see Stevens, 2002). We were able to control for the nested nature of the study by using the "svy" command in STATA. Interpretations for statistical significance were therefore based on alpha levels of 0.05, 0.01, and 0.001.

While propensity score matching might have been another appropriate method for analyzing our data, our analytic models included controls, not only for selection effect variables that were causally prior to one's choice of academic major, but also for variables that were not (e.g., participation in an honors program, extra-curricular involvement, interactions with diverse peers). Since variables not causally antecedent to the independent variable (i.e., professional academic major) are not appropriate as covariates in propensity score matching analyses, we relied on statistical adjustment through regression analysis.

## Results

We computed descriptive analyses to compare the two main groups in our study (students majoring in professional disciplines versus students majoring in traditional liberal arts disciplines). These descriptive analyses are illustrated in Table 3.2.

Table 3.2 demonstrates that the majority of the sample majored in a traditional liberal arts academic discipline (88 percent) rather than in a professional field (12 percent). When examining the sample means for the pretest and posttest levels of the student learning outcomes, students majoring in professional fields had higher improvement during college for seven of the eight outcomes, including: critical thinking, moral reasoning, need for cognition, both measures for intercultural competence, psychological well-being, and socially responsible leadership. Students majoring in traditional liberal arts academic disciplines had a higher mean improvement in positive attitude toward literacy during college. The sample is largely white, female, and continuing-generation college student status.

Results from the regression analyses are summarized in Table 3.3. We found that professional academic majors (when compared to traditional liberal arts academic majors) did not have a statistically significant difference in growth on six of the eight outcome measures (CAAP, DIT-2, NCS, MGUDS, ODC, and RYFF). That is, professional majors and traditional liberal arts majors experienced similar levels of improvement in six of eight liberal learning outcomes. This suggests that the growth in these outcomes—critical thinking, moral reasoning, need for cognition, intercultural effectiveness, and psychological well-being—over four years does not differ by major at liberal arts colleges. Rather, a student's inputs, including

**TABLE 3.2** Descriptive Statistics on Precollege and College Experience Variables by Academic Major using the Wabash National Study of Liberal Arts Education

| | Professional Major (n=304) | | | | | | Traditional Liberal Arts Major (n=2,317) | | | | | |
|---|---|---|---|---|---|---|---|---|---|---|---|---|
| Variables | Mean | SD | Freq. | % | Min. | Max. | Mean | SD | Freq. | % | Min. | Max. |
| Senior-Year Level of Critical Thinking | 63.78 | 4.16 | | | 53 | 72 | 65.53 | 5.36 | | | 47 | 73 |
| Precollege Level of Critical Thinking | 60.68 | 4.76 | | | 51 | 73 | 63.65 | 5.15 | | | 48 | 81.22 |
| | 3.10 | | | | | | 1.88 | | | | | |
| Senior-Year Level of Moral Reasoning | 38.38 | 14.43 | | | 1.82 | 68.06 | 46.45 | 15.07 | | | -2.02 | 81.01 |
| Precollege Level of Moral Reasoning | 30.24 | 13.33 | | | 0.27 | 63.47 | 38.64 | 15.37 | | | -8.84 | 81.22 |
| | 8.14 | | | | | | 7.81 | | | | | |
| Senior-Year Level of Positive Attitude toward Literacy | 3.08 | 0.8 | | | 1 | 5 | 3.54 | 0.73 | | | 1 | 5 |
| Precollege Level of Positive Attitude toward Literacy | 3.09 | 0.69 | | | 1 | 5 | 3.45 | 0.71 | | | 1 | 5 |
| | -0.01 | | | | | | 0.090 | | | | | |
| Senior-Year Level of Need for Cognition | 3.59 | 0.59 | | | 1.5 | 4.72 | 3.78 | 0.59 | | | 1.17 | 5 |
| Precollege Level of Need for Cognition | 3.29 | 0.55 | | | 1.67 | 4.67 | 3.59 | 0.58 | | | 1.44 | 5 |
| | 0.30 | | | | | | 0.19 | | | | | |
| Senior-Year Level of Openness to Diversity/Challenge | 3.76 | 0.7 | | | 1 | 5 | 3.96 | 0.66 | | | 1 | 5 |
| Precollege Level of Openness to Diversity/Challenge | 3.76 | 0.61 | | | 1.29 | 5 | 4.01 | 0.6 | | | 1 | 5 |
| | 0.00 | | | | | | -0.05 | | | | | |

(continued)

TABLE 3.2 Descriptive Statistics on Precollege and College Experience Variables by Academic Major using the Wabash National Study of Liberal Arts Education (continued)

| Variables | Professional Major (n=304) | | | | | | Traditional Liberal Arts Major (n=2,317) | | | | | |
|---|---|---|---|---|---|---|---|---|---|---|---|---|
| | Mean | SD | Freq. | % | Min. | Max. | Mean | SD | Freq. | % | Min. | Max. |
| Senior-Year Level of M-GUIDS | 4.6 | 0.65 | | | 2.53 | 5.93 | 4.75 | 0.64 | | | 1.33 | 6 |
| Precollege Level of M-GUIDS | 4.44 | 0.63 | | | 2.6 | 5.8 | 4.67 | 0.63 | | | 1.33 | 6 |
| | 0.16 | | | | | | 0.08 | | | | | |
| Senior-Year Level of Psychological Well-Being | 4.75 | 0.55 | | | 3.22 | 5.93 | 4.69 | 0.6 | | | 1.37 | 6 |
| Precollege Level of Psychological Well-Being | 4.49 | 0.54 | | | 3.24 | 5.85 | 4.52 | 0.57 | | | 1.65 | 5.91 |
| | 0.26 | | | | | | 0.17 | | | | | |
| Senior-Year Level of Socially Responsible Leadership | 4.17 | 0.42 | | | 1.57 | 4.99 | 4.12 | 0.47 | | | 1.05 | 5 |
| Precollege Level of Socially Responsible Leadership | 3.97 | 0.4 | | | 1.88 | 4.93 | 4 | 0.44 | | | 1.00 | 5 |
| | 0.20 | | | | | | 0.12 | | | | | |
| Covariates | | | | | | | | | | | | |
| Black | | | 8 | 2.63 | 0 | 1 | | | 83 | 3.58 | 0 | 1 |
| Asian | | | 8 | 2.63 | 0 | 1 | | | 121 | 5.22 | 0 | 1 |
| Hispanic | | | 9 | 2.96 | 0 | 1 | | | 115 | 4.96 | 0 | 1 |
| Male | | | 101 | 33.22 | 0 | 1 | | | 997 | 43.03 | 0 | 1 |
| ACT Composite Score | 24.58 | 3.88 | | | 15 | 33 | 27.34 | 4.14 | | | 8 | 36 |

| Variable | | | | | | | | | | | | |
|---|---|---|---|---|---|---|---|---|---|---|---|---|
| High School GPA | 4.61 | 0.51 | | | 3 | 5 | 4.69 | 0.49 | | | 1 | 5 |
| First Generation Status | | | 97 | 31.91 | 0 | 1 | | | 509 | 21.97 | 0 | 1 |
| Precollege Educational Aspirations | 3.91 | 0.88 | | | 2 | 6 | 4.59 | 1.14 | | | 1 | 5 |
| Precollege Academic Motivation | 3.56 | 0.52 | | | 2.38 | 5 | 3.66 | 0.54 | | | 1.25 | 5 |
| Institutional Selectivity | 25.27 | 2.04 | | | 21.13 | 30.93 | 27.25 | 2.59 | | | 21.12 | 31.76 |
| Academic Honors Program | | | 94 | 30.92 | 0 | 1 | | | 570 | 24.6 | 0 | 1 |
| Co-Curricular Involvement | 3.01 | 1.69 | | | 1 | 5 | 3.12 | 1.79 | | | 1 | 8 |
| Professional/Career Success Scale | 2.35 | 0.71 | | | 1 | 4 | 2.27 | 0.69 | | | 1 | 4 |
| Meaningful Interactions with Diverse Peers | -0.27 | 0.82 | | | -1.86 | 1.66 | 0.07 | 0.84 | | | -1.86 | 1.74 |
| Propensity to Enroll in a Pre-Professional Discipline | | | 593 | 22.62 | 0 | 1 | | | 2028 | 77.38 | 0 | 1 |

**TABLE 3.3** The Estimated Effects of Academic Major at Liberal Arts Colleges on Student Learning Outcomes Using Wabash National Study Data

| | Critical Thinking | Moral Reasoning | Need for Cognition | Positive Attitude towards Literacy | Openness to Diversity | M-GUDS | Psychological Well-being | Socially Responsible Leadership |
|---|---|---|---|---|---|---|---|---|
| | n=1,202 | n=1,261 | n=2,574 | n=2,615 | n=2,617 | n=2,497 | n=2,511 | n=2,563 |
| | Coef | Coef | Coef | Coef | Coef | Coef | Coef | Coef |
| Black | -0.1304 | -0.0537 | -0.0934 | -0.1097 | -0.0347 | -0.0854 | -0.1251 | 0.0123 |
| Asian | 0.03716 | 0.0452 | -0.1654 | -0.1697 | 0.0299 | 0.0976 | -0.0726 | 0.0081 |
| Hispanic | 0.0322 | -0.1549 | 0.0552 | -0.1522* | 0.0722 | 0.1116 | 0.0485 | 0.0848 |
| Male | 0.0327 | -0.2390*** | 0.0845* | 0.0366 | -0.0869* | -0.1324** | -0.0860* | -0.1001** |
| ACT Composite Score | 0.2009*** | 0.2111*** | 0.1165*** | 0.0956*** | -0.0060 | 0.0136 | -0.0111 | -0.0309 |
| First Generation Status | 0.1232** | -0.0697 | 0.0126 | -0.0415 | 0.0364 | -0.0139 | -0.0008 | 0.0046 |
| High School GPA | 0.0362 | 0.0264 | 0.0199 | -0.0075 | 0.0346* | 0.0124 | 0.0175 | 0.0174 |
| Precollege Educational Aspirations | 0.0234 | -0.0109 | 0.0109 | 0.0354* | -0.0129 | -0.0052 | 0.0081 | -0.0146 |
| Precollege Academic Motivation | -0.0104 | 0.0058 | -0.0111 | -0.0465 | -0.0386** | 0.0142 | -0.0103 | 0.0545* |
| PRETEST | 0.5301*** | 0.4335*** | 0.5514*** | 0.5339*** | 0.3138*** | 0.4659*** | 0.4776*** | 0.2886*** |

| | | | | | | | | |
|---|---|---|---|---|---|---|---|---|
| Institutional Selectivity | -0.0178 | -0.0029 | -0.0194 | -0.0072 | -0.0135 | -0.0104 | -0.0161 | -0.0134 |
| Academic Honors Program | -0.0701 | 0.0639 | 0.0719 | 0.0246 | 0.0619* | 0.0570 | 0.0632 | 0.0769 |
| Co-Curricular Involvement | -0.0209 | -0.0149 | -0.0040 | -0.0097 | 0.0112 | -0.0160 | 0.0532* | 0.0763** |
| Professional/Career Success Scale | -0.1032* | -0.0866** | 0.0565** | -0.0134 | 0.0210 | -0.00552** | 0.0208 | 0.0240 |
| Meaningful Interactions with Diverse Peers | 0.0198 | 0.0681** | 0.1381*** | 0.1733*** | 0.4318*** | 0.3006*** | 0.1028*** | 0.1422*** |
| Propensity to Enroll in a Pre-Prof Major | -0.1166* | -0.0725 | 0.0501 | -0.0522 | -0.0360 | -0.0325 | -0.0161 | -0.0276 |
| Professional Major | 0.0905 | -0.0645 | 0.0294 | -0.2073*** | -0.0281 | 0.0621 | 0.0874 | 0.1378*** |
| | $R^2 = 0.5380$ | $R^2 = 0.4535$ | $R^2 = 0.3875$ | $R^2 = 0.3998$ | $R^2 = 0.3478$ | $R^2 = 0.4180$ | $R^2 = 0.2831$ | $R^2 = 0.1695$ |

Note: $^{*}p<0.05$, $^{**}p<0.01$, $^{***}p<0.001$.

ACT scores, the pretest, and in the case of critical thinking, a student's propensity to enroll in a professional major, influence growth in each outcome. Additional educational experiences, including meaningful interactions with diverse peers also influence improvement in learning outcomes.

Professional major (when compared to traditional liberal arts academic major) was a significant negative predictor for positive attitude toward literacy (PATL) and significant positive predictor for socially responsible leadership (SRLS). Students who majored in professional disciplines had on average a 0.21 decrease in PATL compared to their peers who majored in traditional liberal arts majors, holding all other variables constant ($p < 0.001$). Students who majored in professional disciplines had on average a 0.14 increase in SRLS compared to their peers who majored in traditional liberal arts majors, holding all other variables constant ($p < 0.001$). These findings suggest that students majoring in professional majors are having fewer gains in positive attitudes toward literacy and greater gains in socially responsible leadership than their peers majoring in traditional liberal arts academic majors.

## Limitations

Our study has several limitations. Our study does not allow for a comparison group of comprehensive, regional, or research institutions. Significantly more students majored in traditional liberal arts disciplines, rather than professional programs. We do not control for this disproportion within our analyses. Further, we have no information about the general education programs at any of our institutions, therefore limiting the findings of major course-taking habits.

## Discussion

Our results lead us to the conclusion that students' majoring in a professional major does not provide significantly more growth on liberal learning outcomes than their peers majoring in traditional liberal arts disciplines. Findings indicated significant differences only in students' positive attitude toward literacy and in students' gains in socially responsible leadership. Students enrolled in a professional major experienced greater growth in socially responsible leadership, while students enrolled in a liberal arts discipline saw improved growth in positive attitude toward literacy. These differences are important and merit discussion. Perhaps students enrolled in professional majors engage in more collaborative learning, while students enrolled in liberal arts disciplines engage with a broader variety of literature. Future research should seek to identify the mechanisms that lead to these differences.

We believe, however, that the similarities between the two groups of students is the most striking finding. Analyses suggest colleges can promote liberal learning outcomes irrespective of a student's chosen major. We therefore do not find support for our hypothesis that a student's chosen major would influence growth in measures liberal learning outcomes. Based on these results, we believe that important learning outcomes are supported not by a student's major, and additional studies should seek to identify the components of liberal arts characteristics that do promote educational growth. Indeed, some research has already sought to answer this question. Pascarella et al. (2013), for example, found that liberal arts colleges expose students to deep learning practices and to good classroom instruction more frequently compared with regional comprehensive and research universities. Other institutional factors then, more than anything else, could explain students' growth in cognitive skills. Our findings reinforce this conclusion. In this instance, the liberal arts curriculum—that is, majoring in a liberal arts discipline—cannot explain growth in students' educational outcomes. Other characteristics of a liberal arts education may potentially provide a better explanation. Breneman (1990) of course notes that a liberal arts college comprises several key characteristics other than a focus in the liberal arts curriculum. These characteristics include a general education program, a focus on teaching, and a residential college experience. Results would suggest that future research should collect data on additional campus characteristics and analyze how these characteristics influence educational outcomes.

Another conceptual explanation for a major's minimal influence on learning outcomes could be Stark and Latucca's (1997) framework of disciplines and fields. The authors point out that fields (including professional) draw theories and methods from parent disciplines. Rather than abandon these disciplines, professional programs at liberal arts colleges may more adeptly integrate disciplines. More research is therefore needed on *how* liberal arts colleges teach professional programs in order to support beneficial learning outcomes. Further research on this point could additionally help to explain differences we saw between groups. Understanding how major programs are taught and structured at liberal arts colleges may additionally explain our two significant findings. Specifically, this research could elucidate why students in traditional liberal arts majors have higher gains in positive attitude toward literacy or students in professional experience greater growth in socially responsible leadership.

A final implication, and one warranting additional research, is the influence professional majors might have on the liberal arts college campus. We wonder whether the addition of professional programs represents an attempt to draw new students and revenue in order to buffer the liberal arts curriculum from external pressures or if this change signifies a broader and more deleterious shift. We certainly acknowledge that colleges must adapt to their environments in order to stay financially afloat. Adaptation should, however, be mission-centered. With declining enrollments in the liberal arts disciplines, colleges can leverage revenues from professional programs to insulate more traditional programs from debilitating budget cuts. Work by Jaquette (2013) and Morphew (2002) has demonstrated that a college's decision to become a comprehensive university is typically preceded by broad curricular change and programmatic expansion. Administrators at liberal arts colleges should remember that change can be a slippery slope. Because colleges in our sample have small populations of professional majors, we cannot be certain that our predictions will hold for colleges that have a larger share, or even dominant share, of professional majors. As they add professional programs, administrators must work to cultivate liberal learning outcomes among and affirm their commitment to protect and sustain the liberal arts disciplines.

## References

Allison, P. D. (1999). *Logistic Regression Using the SAS System: Theory and Application*. Cary, NC: SAS Press.

American Association of Colleges and Universities. (1998). "Statement on liberal learning." *AACU*. Retrieved January 5, 2015, from www.aacu.org/about/statements/liberal-learning.

American College Testing Program. (1991). *CAAP Technical Handbook*. Iowa City, IA: Author.

American Academy of Arts and Sciences. (2016, March). *Bachelor's Degrees in the Humanities*. Retrieved April 1, 2016, from http://humanitiesindicators.org/content/indicatordoc. aspx?i=34.

Astin, A., Astin, H., Boatsman, Bonous-Hammarth, Chambers, Goldberg, L. S., Johnson, C. S., Komives, S. R., Langdon, E. A., Leland, C., Lucas, N., Pope, R. L., Roberts, D., & Shellogg, K. M. (1996). *A Social Change Model of Leadership Development: Guidebook* (Version 3). Los Angeles, CA: University of California, Higher Education Research Institute.

Astin, A. W. (1993). Assessment for excellence: *The Philosophy and Practice of Assessment and Evaluation in Higher Education*. Phoenix, AZ: Oryx Press.

Astin, A. W. & Lee, C. B. T. (1972). *The Invisible Colleges: A Profile of Small, Private Colleges with Limited Resources*. New York, NY: McGraw-Hill.

Astin, A. W. & Sax, L. J. (1998). "How undergraduates are affected by service participation." *Journal of College Student Development, 39*(3): 251–63.

Breneman, D. W. (1990). "Are we losing our liberal arts colleges?" *American Association of Higher Education Bulletin, 43*: 3–6.

Breneman, D. W. (1994). *Liberal Arts Colleges: Thriving, Surviving, or Endangered?* Washington DC: Brookings Institution.

Cacioppo, J., Petty, R., Feinstein, J., & Jarvis, W. (1996). "Dispositional differences in cognitive motivation: The life and times of individuals varying in need for cognition." *Psychological Bulletin, 119*: 197–253.

Committee of the Corporation and the Academical Faculty. (1828). *Reports on the Course of Instruction in Yale College*. New Haven, CT: Yale University.

Delucchi, M. (1997). "'Liberal arts' colleges and the myth of uniqueness." *Journal of Higher Education, 68*(4): 414–26.

Dugan, J. (2006). "Explorations using the social change model: Leadership development among college men and women." *Journal of College Student Development, 47*: 217–25.

Ferrall, V. E. (2011). *Liberal Arts at the Brink*. Cambridge, MA: Harvard University Press.

Ferrall, V. E. (2015, 27 January). "Valediction for liberal arts." *Inside Higher Ed*. Retrieved January 30, 2015, from www.insidehighered.com/views/2015/01/27/essay-offers-valediction-liberal-arts

Flaherty, C. (2015, 29 October). "Liberal arts minus liberal arts professors." *Inside Higher Ed*. Retrieved November 1, 2015, from www.insidehighered.com/news/2015/10/29/wartburg-college-and-other-liberal-arts-institutions-make-drastic-cuts-challenging

Foster, E., Wiley-Exley, E., & Bickman, L. (2009). "Old wine in new skins: The sensitivity of established findings to new methods." *Evaluation Review, 33*: 281–306.

Fuertes, J. N., Miville, M. L., Mohr, J. J., Sedlacek, W. E., & Gretchen, D. (2000). "Factor structure and short form of the Miville-Guzman Universality-Diversity Scale." *Measurement and Evaluation in Counseling and Development, 33*: 157–69.

Hartocollis, A. (2016, 29 April). "At small colleges, harsh lessons about cash flow." *The New York Times*. Retrieved May 1, 2016, from www.nytimes.com/2016/04/30/us/small-colleges-losing-market-share-struggle-to-keep-doors-open.html?ref=topics.

Indiana University Center for Postsecondary Research (n.d.). *The Carnegie Classification of Institutions of Higher Education, 2015 ed.* Bloomington, IN: Author.

Jaquette, O. (2013). "Why do colleges become universities? Mission drift and the enrollment economy." *Research in Higher Education, 54*(5): 512–43.

King, P. M., Kendall Brown, M., Lindsay, N. K., & VanHecke, J. R. (2007). "Liberal arts student learning outcomes: An integrated approach." *About Campus, 12*(4): 2–9.

Kraatz, M. S., & Zajac, E. J. (1996). "Exploring the limits of the new institutionalism: The causes and consequences of illegitimate organizational change." *American Sociological Review, 61*(5): 812–36.

Kraatz, M. S., & Zajac, E. J. (2001). "How organizational resources affect strategic change and performance in turbulent environments: Theory and evidence." *Organization Science, 12*(5): 632–57.

Morphew, C. C. (2002). "A rose by any other name: Which colleges became universities. *The Review of Higher Education, 25*(2): 207–23.

Pak, M. S. (2008). "The Yale Report of 1828: A new reading and new implications." *History of Education Quarterly, 48*(3): 30–57.

Pascarella, E., Edison, M., Nora, A., Hagedorn, L., & Terenzini, P. (1996). "Influences on students' openness to diversity and challenge in the first year of college." *Journal of Higher Education, 67*: 174–95.

Pascarella, E. T., Wang, J. S., Trolian, T. L., & Blaich, C. (2013). "How the instructional learning environments of liberal arts colleges enhance cognitive development." *Higher Education, 66*(5): 569–83.

Rest, J., Narvaez, D., Thoma, S., & Bebeau, M. (1999). "DIT2: Devising and testing a revised instrument of moral judgment." *Journal of Educational Psychology, 91*: 644–59.

Reynolds, C. L., & DesJardins, S. L. (2009). "The use of matching methods in higher education research: Answering whether attendance at a 2-year institution results in differences in educational attainment." In Smart, J. C. (Ed.) *Higher Education: Handbook of Theory and Research* (pp. 47–97). Netherlands: Springer.

Seltzer, R. (2016, 14 June). "The philosophy of what makes a university." *Inside Higher Ed*. Retrieved June 16, 2016, from www.insidehighered.com/news/2016/06/14/questions-raised-about-cuts-liberal-arts-programs-western-illinois.

Shah, B., Laupacis, A., Hux, J., & Austin, C. (2005). "Propensity score methods gave similar results to traditional regression modeling in observational studies: A systematic review." *Journal of Clinical Epidemiology, 56*: 550–9.

Stark, J. S. & Lattuca, L. R. (1997). *Shaping the College Curriculum*. Boston, MA: Allyn & Bacon.

Stevens, J. P. (2002). *Applied Multivariate Statistics for the Social Sciences*, 4th ed. Hillsdale, NF: Erlbaum.

Woodhouse, K. (2015, 28 September). "Closures to triple." *Inside Higher Ed*. Retrieved from October 2, 2015, www.insidehighered.com/news/2015/09/28/moodys-predicts-college-closures-triple-2017.

Zanutto, E. L. (2006). "A comparison of propensity score and linear regression analysis of complex survey data." *Journal of Data Science, 4*(1): 67–91.

# 4

# THE LURE OF LIBERAL ARTS

## Emerging Market Undergraduates in the United States[1]

*Peter Marber*

While the economic, environmental, political, and cultural impacts of globalization have been widely studied and analyzed (Yergin & Stanislaw, 1998; Friedman, 1999, 2005; Marber, 1999, 2003, 2009; Stiglitz, 2003, 2007; Rodrik, 2012; Christoff & Eckersley, 2013; Fukuyama, 2015; Radelet, 2015), the inquiry into the globalization of higher education has been more recent and modest (King, Marginson, & Naidoo, 2011; Pusser, Kempner, Marginson, & Ordorika, 2012; Wildavsky, 2012; Araya & Marber, 2013; Altbach, 2016).

According to the Institute of International Education (IIE, 2015), approximately five million students currently cross borders for tertiary study each year, and it is estimated this number will grow to eight million by 2025 (UNESCO Institute for Statistics, 2015). The US is the leading destination for overseas study: for academic year 2014–15, the IIE reported 974,926 international students enrolled in the US. Of those, more than 85 percent hailed from Emerging Market (EM) countries—low- and middle-income countries in Asia, Africa, Latin America, the Middle East, and the former Soviet Union. The number of international students seeking US *undergraduate* degrees has shown a dramatic increase since the global financial crisis, up from 233,789 in the 2006–07 academic year to 398,824 in 2014–15 (IIE, 2015).

Why are more international students, specifically from EM countries, entering the US for undergraduate degrees? Why are US institutions accepting, accommodating, and even recruiting these students? Over a three-year period, I probed these questions through quantitative and qualitative research with more than 1,200 overseas students from 70-plus countries, as well as 33 higher education experts. While socioeconomic advancement was found to be an important student motivation, the two factors that ranked highest among students' reasons to study in the US were (1) the desire to think and learn differently, and (2) America's flexible, multidisciplinary approach to undergraduate study—both core tenets of the liberal arts philosophy. Students also mentioned noteworthy satisfaction with the residential-extracurricular structure of US undergraduate studies, what may be called a "total" tertiary experience—another element of the American liberal arts tradition. Interviews with 33 higher education scholars, professors, and administrators yielded near universal agreement that key motivations for US schools to host overseas students included not only economic factors but also the strong desire for broader opinions, perspectives, and diversity in school curriculum and culture—again, central features of the liberal arts tradition.

## The Global Growth of Higher Education

Part of the recent growth in the number of foreign undergraduates in the US is linked to larger megatrends associated with globalization. Formerly closed, statist economies have been economically integrated and now compete in a highly interconnected web of supply chains, consumers, and financial markets (Yergin & Stanislaw, 1998; Friedman, 1999, 2005; Marber, 1999, 2003, 2009; Stiglitz, 2003, 2007; Radelet, 2015). In this era, once theoretical "knowledge work" (Drucker, 1966/2006) now commands significant premiums compared to manual labor and manufacturing jobs (US Bureau of Labor Statistics, 2014).

Extensive literature links education to economic growth (Barro, 1991; Becker, 1993; Drucker, 1966/2006; Goldin & Katz, 2010; Schultz, 1971). Indeed, education-based talent and the resulting productivity are generally accepted as essential to economic development (Barro, 1991; Lucas, 1988); therefore, increasing rates of formal and higher education have contributed to, reflected, and now outpaced the expanding global economy, particularly in the late twentieth century (Araya & Marber, 2013; Odin & Manicas, 2004; Radelet, 2015; Slaughter & Rhoades, 2004). According to the UNESCO Institute for Statistics (2015) and the World Bank (2015), total enrolled students in higher education institutions (HEIs) grew approximately six-fold to 183 million from 1970 to 2013, while GDP grew less than three-fold and the world's overall population less than two-fold.

To compete in a globally interconnected, competitive economy, many developing countries have implemented mass primary and secondary school education efforts and now boast record numbers of students seeking university degrees (World Bank, 2015; UNESCO Institute for Statistics, 2015). For example, in China, only 50,000 students were enrolled in tertiary education in the late 1970s. That number reached 24 million in 2012, the largest total worldwide for a single country. Based on scores from the 2012 Program for International Student Assessment, many EM countries now boast some of the world's most academically prepared students, with several regions in China at the top of the list (UNESCO, 2015). At the beginning of the 20th century, higher degrees were considered an elite experience, with only one percent of college-aged populations enrolled in tertiary education (Banks, 2001). Table 4.1 presents recent Gross Tertiary Enrollment Ratio (GTER) trends for different world regions.

**TABLE 4.1** Global tertiary enrollment by region, 1970-2013.

|  | *1970* | *2000* | *2013* |
|---|---|---|---|
| *World* **(total)** | *9.9* | *19.0* | *32.9* |
| North America and Western Europe | 30.8 | 60.0 | 76.6 |
| Central and Eastern Europe | 29.8 | 42.8 | 71.4 |
| Latin America and the Caribbean | 7.0 | 22.8 | 43.9 |
| East Asia and the Pacific | 2.9 | 15.4 | 33.0 |
| Arab states | 6.0 | 18.8 | 38.1 |
| Central Asia | n.a. | 22.0 | 26.1 |
| South and West Asia | 4.2 | 8.7 | 22.8 |
| Sub-Saharan Africa | 0.9 | 4.4 | 8.2 |

*Note*: n.a. = not available. First available GTER data for Central Asia are for 1980 at 24.4%.
Source: Marginson (2016); UNESCO Institute for Statistics (2015)

By 1970, enrollment had grown to 9.9 percent but was still largely the preserve of higher income countries (UNESCO Institute for Statistics, 2015). At that time, GTER exceeded 15 percent in only 19 countries, led by the US, the world's first mass higher education system (UNESCO Institute for Statistics, 2015), at 47 percent. Nearly all the growth since 1970 has come from EM countries. Asia particularly has been expanding rapidly and now enrolls nearly half the world's students.

Accelerating HEI enrollment rates worldwide have transformed higher education from an exclusive privilege into a more common experience. A university degree, perhaps a pipe dream two or three generations ago, is now within reach of many families around the world.

## The Growth of Foreign Study

Parallel to the worldwide expansion of higher education has been the growth of foreign study (IIE, 2015). While students have travelled to learn for centuries, cross-border education has accelerated in the late 20th and early 21st centuries, possibly following the reduction in transportation and communication costs (Gersbach & Schmutzler, 2000; Rodrigue, 2013). The ubiquity of the Internet—and the low cost of staying in touch with families and friends through video chat, text, email, and voice—may also be contributing to this trend (Wooley, 2013).

According to the OECD (2015), in 1975, approximately 800,000 degree-seeking students enrolled abroad from 34 countries. By 2000, this number more than doubled to two million students, and by 2014 there were five million students from 100+ countries seeking degrees abroad. According to the IIE (IIE, 2015) four countries of origin comprise more than half of overseas US undergraduates including China (31.2 percent), South Korea (8.7 percent), Saudi Arabia (7.8 percent), and India (4.1 percent) with 100+ countries comprising the remainder.

This international demand for higher education is unprecedented and will likely intensify as competition for employment increases in a globalizing economy (Olssen & Peters, 2005; Marber, 2009, 2015; Brown et al., 2010; Radelet, 2015; Altbach, 2016). Empowered by successful economic development and by democratized information via the Internet, formerly isolated EM students can make choices about their education and pursue opportunities previously unavailable. In such a brave new world, more young people can cultivate their talents and reap the rewards in more locations than ever before. They have greater freedom to make more individualized decisions about how and where they study, work, and consume.

## Tertiary Supply/Demand Imbalances in Emerging Markets and the US

Privileged classes globally have had access to universities for the last few centuries, but mass tertiary education is a relatively new phenomenon, particularly in EM countries (Schofer & Meyer, 2005; Trow & Burrage, 2010; UNESCO Institute for Statistics, 2015). With rising middle classes in many EMs, families now have disposable income to afford higher degrees (Kharas & Gertz, 2010). However, in many EM countries, capacity is limited (South China Morning Post, 2012; Mishra, 2012; Knobel, 2014; Oxford, 2015). While private sector factories can be built relatively quickly, traditional higher education schools take years—if not decades—to cultivate faculties, curriculums, and facilities. To satisfy demand quickly, many overseas governments have found it more efficient to offer scholarships for students to undertake degrees overseas (Ortiz, 2015; Lu, 2014).

Americans accustomed to a decentralized, variegated higher educational landscape—with a mix of state, community, and independent colleges—might be surprised to learn that most higher education systems around the world are publicly funded and managed, with federal policies organizing and governing them. Some are vestiges of centrally planned economies (McMullen, Mauch, & Donnorummo, 2002) that include large state-run, multi-campus institutions, serving millions of students. Moreover, few EM universities resemble traditional

American residential campuses; students are more likely to be commuters to large city universities.

Many countries require competitive national entrance exams for rationed access to higher education. In China, for example, the central government regulates the number of available university places based on an annual matrix of school and subject quotas tied to scores on the infamous *gaokao*, a grueling two-day national university entrance exam. In some recent years, less than 50 percent of students who have taken the *gaokao* have been granted entrance to Chinese universities. In addition, many students who gain entrance often fail to score high enough for their preferred academic discipline. Because a university degree is seen as the only ticket to upward mobility in a country of 1.3 billion, some Chinese students take the *gaokao* ten or more times (Wong, 2015). Cheating is so rampant that drones and metal detectors are used to help police exam sites (Lus & Whiteman, 2015; Wong, 2015). In India, similar hyper-competition social mobility pressure has been reported, resulting in elaborate admissions schemes involving leaked test questions, rigged answer sheets, corrupt graders, and the organized recruitment of test takers (Biswas, 2015; Mackasill, Stecklow, & Migglani, 2015; Angad & Hafeez, 2015). Comparable phenomena recorded in other countries (Associated Press, 2016; Crone, 2015; *Daily Mail Reporter*, 2012) underscore the high-stakes environment to access higher education in some EM countries.

Questionable quality among EM universities may also be driving students to the US. While many EM countries produce some of the world's most academically prepared students, few systems boast top-ranked institutions in the world's popular league tables (ShanghaiRanking, 2016; THE, 2016). US schools dominate such tables and, in some rankings, comprise more than half of the top 100 places. Any American universities ranked above 100 may be perceived as better than many unranked schools in EM countries, regardless of local prestige.

While the quantity/quality issues in EM higher education systems could push EM students to American schools, other factors make overseas students attractive to US host institutions. Data suggest that American HEIs are grappling with declining in-country demand due to a shrinking school-age population, which is expected to decline approximately 15 percent through 2034 (United States Census Bureau, 2014). This is expected to hurt both private and public institutions that have expanded their fixed costs (e.g., classrooms, dormitories, laboratories), which is partially why tuition costs that have outpaced inflation for decades (Department of the Treasury, 2012). Furthermore, state funding to US public HEIs has declined since 1980, increasing the financial importance of student tuitions to balancing budgets (Department of the Treasury, 2012). Looking forward, an increase of online degree and certificate programs may also draw American students away from traditional residential HEIs (Department of the Treasury, 2012), adding further financial pressure on US schools with large fixed expenses. In most state tertiary schools, out-of-state students, including those from overseas, often pay a premium in tuition. At some schools, international students pay additional fees above those for US out-of-state students (Lewin, 2012). All of these trends, plus the rising academic and financial capabilities of overseas students, makes marketing to and recruiting international students economically attractive for US schools, both public and private.

## Research Findings[2]

The trends noted above were woven into a mix of quantitative and qualitative inquiries over a three-year period from April 2013 through April 2016. Student motivation data were triangulated from (1) primary surveys of 1,210 students from 71 countries at 159 US institutions, (2) follow-up surveys using a 343-student subset, (3) 85 self-authored student essays, (4) eight focus groups conducted with 43 EM students, and (5) semi-structured interviews with 12 EM students. Host school motivation findings were derived from interviews with 33 higher education scholars. With only modest country, gender, and socioeconomic variation, surveyed students sought US undergraduate degrees primarily for (1) new ways of thinking and learning, (2) a more flexible curriculum, and (3) an improvement or preservation of socioeconomic status and prospects. Data also indicate a high rate of student satisfaction with the choice to study in the US and their schools— possibly linked to the residential and extracurricular experience of traditional US undergraduate degrees. The motivations of US host schools were found to be multidimensional and included the desire to (1) expand the quantity and quality of students, (2) broaden sources of revenue, (3) internationalize campus culture and curriculum, and (4) enhance school reputation.

## Uniqueness of American Undergraduate Degrees and Experience

In most US schools, an undergraduate degree typically includes one to two years of broad subject (or "distribution") requirements, followed by more focused study and electives determined after enrolling. This multidisciplinary philosophy, codified first in the famous *Yale Report of 1828* fosters broad inter-relational thinking:

> In laying the foundation of a thorough education, it is necessary that all the important mental faculties be brought into exercise. It is not sufficient that one or two be cultivated while others are neglected. A costly edifice ought not to be left to rest upon a single pillar. When certain mental endowments receive a much higher culture than others, there is a distortion in the intellectual character. The mind never attains its full perfection unless its various powers are so trained as to give them the fair proportions that nature designed.

After sampling several disciplines while completing distribution requirements, US undergraduate students then decide on a more focused "major" to complete their degrees. Whether students ultimately major in humanities or science subjects—or even more contemporary areas like computer science or business management—multidisciplinary requirements are the norm in American undergraduate programs at small liberal arts colleges, larger research institutions, and even many technical schools. Indeed, the US liberal arts tradition of broad distribution requirements followed by more concentrated study extends beyond small baccalaureate-only institutions.

This contrasts sharply to most undergraduate programs outside the US. As noted earlier, a typical international student will take a national test in his or her home country to gain entrance into a state-funded university for a specific academic discipline. Such an approach resembles an American master's degree—a focus on one subject. The ability to sample several subjects first and then decide on a major—and even change the major at a later time—is a unique feature of the US tertiary system. While there are exceptions globally, most schools outside the US require students to apply to universities for a specific major. Outside the US, changing a university major after a mono-disciplinary program has begun largely means starting a new course of study from scratch—with a corresponding loss of time and money. As findings will show, the US liberal arts system of broad study, followed by the freedom to choose or change a major *after* admission, is a key attraction for international students to pursue undergraduate degrees in America.

## Student Motivations to Study in the US: Quantitative Findings

In a 64-question survey, twelve specific prompts investigated student motivations to study in the US. As results in Table 4.2 note, the desire for new ways of thinking, studying, and learning ranked highest (4.18 on a scale of 1–5, with 5 being the strongest), followed by the desire for a more flexible curriculum (4.11). In terms of socioeconomic pull factors, the prestige of a US degree was an important motivator (4.05). Studying abroad to improve one's international career prospects also scored high (3.94)—but not as high as the liberal arts motivations. Modest statistical differences were found between genders and countries. In a further probe of whether family income was shaping such motivations, data shows surprisingly little impact. In a subset survey of 351 students, respondents were asked to identify their family's income as "Below Average," "Average," or "Above Average" relative to the families of their US school peers. Based upon such responses, the subgroup's answers to questions were recomputed and reanalyzed along these three financial categories, reported below in Table 4.2.

Regardless of self-reported income group, respondent motivations were ranked similarly. The strongest motivations for all three income groups were the two strongest for the broader respondent pool: (1) experiencing new ways of

**TABLE 4.2**  Primary survey scores for 12 key student motivations, overall averages, and by income group.

| QUESTIONS (SCALE: 1 is "not important", 2 "less important" 3 "important," 4 "more important," and 5 "very important") | Overall Mean | Below Average Income Mean | Average Income Mean | Above Average Mean |
|---|---|---|---|---|
| I wanted to experience new ways of thinking, studying, or learning. | 4.18 | 4.42 | 4.40 | 4.37 |
| I wanted broader or more flexible curriculum than offered in my home country. | 4.11 | 4.13 | 4.24 | 4.25 |
| Was university reputation, prestige, or ranking important in your decision to study at a foreign university? | 4.05 | 3.88 | 4.12 | 3.97 |
| I wanted to improve my chances for an international career. | 3.94 | 4.00 | 3.93 | 4.01 |
| I wanted access to better facilities (labs, libraries, sports, etc.) than what was available in my home country. | 3.93 | 4.08 | 3.89 | 3.65 |
| I wanted the opportunity to become more independent. | 3.86 | 4.08 | 4.18 | 3.99 |
| I wanted to improve my chances for a better career in my home country. | 3.56 | 3.63 | 3.95 | 3.76 |
| I was interested in and wanted to experience foreign culture. | 3.45 | 3.82 | 4.08 | 3.68 |
| I wanted to learn how to function better in a foreign language. | 3.45 | 2.79 | 3.01 | 2.44 |
| I wanted to build international friendships and networks. | 3.43 | 3.56 | 3.84 | 3.76 |
| There were limited places to study at prestigious schools in home country. | 2.63 | 2.42 | 2.74 | 2.51 |
| The subject I wanted to study was not offered in home country. | 2.44 | 2.33 | 2.58 | 2.17 |

thinking and learning and (2) enjoying a more flexible curriculum. The lowest scored motivations in the Primary Survey—limited places at home or desired subject not offered—were also the lowest for all three income groups in the Secondary Survey. Prestige, the desire to improve career prospects, and wanting to build international networks also scored fairly high, and the scores were fairly consistent across income groups.

In summary, quantitative research on foreign student motivation to earn undergraduate degrees in the US found that the liberal arts philosophy—learning in new and different ways and enjoying a flexible, multidisciplinary curriculum—scored highest, even ahead of socioeconomic advancement.

## Student Motivations to Study in the US: Qualitative Findings

Qualitative data was collected from open-ended questions, essays, and group and individual interviews. Recurring themes were identified and findings were coded using ATLAS-ti and summarized in Table 4.3.

The three top-rated motivations from the quantitative data—new ways of thinking and learning, flexible curriculum, and socioeconomic advancement—were also the top-rated motivations in the qualitative inquiries. While new ways of thinking and learning were mentioned less frequently in the group and student interviews, combined with educational flexibility, these two pillars of the liberal arts philosophy were recorded more than socioeconomic advancement.

A male Pakistani student described his decision to attend a small liberal arts college in New England, echoing the spirit of the Yale Report: "I wanted an education which allowed me to develop intellectually and make me think, rather just train me as an engineer or a doctor." A Hong Kong student at a Southern public research university noted, "In pursuing my studies in the United States, I wish to become more open-minded and receive a general education." Such a sentiment was shared by many students from Eastern Europe, the Middle East, Latin America, and Asia. Respondents frequently cited "liberal arts," "liberal thinking," and "creative thinking." As noted in the Yale Report, American universities foster investigation and debate. Indeed, forming opinions plays an integral role in the US model, and that feature isn't lost on EM students, many of whom cited the free exchange of ideas as an important motivator to come to the US.

The flexibility of the US system—exploring several disciplines before declaring a major—was mentioned in more than half of the responses. A Singaporean male at a Midwestern Big Ten university wrote,

> While this requires more time and money than the Asian mode, I find this more intellectually stimulating and enjoyable. Not only will every student have a chance to explore and study subjects outside of their interest, I believe that such general knowledge will also benefit one when interacting with others in a social setting. Coming to the US has definitely changed how I perceive myself as a student, and made me realize they are endless possibilities. I had my undergraduate degree in Biology, and next year I will be attending law school. Before I came to the US, I would have never dreamed of myself becoming a lawyer.

**TABLE 4.3** Summary of EM student motivation qualitative findings

| Motivations and Considerations | Primary Survey | | Secondary Survey | | Student Essays | | Group and Individual Interviews | |
|---|---|---|---|---|---|---|---|---|
| | Counts | Percentage | Counts | Percentage | Counts | Percentage | Counts | Percentage |
| Socioeconomic Advancement | 7 | 22.6 | 118 | 44.9 | 23 | 34.80 | 23 | 32.9 |
| Educational Flexibility | 6 | 19.3 | 65 | 24.7 | 31 | 47.00 | 39 | 55.7 |
| New Ways of Learning, Thinking, Processing | 18 | 58.1 | 80 | 30.4 | 12 | 18.20 | 8 | 11.4 |
| **TOTAL COUNTS** | **31** | | **263** | | **66** | | **70** | |

Similarly, a male Tanzanian student at an East Coast university wrote, "The idea of flexibility in your study, the liberal arts system and the encouragement of exploration were the reasons I came to the US." A male Singaporean expanded, "The Western education encourages students to explore and develop their interest and pursue the subjects they like. This is very different from the mindset of Asian parents and students as they tend to favor subjects that promise a better financial prospect in long-term."

Perhaps this statement from a Hong Kong student best sums up the spirit of the liberal arts tradition and why so many students are pursuing undergraduate degrees in the US:

> In the United States, a place where ethnicities from all over the world meet, there are people from all continents in a class of twenty. We differ in many aspects, from the language we speak to the way we think. I have never encountered such diversity in Hong Kong, and this assortment definitely enriches the learning environment. All of us have different backgrounds and cultures. We think differently, we work differently, and we see things differently. This educational mix enables individuals with different ideas and innovations to be brought together.... This valuable experience I acquired not only helps me to interact and get along with people, but it gives me an idea that the world isn't as big as it seems, as people from all over the world can actually develop stronger bonds and closer relationships and be brought together closer even by overcoming the racial barrier. Throughout the semesters I spent in the States, I have gained new insight about this highly diverse society.

A student's desire to study a subject they were passionate about was often thwarted by a rigid quota system in their home country. For example, several Chinese students noted that the *gaokao* entrance system often required higher test scores for certain schools and certain subjects. As one female student lamented, "this is very inhumane to me, thinking back now.... Here [in the US] people choose to study what they love, so they have more motivation to keep doing things like research." Because many Chinese professors studied things they were not passionate about, students observed, their lack of enthusiasm carried over into the university culture. One Chinese student noted that China's lack of "very serious scholars" could be traced to a system that forces students into specific channels instead of inspiring them to follow their personal interests.

Many of the students interviewed noted that a typical university experience in their home country was more of a "commuter" experience, whereby the school was only for lectures and classes, after which most students went back to their parents' home at night. The residential American college experience, including living and socializing with other students away from home, was often mentioned as a huge attraction, one more fully appreciated after attending. This "total" college experience was highlighted, too, in the Yale Report. It is an experience that transcends the mere transmission of knowledge from teacher to student. A nurturing enterprise pursued during the transition from childhood to adulthood, it fosters relationships, social unity, maturity, and even a sense of place and belonging:

> College students are generally of an age that requires that a substitute be provided for parental superintendence. This consideration determines the kind of government that ought to be maintained in our colleges. Like the parent–child relationship, it should be founded on mutual affection and confidence. It should aim to effect its purpose principally by kind and persuasive influence, not wholly or chiefly by restraint and terror. Still, punishment may sometimes be necessary. The parental character of college government requires that the students should be so collected together as to constitute one family, that the intercourse between them and their instructors may be frequent and familiar. This renders it necessary that suitable buildings be provided for student residence.

The residential aspect of a liberal arts education is central to the total college experience. Students leave the nest at home and discover a broader world, where they are encouraged to explore new ideas, cultivate new relationships, and develop new thinking skills—all within the safety of a surrogate family.

The pull of the liberal arts philosophy was echoed often in student essays. A Chinese female at Oberlin recounted, "I applied only to liberal arts colleges in the US because I wanted the close knit relationship both between professors and students, and among students in small colleges." Many students valued the "24/7" nature of the American residential college experience. Lectures, parties, and organized sports were all viewed as important attractions at US schools. Another Chinese student at a Great Lakes public university noted, "I'm amazed about the sheer amount of events and lectures on campus. There are so many things to enjoy besides academics." In an amusing exchange at one focus group, a student was asked if he had picked his Midwestern public research university based on its ranking. "Well," he replied, unaware that the question referred to academic ranking, "our football team is top ten, but our basketball team is only top twenty." Indeed, many students who had graduated mentioned returning to their alma maters for big athletic events and reunions. Some graduates said they stay in touch with classmates—who they often regard as "family"—years after graduation by going to sports bars and watching with other alumni as their alma maters play big games.

According to a male Singaporean student at a private research university on the East Coast, this total college experience, academic and extracurricular, helps students

> acquire and hone several important and marketable skills like critical and creative thinking, researching and analyzing skills, and being decisive, which

are important soft skills that are useful in all industries. I am confident that a US education will not only provide me with a strong academic education but will also help me grow as a person, developing both my IQ (Intelligence Quotient) and EQ (Emotional Quotient), which are equally important to me.

This improvement of IQ/EQ observation was also echoed in some questions in the smaller subset survey. In addition to students noting that more than 80 percent were satisfied with their decision to go to their US school, when asked if their US undergraduate experience made them more confident about their future, 25.7 percent noted "much more confident," 51.8 percent responded "more confident," 18.4 percent recorded "about the same" level of confidence, and only 0.3 percent responded "more insecure" about their future.

To summarize, the liberal arts approach of pursuing a general education and flexibly choosing a major was found to be the most important motivation among EM undergraduate students at large and small, public and private US schools, regardless of academic interests. While data also suggest that the total college experience, in and out of American classrooms, contributed to satisfaction with attending their schools, more research would be needed to understand whether this was a motivation before enrolling.

## Host School Motivations

Interviews were conducted with 33 higher education experts, including provosts, admissions professionals, scholars, teachers, and journalists with more than 500 collective years of experience in higher education, including public, private, large, and small schools. Recurring themes were identified and coded, revealing four dominant motivations for HEIs to recruit international students: (1) increasing revenue, (2) improving the applicant pool, (3) internationalizing student perspectives and diversifying campus culture, and (4) enhancing school reputation (Table 4.4).

**TABLE 4.4** Summary count of 33 expert interview observations.

| Host School Motivation/Concern | Count/N | Percentage |
|---|---|---|
| New Revenues | 32/33 | 96.97 |
| Improving Applicant Pool | 31/33 | 93.93 |
| Internationalization | 30/33 | 90.90 |
| Enhancing Reputation | 29/33 | 87.88 |
| Supply-Demand Trends | 26/33 | 78.78 |

All experts interviewed mentioned economic motivations, and often the topic spilled into discussions of improving applicant pools and enhancing school reputation. Most of the respondents mentioned the decline in public funding in the US and the demographic contraction of traditional high school age students. High cost structures and stagnant residential attendance rates have led both public and private US schools to view their offerings as "exports" for foreign markets. As US high school applicant pools wane, more academically and financially capable students emerge from the rest of the world. Concerns for adding new revenue, improving the quality and quantity of applicant pools, and enhancing reputation were said to be survival tactics in an increasingly competitive marketplace of higher education, not only in the US but globally.

However, money is not everything to US schools—at least according to most experts interviewed. Aside from demographic/financial considerations, another frequently mentioned motivation to attract EM students was internationalizing campus culture and curriculum with more diverse students—noted by more than 90 percent of those interviewed.

Thirty-one of 33 experts remarked that most US schools desired a greater socioeconomic, ethnic, and racial mix of students on campus, including those from overseas. "There's a universal belief that more diversified student bodies provide more enriching college experiences," one expert said. That enrichment is multidimensional, providing different perspectives in classrooms, dormitories, libraries, clubs, and dining halls. "It sets up students for the world they're inheriting, which is very different than when I went to school in the seventies," another expert noted. Some stated that many public universities cannot generate diversified student pools from their state's demographic population; certain ethnic groups are just too small. As such, "foreign students diversify otherwise largely Caucasian campuses," one official noted. "They fill a need." Another enthusiastic expert noted of his West Coast community college, "If our [local] students can't visit the world, we'll bring the world to the campus." Contrary to a cynical view of these comments as mere platitudes, experts interviewed appeared earnest in their belief that EM students genuinely improve the holistic educational experience—inside and outside of class—offered by their schools.

The efforts to internationalize American campus culture and perspectives take many forms beyond attracting foreign students to campus. One expert explained how his school established "global centers" in several EM countries, including Jordan, China, India, Brazil, Chile, and Kenya. These centers are partially for recruiting applicants (and overseas faculty), but the expert noted they help "cross-fertilize ideas," "enhance the curriculum," promote cross-border travel and understanding, provide research bases for faculty and students, and allow schools to keep in closer contact with overseas alumni. In total, these efforts—along with other strategies mentioned, such as building overseas branch campuses, offering online programs for international students, and encouraging study abroad and other exchange programs—play a crucial role in diversifying university communities and promoting the liberal arts mission.

## Summary

The US higher education system, firmly anchored by the liberal arts philosophy for over two centuries and yet continuously evolving, has proven to be one of America's most durable exports. Research shows that EM students are enrolling in US undergraduate programs more than ever before, largely attracted by the uniquely American liberal arts education. Moreover, according to HEI experts these EM students, in turn, strengthen liberal arts institutions by contributing their diverse insights and experiences to the educational discourse. It is unsurprising that EM and developed countries around the world, wanting to keep talented students at home, have developed a growing interest in forming their own liberal arts institutions (Godwin, 2015). Far from obsolete, the liberal arts package offered by most US colleges and universities—with broad and flexible paths of study geared toward creativity and critical thinking, mixed with a rich residential-extra-curricular experience—has never been more vital, relevant, and in demand.

## Notes

1 The author would like to thank Peter Gronn, Diane Reay of Cambridge University for supervising and assisting with this research, Their comments and advice has been invaluable in the multi-year study. Thanks also to Lindsey Tan Lim, Yu Ping Chan, Dan Ding, Kamna Mantode, and Adrian Brown for their suggestions and contributions.
2 All quantitative data from the primary survey has been reweighted to reflect the country composition of foreign students as captured by the Institute for International Education for academic year 2014–2015.

## References

Altbach, P. G. (2016). *Global Perspectives on Higher Education*. Baltimore, MD: The Johns Hopkins University Press.

Angad, A. & Hafeez, S. (2015, July 31). "Police bust admission racket in Delhi University, arrest 4, seize forged documents." *India Express*. Retrieved June 1, 2016, from http://indianexpress.com/article/cities/delhi/delhi-university-admission-racket-busted-four-held/.

Araya, D., & Marber, P. (Eds.). (2013). *Higher Education in the Global Age: Policy, Practice and Promise in Emerging Societies*. New York, NY: Routledge.

Associated Press. (2016). "Kenya dissolves exam board for cheating, arrests to follow." *Newsmaxworld*. Retrieved June 1, 2016, from www.newsmax.com/World/Africa/AF-Kenya-Education/2016/03/24/id/720726/.

Banks, A. (2001). *Cross-National Time-Series Data Archive*. Binghampton, NY: Computer Systems Limited.

Barro, R. (1991). "Economic growth in a cross section of countries." *Quarterly Journal of Economies, 106*: 407–43.

Becker, G. (1993). *Human Capital: A Theoretical and Empirical Analysis, with Special Reference to Education*. Chicago, IL: The University Press of Chicago.

Biswas, S. (2015, July 8). "Vyapam: India's deadly medical school exam scandal." *BBC*. Retrieved June 1, 2016, from www.bbc.com/news/world-asia-india-33421572.

Brown, P., Lauder, H., & Ashton, D. (2010). *The Global Auction: The Broken Promises of Education, Jobs, and Incomes*. Oxford, UK: Oxford University Press.

Christoff, P., & Eckersley, R. (2013). *Globalization and the Environment*. Rowman & Littlefield Publishers.

Crone, J. (2015). "Putting his love to the test: Boyfriend, 20, caught dressing up as his 17-year-old girlfriend so he can take her exams." *Daily Mail*. Retrieved June 1, 2016, from www.dailymail.co.uk/news/article-3117089/Putting-love-test-Boyfriend-20-dresses-17-year-old-girlfriend-exams.html#ixzz4E0ncfmo9.

Daily Mail Reporter (2012). "The ultimate cheat sheet: Examiners 'catch student with 35ft-long paper containing 25,000 answers wrapped around his body.'" *Daily Mail*. Retrieved June 1, 2016, from www.dailymail.co.uk/news/article-2158248/Kazakh-exam-student-caught-35ft-long-cheat-sheet-containing-25-000-answers.html.

Department of the Treasury. (2012). *The Economics of Higher Education*. Washington DC: US Department of the Treasury.

Drucker, P. (1966/2006). The Effective Executive: The Definitive Guide to Getting the Right Things Done. New York: HarperCollins.

Friedman, T. (1999). *The Lexus and the Olive Tree: Understanding Globalization*. New York, NY: Farrar, Straus and Giroux.

Friedman, T. (2005). *The World Is Flat: A Brief History of the Twenty-First Century*. New York, NY: Farrar, Straus and Giroux.

Fukuyama, F. (2015). *Political Order and Political Decay: From the Industrial Revolution to the Globalization of Democracy*. New York, NY: Farrar, Straus, and Giroux.

Gersbach, H., & Schmutzler, A. (2000). "Declining costs of communication and transportation: What are the effects on agglomerations?" *European Economic Review*, 44(9): 1745–61.

Godwin, K. A. (2015). "The worldwide emergence of liberal education." *International Higher Education*, (79): 2–4.

Goldin, C., & Katz, L. (2010). *The Race between Education and Technology*. Cambridge, MA: Belknap Press.

Institute of International Education (IIE). (2015). Open Doors Data. International Students: Academic Level and Place of Origin. Retrieved June 1, 2016, from www.iie.org/Research-and-Publications/Open-Doors/Data/International-Students/By-Academic-Level-and-Place-of-Origin.

Kharas, H., & Gertz, G. (2010). "The new global middle class: a cross-over from west to east." *Wolfensohn Center for Development at Brookings*, 1–14.

Kimball, B. (2014). "Revising the declension narrative: liberal arts colleges, universities, and honors programs, 1870s–2010s." *Harvard Educational Review*, 84(2): 243–64.

King, R., Marginson, S., & Naidoo, R. (Eds.). (2011). *Handbook on Globalization and Higher Education*. Cheltenham, UK: Edward Elgar Publishing.

Knobel, M. (2014). "Brazil's shortage of professors." *InsideHigherEd*. Retrieved June 1, 2016, from https://www.insidehighered.com/blogs/world-view/brazils-shortage-professors.

Lewin, T. (2012). "Taking more seats on campus, foreigners also pay the freight." *The New York Times*. Retrieved June 1, 2016, from www.nytimes.com/2012/02/05/education/international-students-pay-top-dollar-at-us-colleges.html?_r=0).

Lu, Z. (2014) "Scholarships drive growth of students from Kuwait." WES Research & Advsiory Services. Retrieved June 1, 2016, from http://wenr.wes.org/2014/09/scholarships-drive-growth-in-students-from-kuwait/.

Lucas, R. (1988). "On the mechanics of economic development." *Journal of Monetary Economics*, 22: 3–42.

Lus, S. & Whiteman, H. (2015). "China's university entrance exams: Would you pass the test?" *CNN.com*. Retrieved from June 1, 2016, www.cnn.com/2015/06/08/asia/china-gaokao-national-exams/.

Mackasill, A., Stecklow, S., & Migglani, S. (2015). "Special report: Why India's medical schools are plagued with fraud." *Reuters*. Retrieved June 1, 2016, from www.reuters.com/article/us-india-medicine-education-specialrepor-idUSKBN0OW1NM20150617.

Marber, P. (1999). *From Third World to World Class: The Future of Emerging Markets in the Global Economy*. New York, NY: Basic Books.

Marber, P. (2003). *Money Changes Everything: How Global Prosperity Is Reshaping Our Needs, Values, and Lifestyles*. Upper Saddle River, NJ: FT Prentice Hall.

Marber, P. (2009). *Seeing the Elephant: Understanding Globalization from Trunk to Tail*. Hoboken, NJ: John Wiley.

Marber, P. (2015). *Brave New Math: Information, Globalization, and New Policy Thinking for the 21st Century*. New York, NY: World Policy.

McMullen, M. S., Mauch, J. E., & Donnorummo, B. (2002). *The Emerging Markets and Higher Education: Development and Sustainability*. New York, NY: Routledge Falmer.

Mishra, A. (2012). "Poor quality and too few seats push 600,000 students abroad." *University World News*, Issue No. 238. Retrieved June 1, 2016, from www.universityworldnews.com/article.php?story=20120907132825451.

Odin, J. K., & Manicas, P. T. (2004). *Globalization and Higher Education*. Honolulu, HI: University of Hawaii Press.

Olssen, M., & Peters, M. A. (2005). "Neoliberalism, higher education and the knowledge economy: From the free market to knowledge capitalism." *Journal of Education Policy*, 20(3): 313–45.

Organization for Economic Cooperation and Development (OECD), Center for Educational Research and Innovation. (2015). Education Indicators at a Glance. *OECD*. Retrieved June 1, 2016, from www.oecd-ilibrary.org/education/education-at-a-glance_19991487

Ortiz, A. (2015). "Latin America: Government scholarships as the driver of student mobility and capacity building." *WES Research & Advisory Services*. Retrieved from http://wenr.wes.org/2015/04/latin-america-government-scholarships-driver-student-mobility-capacity-building/.

Oxford University, International Strategy Office (2015). "International Trends in Higher Education." University of Oxford. Retrieved June 1, 2016, from www.ox.ac.uk/sites/files/oxford/International%20Trends%20in%20Higher%20Education%202015.pdf.

Pusser, B., Kempner, K., Marginson, S., & Ordorika, I. (2012). *Universities and the Public Sphere: Knowledge Creation and State Building in the Era of Globalization*. New York: Routledge.

Radelet, S. (2015). *The Great Surge: The Ascent of the Developing World*. New York: Simon & Schuster.

Rodrigue, J. P. (2013). *The Geography of Transport Systems*. New York: Routledge.

Rodrik, D. (2012). *The Globalization Paradox: Democracy and the Future of the World Economy*. New York: W.W. Norton.

Schofer, E., & Meyer, J. (2005). "The worldwide expansion of higher education in the twentieth century." *American Sociological Review*, 70: 898–920.

Schultz, T. W. (1971). *Investment in Human Capital*. New York: Free Press.

ShanghaiRanking. (2016). Academic Ranking of World Universities. Retrieved June 1, 2016, from www.shanghairanking.com/index.html.

Slaughter, S., & Rhoades, G. (2004). *Academic Capitalism and the New Economy: Markets, State, and Higher Education*. Baltimore, MD: The Johns Hopkins University Press.

*South China Morning Post* (2012). "Universities brace for overcrowding" *South China Morning Post*. Retrieved from www.scmp.com/article/990531/universities-brace-overcrowding.

Stiglitz, J. (2003). *Globalization and Its Discontents*. New York, NY: W. W. Norton & Co.

Stiglitz, J. (2007). *Making Globalization Work*. New York, NY: W. W. Norton & Co.

Times Higher Education Rankings (THE). (2016). World University Rankings. Retrieved June 1, 2016, from www.timeshighereducation.com/world-university-rankings.

Trow, M., & Burrage, M. (2010). *Twentieth-Century Higher Education: Elite to Mass to Universal*. Baltimore, MD: The Johns Hopkins University Press.

UNESCO Institute for Statistics. (2015). The First Stop for Education Data. Retrieved June 1, 2016, from www.uis.UNESCO Institute for Statistcs.org/Education/Pages/default.aspx.

United States Census Bureau. (2014). Current Population Estimates. Washington, DC. Retrieved June 1, 2016, from www.census.gov/topics/population/data.html.

United States Bureau of Labor Statistics. (2015). "Employment projections." Retrieved June 1, 2016, from www.bls.gov/emp/ep_chart_001.htm.

Wildavsky, B. (2012). *The Great Brain Race: How Global Universities Are Reshaping the World*. Princeton, NJ: Princeton University Press.

Wooley, S. (2013). "Constantly connected: The impact of social media and the advancement in technology on the study abroad experience." *Elo Journal of Undergraduate Research in Communications*, 4(2): 4/4.

Wong, T. (2015). "China's gaokao: High stakes for national exam." *BBC*. Retrieved June 1, 2016, from www.bbc.com/news/world-asia-china-33059635.

World Bank. (2015). World DataBank. Retrieved June 1, 2016, from http://databank.worldbank.org/data/home.aspx.

Yergin, D., & Stanislaw, J. (2008). *The Commanding Heights: The Battle between Government and the Marketplace*. New York: Simon and Schuster.

# 5

# NEXT-GENERATION CHALLENGES FOR LIBERAL EDUCATION

*Jesse H. Lytle and Daniel H. Weiss*

## Introduction

In January 2014 President Barack Obama visited a General Electric plant in Waukesha, Wisconsin. In a speech to the assembled workers at the gas engines facility, he suggested, "folks can make a lot more, potentially, with skilled manufacturing or the trades than they might with an art history degree." While the President went on to qualify his tongue-in-cheek comment, allowing that he did in fact "love art history," he was only the latest public figure to portray the liberal arts as an ineffectual way to prepare oneself for economic advancement and a useful role in society.

The popular media sometimes describe the liberal arts as intellectual navel gazing. To be fair, the work undertaken in a liberal arts classroom sometimes does seem a world away from the pressing demands of the day. When that narrative is spiced with anecdotes like the near closing of Sweet Briar College or stories of unemployed graduates with crushing student debt, one might be forgiven for wondering whether the liberal arts are fated for oblivion.

Simultaneously, though, the flow of students into leading liberal arts colleges and universities in the U.S. shows no signs of abating, while countless institutions around the world seek to assimilate the western liberal arts tradition into their local curricula. Clearly, there is still healthy demand for liberal education and a host of institutions eager to meet it.

The arguments in support of liberal arts education in the United States were first mustered by the nation's founders who believed deeply in the value of an educated citizenry for both personal well-being and an enlightened democracy. As John Adams wrote, "Laws for the liberal education of youth, especially of the lower class of people, are so extremely wise and useful, that, to a humane and generous mind, no expense for this purpose would be thought extravagant." It was through their inspiration that a national movement, now into its third century, created the most extensive and comprehensive system of higher education that the world has known. This system was dedicated foremost to advancing as widely as possible the benefits of a liberal education.

Yet, liberal arts education, an approach built on lofty ideals, has never been free from the criticisms of pragmatic Americans. Idealization of the "self-made man" extends as far back, somewhat paradoxically, as the hunger to build a nation of robust political and economic systems that serve as context for individual liberties. Since its colonial roots, American higher education has been asked to inhabit this paradox by serving simultaneously as a conservative force—a contributor to social order and economic organization—and as a liberating one—a vehicle for individual self-determination and mobility.

The colleges and universities that have subscribed to the intellectual and pedagogical tenets of liberal education have throughout their existences lived out fundamental tensions rooted in that paradox, for example reconciling the competing goals of broad access versus selectivity and excellence, or instrumental learning versus learning for learning's sake. With the benefit of hindsight, one might conclude that these tensions have ultimately been creative ones, resulting in the reality that today's leading liberal arts colleges and universities are significantly overrepresented among the most sought-after and prestigious institutions of learning in the world, whose graduates go on to lead lives of personal and material satisfaction and consequence.

Such retrospective validations of the liberal arts model should reasonably inspire confidence in its adaptability and the institutional strength of the colleges and universities that have evolved through centuries of thoughtful, incremental changes. This is not to suggest, however, that current criticisms are entirely unfounded or that the endurance of the liberal arts is guaranteed. In the wake of the Great Recession, the American system of higher education has seen significant economic, social, and technological change, which has created a "new normal," with a next generation of challenges to sustaining the liberal arts project.

This confluence of pressures on the liberal arts sector of higher education includes:

- The business model—a problem of cost and affordability—that relies on ever-escalating fees that are mediated by an opaque pricing system.
- The transformational impact of technology on every aspect of the enterprise, from research and teaching to student life, communications, and management.
- A demographic shift in the United States, which will soon result in a majority non-white population of high school graduates, many of them representing the first generation in their families to attend college.
- Expanding models of knowledge and the emerging emphasis on design rather than mastery.

- New models of community that embrace both diversity and inclusivity.
- Increasing consensus about the need for reinvigoration of civic and moral life.
- Rising public skepticism about the liberal arts, which might be summed up by Obama's implicit criticism in Waukesha: why should one spend so much for a liberal arts degree when it doesn't obviously lead to a good job?

Ultimately, these disparate pressures may be grouped into three categories of challenges: *economics*, *value*, and *community*. The *economic* challenges revolve around how the liberal arts' resource-intensive educational model can remain an affordable option for students. Questions around *value* relate to the real and perceived benefits of a liberal education to students and to society. Finally, changes in society at large stress the intentional *community* that is a foundation of the liberal arts model.

Because higher education is currently undergoing dramatic change, and because we know that liberal education remains a highly effective model, these pressures offer colleges and universities the chance to change with the times and to improve the value of the educational experience. This will benefit not just students and the institutions at which they work; it will benefit a world that has been bettered by liberal education since its emergence as a formalized approach to learning centuries ago.

Before we proceed farther, it is helpful to distinguish between "liberal education" and "liberal arts colleges." Liberal education is often associated (if not synonymous) with liberal arts colleges: that is, an institution that in the mind's eye sits amid rolling hills aglow with autumn leaves, where colonial spires pierce frosty air and stone buildings surround a central campus green. And that's certainly a place, a setting, where liberal education has long been provided. But today one can get a liberal education almost anywhere. Indeed, given all the "honors colleges" at our state universities, to say nothing of new takes on the liberal arts at universities around the globe, liberal education now happens in places where it probably never snows on the roofs of campus buildings, and institutional histories are recorded in years rather than centuries.

## Economics

Wherever liberal education is practiced, whether on our colonial-spired campus, at an honors college, or even mediated by a technological interface (at least in part—more on that below), it generally carries some consistent economic baggage stemming from its aims and pedagogy.

*Scale*: Liberal arts education, at its core, is labor intensive and resists economies of scale. It relies on dialogic exchange, intensive mentoring, challenging others' ideas, and having one's own ideas challenged. As such, liberal education requires substantial personal interaction, translating into low student/faculty ratios and small groups learning together. Even when conducted among sizable populations, good educational practice creates pressure toward smaller learning communities, whether it's a discussion section of a large lecture class or a residential college nestled within a sprawling university campus.

*Academic breadth*: A full liberal education requires exposure to a broad range of disciplines across the arts, humanities, social sciences, and natural sciences. Not only are faculties constructed to engage with relatively small groups of students, but they must represent a broad range of expertise, and, further, they require an expensive infrastructure of spaces and tools: labs, practice rooms, studios, computers, instrumentation, libraries, academic support services, and more. The degree to which the cost of these resources can be moderated by scale is limited.

*Educating the whole person*: A liberally educated individual is not just a well-developed intellect on legs, but rather a *whole person* who has productively engaged issues of character, morality, community, identity, and perhaps spirituality. Such development fruitfully occurs within the classroom but perhaps even more so in co-curricular and extracurricular venues that, too, come with a price. These include student affairs and support services, residential programs, campus organizations, and the like. One could argue about how essential any one of these specific components might be, but they have been fully embraced by institutions and students alike and are thus 'table stakes' in the educational marketplace in which liberal arts institutions compete.

*On-site learning*: Between the physical resources that undergird the curriculum and the human dimensions of liberal education that are facilitated by physical gathering, the "disruptive innovation" promised by MOOCs and other technological advances has yet to challenge the traditional form of liberal education and appears unlikely to do so. While one might anticipate further technological leaps that could diminish the need for physical infrastructure, for now it's difficult to imagine maintaining the integrity and richness of a chemistry lab, collaborating on a sculpture, ushering rats through a maze, or learning to live with someone different than you via technological mediation.

With these cost pillars fairly securely in place, liberal education is, and will likely remain, an expensive enterprise. Yet, at the same time, we all recognize that continued cost growth, an inevitable byproduct of this educational model—and with it the associated growth in tuition—is not sustainable. Although this disconnect between cost and price may seem intractable, it is the market that ultimately determines the optimal relationship among costs, pricing, and perceived value. Hence colleges, like other more commercial enterprises, must compete in the marketplace on the basis of perceived value. As a result, they must be sensitive to the vicissitudes of the market and be ready to adjust prices, and therefore costs, accordingly. Put differently, if a group of selective liberal arts colleges began to experience declining applications or other existential threats they would attempt to restore the right market balance, either through cost reductions, revenue increases, or some combination. If we assume the fundamental economic law of supply and demand is at work in higher education, and there is no reason to believe otherwise, colleges are investing in their institutions and passing these costs on to their students because the market values the quality of education that is being provided. If they didn't, then colleges would, en masse, continue to seek a better balance between costs and perceived value.

What is new for higher education, though, in the wake of the Great Recession, is revenue constraint. For the first time in modern history, the cost of tuition at many selective colleges and universities now exceeds the median US household income. There is no indication that family income will keep pace with liberal education's cost structure on its own. Threatened with price-point saturation, institutions will be unable to continue to raise tuition well in excess of inflation as they have done in the past. Meanwhile, other revenue sources are unlikely to fill the gap: weakened financial markets depress endowment returns; philanthropy continues but donors face the same economic constraints; and public subsidies and grants are also on the wane.

In this context, maintaining an optimized balance of costs and value—in dynamic tension with competitors and consumers—is the next-generation challenge for liberal arts institutions. Colleges and universities will need disciplined planning and budgeting, of course, but they will also require the full good-faith engagement of their shared governance models so that colleges can work across traditional organizational boundaries in order to pursue mission-optimizing innovations and adaptations.

## Value

Given the cost structures above, liberal education is unlikely to compete on price with other forms of higher education. One can therefore expect only heightened scrutiny of the value that liberal education can deliver. The evidence of the market's interest in understanding the value proposition of liberal education is abundant enough in the industry of college rankings and other imputed arbiters of quality, eagerly gobbled up by the public. As skeptical as educators generally are about the merits of college rankings and rating systems, in aggregate they offer a rich study in the value proposition of liberal education as viewed by the marketplace. Perhaps more accurately, they are a study in how elusive and contested its "value" remains, despite significant efforts to define and measure it.

At its most superficial level, the instrumental value of liberal education is evident and can theoretically be measured. We know, for example, that in aggregate college graduates earn more over their lifetimes than peers who do not hold college degrees. Recent efforts have been made to calculate graduates' salary differentials among individual institutions, although close inspection reveals unreliable data. Similarly, measures of graduates' aggregate debt load are available, but imperfect since many students and families choose different strategies to finance education. Still, what matters is that a straight financial "return-on-investment" measure has currency in the marketplace as a representation of the value of liberal education.

Setting aside the assumption that dollar earnings are a meaningful educational outcome, one can also find data on graduates' professional milestones: access to graduate and professional schools, fellowships and prizes, or resulting status as PhDs, MDs, or CEOs. College graduates' unemployment rate is significantly lower than those with only a high school diploma. Among the most selective institutions in the country, which overwhelmingly offer undergraduate programs centered on the liberal arts, one of the most striking differentiators between themselves as a cohort and less selective institutions is the extent to which their graduates who go on to post-baccalaureate education out-earn the graduates of all other market segments (Zemsky et al., 1997). One could reasonably conclude that a primary competitive advantage of highly selective institutions is the access they provide to elite post-baccalaureate options. Indeed, one might wonder how many fewer families would be willing to accept the steep tuitions of selective liberal arts institutions if the promise of an Ivy League law, business, or medical degree were not gleaming on the horizon.

As with any outcome data along these lines, it is hard to draw sound conclusions about the effects of undergraduate education itself; reliable data is hard to come by, and one can never be sure how much to attribute to individuals who already carry certain talents and predispositions versus the formative impact of an educational experience. One could attempt to discern proxies for the benefits delivered by education: that someone earning a high salary likely carries a set of attributes—honed, one could speculate, by a liberal education—that are valued in the labor market, or that a physician probably received a solid undergraduate pre-med course of instruction. One might also speculate about the social value generated by such individuals' career achievements. Even if we accept such speculation as probable, is professional advancement the full extent of the benefit of their educations?

At this point it bears returning to liberal education's history. It is an interesting characteristic of higher education in America that its development and intended core purpose were first envisioned by the founders who believed deeply that a functioning democracy and productive society depended fundamentally on an educated citizenry. It was primarily for this reason that their inspiration resulted in the dramatic proliferation of American colleges in the first decades of the 19th century. These pioneering institutions shared a belief that what was needed most to build the new nation was not vocational training but a grounding in liberal arts and sciences so that citizens could acquire the critical thinking necessary for the professions and the social leadership skills necessary to build democratic communities and the social order.

This educational vision encompasses, then and now, more than a curricular inventory and more than a set of concrete professional outcomes for students. Liberal education is the process whereby one acquires critical skills, accumulates knowledge, and learns how to navigate individually and socially in a complex and rapidly changing world. Liberal education is generally regarded as an approach that requires students to gather, analyze, and synthesize information in myriad ways that are appropriate to vast and varying areas of study. In so doing, they acquire diverse problem-solving skills in addition to specific knowledge, such that long after facts have faded from memory the strategies developed in the course of mastering material are appreciated in their own right as tools for navigating the long voyage of life.

The crucial question concerns whether those purposes are relevant to our needs today. If college is preparation for life, for what kind of life are we preparing students? When seen in retrospect, the historical exigencies are clear. But what is the contemporary need—and value—of an approach that was developed when our nation was in its infancy and preoccupied with other concerns than those of our day, including economic prosperity and technological prowess?

What does it mean to be liberally educated? What kind of skills, knowledge, and capacities do we expect of students pursuing a liberal education? Wherever it is practiced, the educational experience might be described in terms of six core elements:

*Foundational skills*: This involves the capacity to read, think carefully and critically, analyze data, and structure an argument; synthesize information in order to draw conclusions; and then communicate effectively, both verbally and in writing.

*The question of curriculum*: What should an educated person actually know? This question has been debated within and across our institutions of higher learning since the founding of Harvard and William & Mary in the 17th century. To be sure, there are various approaches that have proven enormously effective, ranging from great books programs, such as those at St. John's or the University of Chicago, to the "open curriculum" practiced at Brown and others since the late 1960s. The assumption among most liberal arts institutions is that study in any *particular* field is of no more importance—and, arguably, is less important—than being exposed to, and being expected to engage with, a wide *range* of issues and topics that define what it means to be human and that reflect the culture and character of the times. Indeed, the *question* of what is worth knowing, and the underlying arguments mustered in favor of various answers are of greater importance than any particular point of view.

*Critical literacies*: Under this system, such broad exposure to fields of knowledge is inextricably linked to the process of study that diverse fields demand. Thucydides? Kant? Lady Gaga? The "what" of content—whether the philosophical foundations of our civilization or pop cultural phenomena that give insight into contemporary values and concerns—melds with the "how" it is studied. Known as "critical literacies," these are the nexus between what is knowable and how we develop and use the skills by which we come to know: the methodologies, modalities, analysis, and synthesis that provide ways of knowing. Command of this vital, distinctive, and life-enriching capacity requires familiarity with concepts and, ideally, various approaches and kinds of literacies, which comes only from studying a diversity of subjects.

*Ethical reasoning and social responsibility*: For students to engage in a life of discovery and purpose, they must examine how to make their own moral judgments while learning about the ethical reasoning of others, both as individuals and in community. How do communities constitute values, meaning, religion, politics, ideology? What is the role of art and humanities in developing a narrative imagination of how one might live, make ethical decisions, or cultivate community? What are models of social leadership to develop the common good? Liberal education is, by its very definition, teaching persons the responsibilities—both socially and individually—of protecting, preserving, and expanding freedom.

*Thinking, adapting, navigating*: If the ultimate purpose of a liberal education is to provide graduates with the capacity to lead full, rewarding, and enriching lives, they must know how to adapt to an ever-changing environment. Because the differences across areas of study and the means by which we study them are real and demand different approaches, students inevitably acquire diverse skills as they solve problems across a variety of fields. Ultimately, no educational approach is more true to life.

*Collaborating, connecting, working in teams*: Because liberal education has always focused on individuals in community, and its mission has been defined both in social and individual terms, it has always implied that education is about shaping collaborative as well as individual skills. Because of the broad-based education across a wide variety of fields, liberal education has always enabled students to connect fields of knowledge among the domains, often focused on specific problems, new designs, or cultural performances. But the current environment makes explicit the need to educate people who know how to make connections in multiple ways through knowledge, ethical reasoning, and social relations and among diverse cultural forms. The ability to collaborate with diverse teams in a society or globally is sorely needed today and among the most enduring benefits of a liberal education.

We suspect that educators, students, and observers alike will find some resonance with the inventory above. Hints of it could probably be found in any college's marketing materials as it seeks to explain its virtues to its various audiences. That the elements above are not the ubiquitous foundation of college ratings is striking, and could be explained in at least two ways. One explanation is that the educational elements that institutions believe to be of high value are not, in fact, what the market understands to be of high value, and it's simply a happy coincidence that students derive the benefits they are seeking by going through the course of study that a college prefers to deliver en route to a credential. There is perhaps some awkward truth behind this for some students whose academic experiences are (at least superficially) unrelated to their careers and later lives: the oft-invoked art history degree. But it is also the nature of educational research that we can never empirically know the "treatment effect" of someone's college education, since there are no "control groups" for students living their lives.

Indeed, this speaks to the other explanation about why the core elements of liberal education do not dominate college rating schemes: many elements of the liberal arts are hard to assess objectively (let alone quantify), the rest impossible. The raters and rankers surely have not—if they've tried—figured it out. To be fair, educators have not done much better, if the goal is to identify clear, digestible measures that reveal the intellectual, personal, and social benefits of a liberal education. As with career outcomes, proxies abound: graduates' GRE scores, voting records, volunteering patterns, and the like. Scholarship like *Academically Adrift* (Arum & Roksa, 2010) offers data-rich glimpses into undergraduate learning, not always with flattering results. But how can we really discern how many diverse habits of mind, for example, a student has developed and the extent to which their liberal education aided that development?

Perhaps the most significant effort to understand the effect of liberal education on students can be found in the flourishing assessment movement, which is now thoroughly embedded in accreditation processes and as a result is being increasingly institutionalized. The rationale driving assessment is clear—colleges and universities should know how well they are delivering on their educational promises and share that information with those who can use it—but whether the movement is bearing fruit commensurate with its energy is broadly contested. Some progress is evident in institutional assessment of local "student learning goals" particularly within discrete subject areas or defined skill sets. But for institutions that place a premium on less tangible elements of liberal education—take, for example, *adaptability*, or *learning to learn*—current assessment techniques seem wholly insufficient to the challenge. Assessing the character and causality of intellectual traits and dispositions is necessarily subjective, while fruits of good education may not ripen until well into a graduate's later life. Whether the assessment data that is being amassed across higher education can be made compelling to the marketplace remains an open question.

So, where does that leave today's colleges and universities that have embraced the ambitious and important tenets of liberal education, whose educational model is fundamentally expensive, and whose audiences increasingly crave assurances of value that are difficult to articulate? We return to our understanding of the place of a liberal arts institution in what is, ultimately, a competitive market.

In the higher education marketplace, it is clear that outcomes matter, and that the nuances of liberal education are difficult to convey to consumeristic audiences. On the other hand, a quick perusal of the college ratings reveals that inputs matter, too. Why should this be? Isn't education about students' journeys from wherever they began to somewhere more developed, more prepared, more enlightened?

As researchers from the University of Pennsylvania's Institute for Research on Higher Education first argued, the higher education marketplace is more usefully understood through a lens of student types than through institutional types. In matters of college choice, student segments of the market, in aggregate, do not meaningfully consider categories like "big" or "small," "public" or "private," "liberal arts" or "other." Rather, data reveal that students of certain characteristics—say, students who are likely to graduate within five years of matriculation—tend to seek out certain sets of schools that despite differences in structure or character tend to produce certain sets of outcomes: their students tend to graduate within a certain timeframe, tend to go on to advanced degrees at a certain rate, and the like (NCPI, 2001). Through this framework one can understand why UC Berkeley (large, public, comprehensive, urban, west coast) would compete for students with Haverford College (small, private, liberal arts, suburban, east coast) more than the University of Nevada, Reno, with which it shares many more superficial characteristics. In that sense, student "inputs" define the market.

Complementary economic research offers a perspective on why this should be. We can understand a student as both an educational consumer and a contributor to the quality of peers' educations (Winston & Zimmerman, 2003). As economist Gordon Winston writes, "students educate students so the school that wants to produce high quality education will have to enroll high-quality students, not to act as passive buyers of the school's educational services, but as factors of its production" (Winston, 2003). In Winston's formulation, in order to attract the students an institution wants, it must show evidence of already having enrolled other desirable students. This offers an economic explanation for why, counterintuitively, colleges are willing to subsidize the attendance of many students while turning away others who are willing to pay full price. It also explains why the financial investments that colleges make to attract and retain students, not just by funding educational programs but also financial aid or even amenities—the infamous climbing wall—are rational, competitive decisions that in fact support educational quality and mission fulfillment. By extension, financial wherewithal (another commonly tracked "input") allows institutions to attract the students they want, secures them stronger market positions, and moves them toward the head of the class in rankings and ratings en route to further fulfillment of their missions.

The key lesson is that liberal arts institutions are competing against diverse colleges and universities—but for the same cohorts of students. An expensive, selective liberal arts college may well compete against an expensive, selective technology school, or conservatory, each institution seeking capable 18–22 year-olds, competing on the basis of such factors as campus life or access to elite advanced degrees. Meanwhile, a lower-cost, open enrollment liberal arts college might compete against a community college or comprehensive university, and would need to provide local students of many ages convenience, a good price, and direct links to the labor market. It is in the context of intra-segment competition that the establishment and communication of a value proposition matters most.

Colleges, liberal arts or other, cannot assume that potential students immediately see value in their distinctive approach to education or the outcomes they are likely to provide. This uncertainty presents two institutional imperatives. First, there is the technical matter of effective marketing and communications—a challenge that should not be understated given the notorious difficulty of explaining the liberal arts to a short-attention-span public, further problematized by academia's traditional resistance toward "corporate" practices. Signs of institutions' increasing market savvy and willingness to take risks to appeal to potential students are everywhere, though, from billboards to YouTube and Twitter. Outcomes matter to the market; so too do inputs. In choosing a college, does the market also need to understand what happens in the educational experience itself, or will "fit," "prestige," and an inventory of lifestyle choices perhaps suffice? These sorts of divergent perspectives on liberal education's real value proposition represent fault lines among devoted educators, savvy marketers, and increasingly consumeristic students and families. In the end, though, it's not clear that any of these perspectives are necessarily incongruous: a college education is arguably "all of the above."

The second imperative for colleges around value is the adaptive challenge of maintaining alignment between educational programs and the needs of students and society at large. Despite old saws about the liberal arts' anachronism—with catalogs that still include the likes of Aristotle, Chaucer, and Marx—curricular evolution within liberal education has of course been a constant. New disciplines, increasing interdisciplinarity, and pragmatic skill-building join time-proven areas of study to define a contemporary liberal education. But it is also certainly the case that the evolution of venerable academic institutions is not as fast as in many other market-dependent industries. Academic governance and the tenure model serve as conservative forces to the extent they allow for only incremental change and often operate in separate silos from an institution's "market sensors," located in places like admissions and career services. These very same plodding academic governance structures also, arguably, serve to preserve educational quality, integrity, and values.

The next-generation challenge is whether liberal arts institutions will develop and acculturate adequate sensory capabilities to understand the evolving needs of their rapidly changing markets, and whether they can innovate fast enough to respond with compelling educational experiences that lead to the outcomes that students, families, graduate and professional schools, and employers are seeking.

## Community

The third and final defining challenge for liberal education is that of sustaining an intentional intellectual community as a productive learning environment in the face of societal change. There are two notable headwinds. First, the demography of college communities is a world away—literally, in the case of schools at the forefront of globalized education—from where it was a generation or two ago. Daily life on campus, though, suggests that there is much yet to be done before the premise of diversity fulfills the promise of genuinely inclusive learning communities. The second headwind centers on mounting tensions around the free and open exchange of ideas.

One of the great triumphs of the last half-century has been the diversification of all segments of higher education. While this work is still very much underway, by any measure student bodies look little like they have in the past. Resulting from a confluence of new public policies, institutional efforts, and social change, higher education is far more open to students of different ethnicities, religions, nationalities, gender identities, abilities, and socioeconomic status than it once was. The professoriate, as a downstream function of the student body, has also diversified significantly, with good reason to think that trends toward pluralism will continue apace.

But expansion of access to higher education has seldom come easily for institutions or for new kinds of students. From women in the early days of coeducation, to Jews black-balled at Ivy League institutions, to the Civil Rights movement and the subsequent struggle over affirmative action, grand notions of social inclusion have felt the friction burn when they've arrived on campus.

A college campus is, after all, an intentional community where students and others are convened around a set of common goals: namely learning together and from each other. Difference is ostensibly to be celebrated, but there is also a fundamental need for normative values and behaviors that provide a community its connective tissue. Not surprisingly, as new identities, cultures, beliefs, and learning objectives join the mix, those normative assumptions are not always shared.

In 2012, in the wake of high profile incidents of perceived racial injustice— from Sanford, Florida to Ferguson, Missouri—the Black Lives Matter movement began to sweep across the nation. What emerged as the next generation of civil rights activism in America found resonance among college students and led to a fresh set of critiques of the academy. Through civil disobedience and organized advocacy, students mobilized around a set of causes that echoed many themes of 1960s but with new salience. Fueled by a social-media-enabled solidarity and visibility, students at countless colleges and universities issued sets of demands to institutional leadership, seeking apologies for perceived mistreatment, louder voices in decision-making, increased recruitment of students and faculty of color, new support for marginalized students, sensitivity trainings for various community members, and more. While local circumstances varied, the emergent theme was that even though the door to higher education was open to many different people, the lived experience on campus remained unsatisfactory for many community members. For communities long committed to equity and social justice, these failures have been painful realizations on all sides.

In today's new era of campus diversity, even the most well-intentioned communities are encountering deep discomfort as tensions new and age-old are brought to the fore. Conflicts around race, ethnicity, and class, while long a part of the American lexicon, continue to be felt poignantly on campus with contemporary inflections. Aggressive recruitment and financial aid has allowed more low-income students to gain admission, only for them to find that they struggle with college's hidden costs, from books to social life to commuting. Effective treatments for mental illness and learning disabilities propel more students toward higher education, but not all colleges are equipped to provide adequate support. The changes required to meet these challenges are significant, and range from the elusive—for example the personal engagement required by all community members to build bridges across what can feel like chasms of difference—to the pragmatic—like providing adequate support systems for different student populations.

Many students describe a sense of alienation on campuses that seem foreign, where they do not feel respected, or where they do not encounter a climate that facilitates their success. This contributes to the second headwind facing the intentional community: the need to reconcile the sense of safety, respect, and dignity that allows individuals to reap fully the benefits of a learning community, with the unconstrained academic search for truth. To wit, frequent demands from students include "safe spaces" and stronger institutional stances against hate speech or insensitive speech. Such demands are problematic for colleges and universities because they quickly come into tension with the free and open exchange of ideas.

This problem is increasingly evident across the country as committed educators run afoul of changing standards on a regular basis. It has led to controversy around provocative language, trigger warnings, speech codes, and accusations of "thought policing." Controversial campus speakers have not just been protested, but in some cases disinvited at the urging of students, prompting criticisms that today's students are intolerant of dissenting views. On campuses that still tend to lean toward the left, unwillingness to hear conservative views has been thought to have a chilling effect on the open inquiry the academy is supposed to represent. Faculty, too, have not been spared, as some who have spoken out on controversial issues have drawn censure. Such conflicts have been exacerbated by social media, which can be inflammatory in its rapid dissemination of information to broad audiences, opening individuals and institutions up to heightened scrutiny and new reputational risks.

The problem can't simply be attributed to arrogant students or misguided educators. Beneath these conflicts are fundamental questions about which there is not yet consensus: do students have the right not to be offended? Do faculty members have the right to say anything in the name of academic freedom? How do we foster empathy if we don't disagree with others or challenge stereotypes? If education fundamentally rests on creating some level of discomfort in learners that leads to new thinking, how does a community find a productive discomfort that works for everyone?

This is a next-generation problem on which many liberal arts institutions are beginning to reflect and experiment. Some communities are seeking more direct engagement from the beginning, starting with orientation processes that develop an intentional framework through which new students understand their role in the academic enterprise. How does one receive views different from one's own?

How does one address conflict? Simultaneously, faculty are engaging in work to prepare themselves for the different experiences and needs that diverse students are bringing to their classrooms. This project is fostering fresh collaboration on campuses as student affairs professionals—who have long been on the front lines of demographic changes—are increasingly critical to helping members of the campus community negotiate difference and turn discomfort into learning opportunities. Generations of diverse alumni, too, have much to add about the roots and long-term consequences of today's lived tensions on campus. The stakes are high as colleges and universities negotiate how to support their diverse students without backing away from their fundamental commitment to the unfettered search for truth.

## Conclusion

In sum, liberal education's next-generation challenges around economics, value, and community are not categorically new. But the fundamental pressures around cost structure, demography, technology, and culture are now such that technical changes are likely insufficient to provide long-term sustainability of their missions. The kind of adaptive change that will maintain fiscal equilibrium, alignment with the market, and inclusive communities will require more organizational nimbleness than many colleges are used to. Strict adherence to command-and-control hierarchies built around functional silos can keep institutions from bringing to bear the organizational capacity spread across the faculty, student support areas, market-attuned revenue arms, back office functions, external supporters, and the students themselves. Colleges and universities that harness the distributed intelligence and energy of their communities will be well positioned to meet these challenges and shape what liberal education looks like for generations to come.

## References

Arum, R., and Roksa, J. (2010). *Academically Adrift: Limited Learning on College Campuses.* Chicago: University of Chicago Press.

National Center on Postsecondary Improvement (NCPI). (2001, March/April). "Resurveying the terrain: Refining the taxonomy for the postsecondary market. *Change.* Retrieved June 1, 2016, from www.thelearningalliance.info/Docs/Jun2003/DOC-2003 Jun18.1055949966.pdf.

Winston, G. (2003, January). "Toward a theory of tuition: Prices, peer wages, and competition in higher education." Retrieved June 1, 2016, from http://sites.williams.edu/wpehe/files/2011/06/DP-65.pdf.

Winston, G. and Zimmerman, D. (2003, January). "Peer effects in higher education." Retrieved June 1, 2016, from http://sites.williams.edu/wpehe/files/2011/06/DP-64.pdf.

Zemsky, R., Shaman, S., and Ianozzi, M. (1997, November/December). In Search of Strategic Perspective: A Tool for Mapping the Market in Postsecondary Education. *Change.* Retrieved June 1, 2016, from www.thelearningalliance.info/Docs/Jun2003/DOC-2003 Jun18.1055951725.pdf.

## PART II

# Liberal Arts around the World

# 6

# PRÉCIS OF A GLOBAL LIBERAL EDUCATION PHENOMENON

## The Empirical Story

*Kara A. Godwin*

Today there is little doubt that interest in liberal education has extended beyond the United States. This book is excellent evidence of rising programs and percolating discourse about liberal education in places where it has rarely existed before. Further illustrations of this global phenomenon are apparent at international conferences, in country-specific case studies, and through increased public and private funding for liberal and general education programs (outside the U.S.), and in China and Hong Kong, through national policies that mandate elements of liberal education be implemented across tertiary systems. New and renewed innovations in liberal education are disrupting traditional university systems and understanding about higher education. It is an exciting time.

What has been lacking, however, is a comprehensive understanding of liberal education's global contours. That is, a broad and empirical portrait of this growing trend. Where does liberal education exist around the world and how might its emergence differ from region to region? What can be gleaned about liberal education's contemporary chronological development that informs our understanding of its function and future? In what format are liberal arts initiatives evolving? What are the similar and diverging characteristics of programs and institutions? What are the rationales for developing new programs? Why is there growing global interest in liberal education and why now? The discussion that follows addresses these questions. It offers a global profile—a foundation—on which policy makers, institutional leaders, and scholars might situate individual liberal education initiatives. Throughout, this story raises challenging questions about the meaning of the data, and in conclusion, critical considerations for liberal education's impact on access and equity, cultural hegemony, and neoliberal tendencies worldwide.

## A Phenomenon and a Global Trend

The increasing global interest in liberal education is a striking phenomenon because the liberal approach to undergraduate education (an overarching educational philosophy as well as a curricular model) is a stark contrast to traditional postsecondary frameworks in much of the world. Excluding the U.S., higher education has been organized around professional studies for centuries. A utilitarian, human capital philosophy defines most tertiary systems worldwide. Societies predominately view higher education's purpose as a means for creating a labor force, a source for staffing needed positions in industry, health care, schools, and public services. Students, as a result, participate in curricula focused almost exclusively on their specific field of study. In contrast to liberal education, this approach to postsecondary training is commonly called "specialized," "career-focused," or "vocational," and it is the global norm.

Liberal education, however, is focused on a broad foundation of knowledge rather than a specific profession. Its central tenet is to empower learners with a mind and skill set that enables them to be critical members of society prepared to address complexity, diversity, and change (Association of American Colleges & Universities; Godwin, 2013). Despite many variations and debates about the definition of liberal education, its essence depends on three components. First, liberal education is multidisciplinary. It provides broad exposure to the arts, humanities, social sciences, natural sciences, and increasingly, STEM fields (ideally, interrelating disciplinary ways of knowing and questioning). Second, liberal education has a "general education" component. That is, within a given program, the broad curriculum approach is required of all or most students. Finally, it strives to engender elemental skills that include critical thinking, problem-solving, analysis, communication, global citizenship, quantitative and qualitative literacy, and/or a sense of social responsibility.

Despite historical roots in Greek, Chinese, Indian, and Egyptian traditions (Godwin & Altbach, 2016), contemporary liberal education is recognized as a distinctly American construct (Becker, 2003; Nussbaum 1997, 2004; Rothblatt, 2003). The U.S. is regularly regarded as liberal education's "home" not only for its designated liberal arts colleges, but also because general education (requirements that all or most students must take courses from a variety of disciplines) is common practice across the majority of public and private institutions. Compared to tertiary systems in other countries, even state institutions in the U.S. incorporate elements of a liberal education philosophy. Among other characteristics, this makes American higher education an anomaly among systems worldwide.

With this contrast in mind, the discussion below illustrates that the global liberal education phenomenon is more than a coincidence of experimental programs. For two reasons, it is a small but important international trend. First, the emerging geographic expanse of liberal education is vast. Programs can now be found in every region of the world, a declaration that could not be made just a few decades ago. Second, the growing numbers of liberal education initiatives is contemporary.

As the chronological data illustrate, more than half of the world's liberal arts initiatives (excluding the U.S.) were founded since 1990 (Godwin, 2013).

## Where, When, and How (In What Format) Is Liberal Education Emerging Globally?

The international emergence of liberal education was first identified as a trend based on analysis of the Global Liberal Education Inventory (GLEI), a worldwide database of liberal education initiatives and their defining characteristics. Among other data, the inventory includes program location, founding date, public/private status, language of instruction, number of students and faculty, institutional partnerships, accreditation, religious affiliations, and gender (all-male or all-female institutions, gender-segregated programs, etc.). While a forthcoming and more comprehensive publication provides deeper regional analysis, this discussion is a brief overview of predominately global data. When the GLEI is analyzed by individual country, the results are more nuanced and reveal significant differences in liberal education between regions and between national tertiary systems.

Excluding the U.S., in 2013 there were 183 liberal education programs dispersed across 58 countries.[1] Figure 6.1 illustrates the regional distribution of liberal education programs excluding the United States. Figure 6.2 shows the worldwide distribution of liberal education including the 365 liberal education or "Arts and Science" institutions (the majority commonly known as "liberal

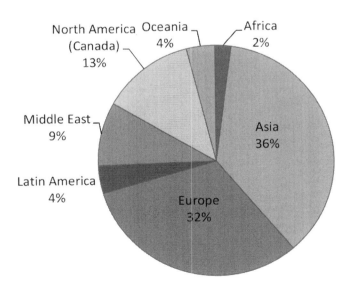

**FIGURE 6.1** Distribution of liberal education as a percent of all programs worldwide excluding the United States. Based on analysis and calculations from the Global Liberal Education Inventory.

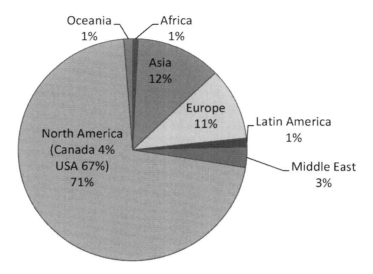

**FIGURE 6.2** Distribution of liberal education as a percent of all liberal arts programs worldwide including the United States. Calculations for the U.S. were based on 365 liberal education or "Arts and Science" institutions (the majority commonly known as "liberal arts colleges") as reported by the U.S. Carnegie Foundation for the Advancement of Teaching (2010). Actual number of U.S. programs is much greater but not easily identified. All other data is based on analysis and calculations from the Global Liberal Education Inventory.

arts colleges") in the U.S. as classified by the Carnegie Foundation for the Advancement of Teaching (2010). (It is important to recognize that there are more than 365 liberal education programs in the U.S. However, because most programs are embedded in research universities, they are difficult to identify. The actual share of U.S. liberal education programs worldwide is much higher than indicated in Figure 6.2.)

Notably, there are a few countries that have a "substantial" liberal education presence, and many countries where there are only one or two liberal education programs. For example, Canada has 21 liberal education programs, more than any other country excluding the U.S. outside of North America, India, the U.K., and Japan have the next highest number of programs (13 or 14 initiatives each). At the upper end of the distribution analysis, only two percent of countries (5 total including the U.S.) have more than 10 liberal education programs. At the lowest end, 45 countries have only one or two GLEI programs each. In sum, the vast majority of GLEI countries, nearly 80 percent of them, have just one to three initiatives in their higher education systems.

Why is this significant? "Crowding at the bottom" of the global distribution dilutes the potential for liberal education to influence the mainstream postsecondary sector more broadly. Because liberal education is a foreign concept in most postsecondary systems, a greater number of programs in one country could increase the reputation and perceived legitimacy of the liberal education philosophy. Especially in places where the government must approve or certify (both public and private) tertiary programs, a larger presence of GLEI initiatives could improve the way policy makers, higher education participants, and the public understand, allocate resources to, and wage political and social support for liberal education. In places like the Netherlands (with six programs), Australia (with seven programs), and the U.K. (with 14 programs), for example, liberal education is gaining enrollment as perceptions improve. Further, the number of liberal education graduates is positively related to the potential impact of this education philosophy on social, political, and cultural conditions—a core impetus for us to care about this phenomenon. A greater concentration of programs could strengthen the chances that the liberal education ethos will be accepted as a legitimate alternative to traditional universities.

## *Brief Regional Summaries*

**Asia.** One of the most surprising results from the 2013 GLEI analysis is that Asia—not Europe—has a stronger presence of liberal education than any region beyond North America. Asia accounts for 36 percent of liberal education programs outside the United States. Three-fourths of the Asian liberal arts programs are in China, India, and Japan, while only a few but important initiatives are in emerging and alternatively developed Bhutan, Afghanistan, and Bangladesh. Central government interest in improving critical thinking and creativity in China is driving liberal education reform that contrasts the country's traditional curriculum. Also in the region, an unprecedented system-wide mandate for liberal education is taking place throughout Hong Kong's public higher education system. General and liberal education initiatives, along with changes to the degree cycles, are being implemented at all Hong Kong public institutions.

**Europe.** In Europe, which accounts for 32 percent of programs outside the United States, liberal education can be loosely distinguished between developments in the western and eastern subregions. In the west, liberal education reforms are often affiliated with the Bologna process and the need to better define the content of first-degree undergraduate education. New programs like those in the Netherlands, for example, were created to diversify higher education and encourage an echelon of excellence in an otherwise egalitarian system. Conversely, liberal education is more closely related to shifts in political power and post-Cold War emerging democracies in eastern states where experiments with new educational philosophies are gaining acceptance. The University of Warsaw's Artes Liberales program and the Collegium of Inter-Faculty Individual Studies are notable examples.

**Middle East and Arab Countries.** The Middle East and Arab countries only account for 9 percent of GLEI initiatives, but attract much attention as an unusual destination for education that encourages critical thinking. In this region, liberal education is commonly called "American-style" education and, from the public's point of view, is often synonymous with quality. Its market success as a naming convention, however, does not reflect the frequent cultural challenges posed by gender segregation and the prominence of religious law. At the same time, the Middle East is home to nine liberal education programs exclusively for women, many of these "guided by the conviction" that their graduates will "play transformative leadership roles in society" (Agarwal & Srinivasan, 2012, p. 69).

**Latin America.** Based on the GLEI, liberal education is comparably less prevalent in Latin America (7 programs or 4 percent of those outside the United States), Africa (4 programs or 2 percent), and Oceania (7 programs or 4 percent). Latin America's liberal education initiatives are often affiliated with the Catholic Church and unlike many of the inventory's programs, none of them use English as their language of instruction (discussed in more detail below). Nonetheless, the region is home to one of the world's most important liberal education experiments. The ProFIS program at Brazil's University of Campinas offers a liberal education curriculum to graduates from some of the country's most underprivileged secondary schools as an entrée to the university that would otherwise be academically unattainable.

**Africa.** While small in number, African programs offer unique postsecondary opportunities in places where higher education is strained by demand and where founders hope the philosophy will impact economic and social development in Kenya, Morocco, Ghana, and Nigeria. Ashesi University in Ghana, for example, has had an innovative and positive impact on perceptions of liberal education in emerging market country contexts.

**Oceania.** In Oceania, Australia is the only country with liberal education initiatives. Unlike most regions where liberal education plays a sub-prominent role within national higher education systems, the top-ranked University of Melbourne has developed a liberal arts undergraduate curriculum. That the University's approach has been nicknamed the "Melbourne Model" and is now emulated by other high-ranking, world-class institutions is a significant development in the global liberal education phenomenon.

**North America.** Finally, because the United States was excluded from the GLEI, Canada is the only country representing North America. Canada has 21 programs, more than any other single country. On the whole, however, it has had little influence on the dialogue and activity around recent global liberal education developments. Canada has a longer history of liberal education than most countries, but only three new liberal arts initiatives have emerged since 1990. Two of these, the U4 League, a consortium of four long-standing liberal education institutions, and Quest University, which delivers a unique curriculum in a diverse academic culture, could set new precedents for liberal education in Canada and more broadly beyond national boarders.

## Chronology

Liberal education's worldwide chronological development is dramatic. Evidence from the GLEI illustrates a distinct increase in liberal education programs and the global distribution of those programs over the last 15 years. With Canada/North America as an exception, since 2000 the number of liberal education programs has grown in every other region. Figure 6.3 illustrates the historical presence of liberal education and the founding of new programs over time. The darkest line represents the number of new programs developed in each time period. The lighter line represents the total (cumulative) number of programs in existence during the same span of years. Figure 6.4 illustrates the chronological growth of liberal education by region.

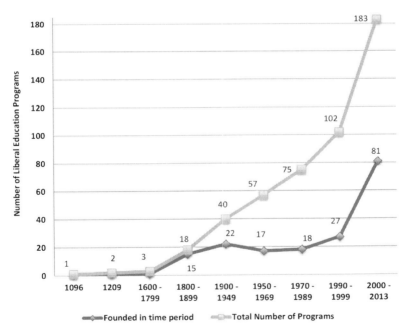

**FIGURE 6.3** Number of liberal education programs founded and cumulative number per time period. Points on the darkest line indicate the number of programs founded in the corresponding span of years. Points on the lighter line indicate the total number of programs in existence for the same period. Note that the year intervals vary and are not consistent for each period. The time periods were created to illustrate the significant changes in liberal education program development based on their chronology. Based on analysis and calculations from the Global Liberal Education Inventory.

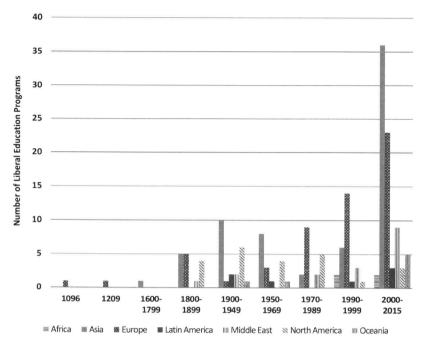

**FIGURE 6.4** Number of liberal education programs found in each region over time (excluding the U.S.). Based on analysis and calculations from the Global Liberal Education Inventory.

Given that the number of higher education providers has increased everywhere in response to swelling demand for postsecondary training (known in the study of higher education as "massification" (Trow, 2006; see also Marginson, 2016), interpretation of the GLEI chronological data should be tempered. However, the stark contrast between liberal education and traditional specialized university curricula as described above makes the global liberal education phenomenon a unique development irrelevant of burgeoning higher education providers. Outside the U.S., liberal education remains an atypical approach to higher education, one that could impact the labor market, politics, and culture differently than conventional university programs. Thus, its chronological development characterizes the increasing interest in liberal education as a distinctly contemporary international trend.

## Location

The GLEI includes data about the geographic location of liberal education programs, that is, whether they reside in rural, small towns (population of 30,000 or less), suburban (metropolitan area directly outside a major city), or urban areas.

This information allows researchers to identify patterns or outliers related to a programs' proximity to rural or metropolitan settings. Like most postsecondary institutions around the world, GLEI programs are located predominately in urban locations. Ninety-two percent of liberal education initiatives are in urban or suburban areas.[2]

When examining liberal education access, this is an important but frequently overlooked finding. As Altbach, Reisberg and Rumbley (2009) emphasize, the location of higher education institutions is "easily underestimated" as a component of inequality (p. 40). Research illustrates that the urban concentration of higher education programs and the deficit of rural institutions is a barrier to postsecondary access (Dassin, 2011; Duczmal, 2006; Yang, 2010). This is also likely to be true of initiatives offering a liberal education. Of degree-granting liberal education programs, only 8 percent or 14 programs (4 private and 10 public) are in rural areas or small towns. Most can be found in Canada and Asia. The concern with these statistics is that students from rural areas often come from disadvantaged secondary schools and families with fewer social and economic resources. Many students are unable to travel to larger metropolitan areas in order to attend university. Especially in Australia (Center for the Study of Higher Education, 2008), Africa (Bradley, 2000), and parts of Asia (Yang, 2010 for example), indigenous populations are also more likely to live in rural areas.

The tendency for liberal education programs to concentrate in large metropolitan areas, however, is likely to persist. Where new programs are developing as subsidiaries of existing research universities, they will also be established disproportionately in urban locations. Cities offer access to the greatest number of people as well as ancillary resources. Museums, libraries, music, and cultural centers are especially pertinent to liberal education. Further, public transportation, greater ingress to technical infrastructure, and more options for non–university (and university-sponsored) housing are assets for attracting international students and faculty. It is notable, however, that half of rural and small town liberal education initiatives were founded after 1995. Like higher education in general, the location of liberal education programs will impact accessibility as well as the profile of students who can participate. It requires future vigilance if the global liberal education trend continues.

## Public/Private Status

Outside the U.S., tertiary education is usually a function of the national government, often through a ministry of education. Many of the most prestigious institutions are state-led and publically funded research universities and students receive some degree of government financial support to pursue postsecondary education. However, in the last two to three decades, as demand for tertiary training has surpassed supply (both the number of student seats and providers available), private higher education has increased in importance and magnitude. Given perpetual debate about the purpose of higher education, liberal education's status as a public or private entity matters greatly. It can dictate a variety of program opportunities and challenges including funding sources, decision-making autonomy, accreditation, leadership, and reputation. Public sector liberal education is a particularly salient concern because it signals government tolerance (though not necessarily support) of a particular education philosophy, that is, education that engenders critical thinking about social, political, and cultural conditions— conditions often influenced or controlled by the government itself.

Taking all regions into account, liberal education programs are split almost evenly between the public and private sectors. Of 172 degree-granting programs in the GLEI, 46 percent of liberal education initiatives are public and 54 percent are private. The findings indicate that liberal education is emerging in both sectors and by relatively similar proportions.

Analyzed by region and by founding date, however, the results are more varied and illuminating. Figure 6.5 illustrates the number of public and private programs for each region. Although liberal education is divided almost evenly between public and private programs globally, there are more significant gaps between sectors, respectively congruent with the overall higher education systems, when analyzed by region. For example, liberal education programs in the Middle East, where the number of private tertiary providers is growing rapidly, are also predominately private (though most of them receive public funding). In Canada and

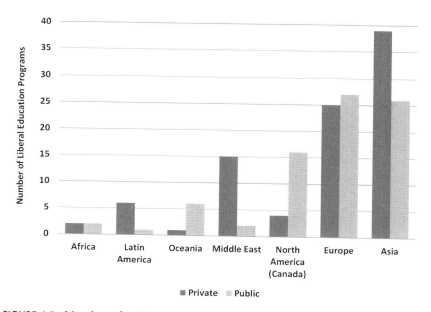

**FIGURE 6.5** Number of public and private liberal education programs by region. Calculations for private programs include one for-profit program; all other private programs are non-profit. Based on analysis and calculations from the Global Liberal Education Inventory.

Western Europe (subregion not delineated in the graph), liberal education's public presence parallels higher education systems that continue to favor the pubic sector. In Asia, the results are split. In general, liberal education follows the path of rapidly developing private initiatives. However, statewide policy changes in Hong Kong (and many public Chinese institutions) simultaneously drive up the ratio of public liberal education initiatives.

Given the landscape of privatization in higher education and the rapid development of private programs everywhere, analyzing liberal education founding dates in conjunction with public/private program designations produces surprising results. Figure 6.6 illustrates that since 2000, 20 percent more public liberal education programs have been founded than private. This is unexpected. Because liberal education programs account for a minute share of global tertiary enrollments, we might expect the most recent initiatives to originate through independent and small private institutions in accordance with umbrella international higher education trends. Instead, the GLEI reveals that the majority of recent programs are either incorporated into large public research institutions, are subsidiaries or "university colleges" associated with a public institution, or are part of system and university-wide policy changes like those in Hong Kong, China, and Australia.

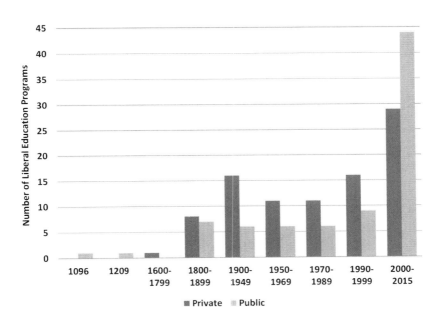

**FIGURE 6.6** Number of public and private liberal education programs by founding date. Calculations for private programs include one for-profit program; all other private programs are non-profit. Based on analysis and calculations from the Global Liberal Education Inventory.

Liberal education's significant presence in the public sector is remarkable. Given liberal education's broad and holistic philosophy, its central purpose contradicts the dominant human capital model that generally defines public tertiary systems globally. However, it is reminiscent of calls for reform and resources for higher education in emerging markets and developing countries promoted by the World Bank–UNESCO joint Task Force on Higher Education and Society convened in 2000. Authors of their final report, *Higher Education in Developing Countries: Peril and Promise*, would be pleased to hear that many of the newest liberal education programs have emerged in the public sector. They described higher education as "reflecting and promoting an open and meritocratic civil society," playing a role that promotes inclusive values that are more "public" than other social organizations and communities (p. 44). Liberal education philosophy uses academic inquiry and interdisciplinarity to develop citizens who will be critical of the society in which they live. While private universities may have more freedom to experiment with curricula and promote arts and humanities (less popular fields), the Task Force made recommendations that centered on the public sector and specified provisions for liberal education in developing regions.

## Program Partnerships and Affiliations

There are several reasons to explore program partnerships and institutional affiliations within the global liberal education phenomenon. First, because liberal education is traditionally not well understood outside the U.S. and is considered a distinctively American tradition (Tymowski, 2010), it is logical to expect that non-U.S. programs might consult or partner with U.S. institutions to learn about the content and administration of such programs. Second, challenges caused by the relative anomaly of liberal education might be assuaged with organizational partnerships. Institutional affiliations might help liberal education programs garner financial support, improve name recognition, or bolster institutional legitimacy. Finally, in the same way that comparative and international education researchers have attempted to understand the flow of students and scholars worldwide (see, for example, Banks and Bhandari, 2012; Bhandari and Blumenthal, 2011), or the "center and peripheries" (Altbach, 2002) of higher education knowledge production and leadership, analyzing GLEI program partnerships helps to identify relationships between countries and regions. Doing so illuminates a more complete profile of liberal education in a global context as well as the movement of higher education knowledge, power, and players.

Analysis of the GLEI data unveiled two unexpected findings related to liberal education program partnerships and affiliations. First, because the higher education news stream and much of the dialogue in the field frequently refer to international partnerships when discussing liberal education, it is surprising to learn that more than half of the GLEI programs do *not* have an affiliation with another institution. Fifty-seven percent of degree-granting liberal education programs operate "independently" without a formal (and publicized) institutional partnership in their own country or abroad. However, although the number of independent programs exceeds those with partnerships, independent liberal education initiatives have decreased over the last 50 years and reflect a recent proclivity for institutional cooperation.

## *Liberal Education Programs with Affiliations*

While 57 percent of GLEI programs are not formally affiliated with another institution, a significant portion, 72 programs (or 43 percent) are part of a formal organizational relationship. As globalization has waged greater and greater influence on higher education, the number of liberal education programs that are buttressed by a relationship with another university has increased. Sixteen of these programs, like Amsterdam University College, Habib University in Pakistan, and United International College in China, have at least two partnerships. In total there are 88 relationships between GLEI liberal education programs and other institutions, programs, or organizations.

The second surprising finding related to affiliations is that most liberal education partnerships are *not* international. Sixty-one percent of GLEI partnerships are domestic, between two institutions in the same country. Canada, where 11 liberal education programs are affiliated with large research universities, has the highest number of domestic partnerships. In some cases like the Faculty of Arts Program at the University of Prince Edward Island, the liberal education program is housed within an academic department at a public research university. In other instances like Glendon College and St. Thomas More College, the liberal education program operates like a "university college." In this arrangement the "college" is an undergraduate subsidiary of a large research university that oversees programs and sometimes awards degrees, but allows the college to operate as an independent entity. In this example Glendon College is affiliated with York University, and St. Thomas More College with the University of Saskatchewan.

Among the 88 partnerships between liberal education programs and other institutions, only 33 percent are with universities in the United States, by far the most for any single country. The impetus for liberal education programs to align with U.S. institutions is conspicuous. The history and experience of liberal education in the U.S. is long and pervasive. In addition to the institutions classified by the Carnegie Foundation as "small liberal arts colleges," most large research universities have a general (though not necessarily liberal) undergraduate curriculum requiring some study in various disciplines. Also, the size, diversity, and global prestige of the U.S. higher education system are well known. Many countries and universities that wish to ascend the world university rankings emulate organizational strategies, curricula, and institutional policies of the most highly ranked (U.S.) institutions. So while the number of liberal education partnerships with U.S. institutions is smaller than expected, the existence of those affiliations is logical and potentially beneficial for non-U.S. programs.

## Languages of Instruction

There are only 16 different languages represented among the 172 liberal education degree-granting programs spanning 58 countries in the GLEI. These include Bulgarian, Chinese, Czech, Dutch, English, German, Hebrew, Japanese, Korean, Lithuanian, Polish, Portuguese, Russian, Spanish, Swedish, and Thai. English is overwhelmingly the dominant language of instruction. Based on the GLEI 81 percent of non-U.S. liberal education programs use English as the teaching medium. Approximately 67 percent of the programs that use English are in non-native English speaking countries.

English is increasingly viewed as the *lingua franca* for administration, leadership, and research in higher education. Its use as a teaching medium is also growing. The GLEI results raise critical questions about the role of English in the international evolution of liberal education. On the one hand, the universities that "dominate the academic community" use English. These are the same institutions that produce the most influential and greatest volume of research (Altbach, Reisberg, & Rumbley, 2009, p. 11; Sadlak and Liu, 2007).

However, liberal education worldwide is developing on the periphery of mainstream tertiary systems (Godwin, 2013; Peterson, 2012a). If liberal education is to be legitimized internationally, then following the lead of the most successful universities, including their use of English, is likely a critical component for doing so. That is, if a broader curriculum and 21st-century skills like critical thinking, multidisciplinary inquiry, global citizenship, and analytic aptitude are to have a role in world-class education, if the general public is to have a better understanding of liberal education as a first-rate alternative to traditional career-specific university programs, and if liberal education is to survive in the globalized higher education market, it is expected (if unfortunate) that English will be the dominant medium for delivering that education.

Conversely, the GLEI analysis prompts us to ask whether the massive shift toward English in higher and liberal education signal a form of cultural hegemony. Do English-medium liberal education programs dissuade program developers and faculty from working toward a non-Western canon appropriate for liberal education in new cultural contexts? Does the use of English preclude programs from liberal education's seminal mission to embrace the culture, heritage, and social evolution that language preserves? What does electing not to use English as the language of instruction, as seen in Latin American, mean for programs' long-term sustainability?

## Why Has Liberal Education Emerged Globally and Why Now?

Reasons for the global liberal education phenomenon vary from country to country and are multifaceted. A few distinct patters, however, have emerged and can be loosely categorized into a three-tier "rationale schema." An important feature of this schema and a reality of liberal education's development globally is that rationales overlap, change, and can coexist. Explanations for the increasing number of liberal education programs include (1) *global rationales* that reflect global trends and pressures on higher education that reverberate across regions and countries; (2) *national/regional rationales* stemming from state or local social, economic, and educational policies; and (3) *local rationales* that result from institutional, programmatic, or individual strategic plans and academic initiatives.

## Global Rationales

Contemporary conditions, or "new realities" (Task Force, 2000) in society and higher education are catalysts for curricula experiments and alternative approaches to undergraduate education worldwide. They make up the *global rationales* for increasing interest in liberal education at the macro level. Global rationales affect all countries and tertiary programs, but to varying degrees and with a variety of outcomes. Global rationales include the following:

- Globalization or "the flow of technology, economy, knowledge, people, values, [and] ideas … across-borders." The impact on each country differs due to "individual history, traditions, cultures and priorities" (Knight & de Wit, 1997, p. 6). In addition to its intimate relationship with the other rationales below, globalization demands graduates with intercultural competence who can function effectively across cultures and in diverse work environments.
- Evolution from an industrial to a knowledge economy, that is, social and economic conditions that are driven by knowledge and technology rather than industrial production. Technological advances have led to subsequent calls for a "broader epistemic base" (Gürüz, 2012, p. 206), a new kind of human capital, and interdisciplinary problem solving. Policy makers, academic leaders, and portions of the general public recognize the need for a more malleable work force, one that can adjust to rapid technological changes and new innovation. Global advances in science and the social sciences are blurring the lines between disciplines, industry classifications, and certainly geographic boundaries. Scientists and academics are increasingly cognizant of the need for interdisciplinary thinking, workplace collaboration, and intercultural competence.
- Dramatic shifts in higher education demand from "elite" members of society to the "masses," also known as massification (Trow, 2006), with a need to differentiate program offerings as well as increase the number of tertiary providers as a result.
- Neoliberal competition, marketization, and privatization. With massification has come global competition for students, scholars, and resources as well as the race for higher rankings across institutions. Privatization or the evolution of new private for-profit and not-for-profit providers has meant an influx of

private funding, and the increasing commercialization of universities, research and development, and market-oriented stakeholders.

## National/Regional Rationales

The next level of rationales pertains to events, policies, imperatives, and social changes at the state or regional level. *National/regional rationales* examples include the following: declarations from an education ministry like those that implemented general education requirements across all Hong Kong universities; a movement toward developing graduates with more critical thinking skills in China; domestic economic or political shifts like the evolving democratic movements in Poland; and broader regional initiatives like the Bologna Process in Europe.

## Local Rationales

*Local rationales* at the micro level are sometimes difficult to identify because in discussions about why a particular liberal education program was founded, local rationales are frequently intermingled with the pronounced forces of global and national rationales. Local rationales motivate the creation of liberal education programs from the institution, program, course, or individual (faculty, staff, student, policy maker, entrepreneur, etc.) level. The idea for Ashesi University in Ghana came from an African entrepreneur formerly educated in the United States, for example. Collegial relationships between faculty at St. Petersburg University in Russia and Bard College in New York became the foundation for Smolny College. The few branch campuses that spawned from older institutional partnerships and exchanges are also examples of micro rationales for liberal education.

## Conclusion

Despite there being nearly 200 liberal education programs outside the U.S., career-focused higher education continues to prevail. With few exceptions like Hong Kong University of Science and Technology and Australia's Melbourne University among others, liberal education's development remains a phenomenon occurring on the periphery of—without a great deal of influence on—mainstream, world-class higher education where attention, resources, and research knowledge are concentrated. The number of programs and the number of students enrolled in liberal education are minute compared to traditional postsecondary degrees.

In a 2012 *Chronicle of Higher Education* article, Patty McGill Peterson (2012b) described liberal education programs as mere "islands in an uneven global sea of undergraduate education" (para. 2). She asked exactly the right question: Can liberal education develop "deep indigenous roots?" Are "independent" liberal education programs, for example, sustainable in the competitive, neoliberal university environment? Can liberal education play the visionary role in economic and human development recommended by the Task Force on Higher Education and Society over a decade ago?

It should be noted that the lack of liberal education curricula worldwide does not necessarily mean that the majority of higher education systems do not desire outcomes similar to those identified by GLEI programs. Authors who write about Turkey, India, and China, for example, places where higher education has a long tradition of specialization, point to historical rhetoric about national education initiatives that sound very much like liberal education. As Gürüz (2012) declares in his discussion about Turkey, "no clause in this [1981 national law] article precludes a liberal arts education" (p. 207). In fact, he explains, it contains phrases like "independent thinking with a broad worldview" and "respect for human rights," which imply a liberal education objective. Gürüz makes an important observation when he says that ultimately the phrases from the Turkish national article "stem from a traditional view of higher education's nation-building role rather than a philosophy of curriculum" (p. 207). Many would argue (as authors have done in this book) that in the global knowledge economy, liberal education has never been more essential.

There is cause for excitement in having established concrete, empirical data about the trends and key characteristics of liberal education, as well as the movement itself toward an alternative education philosophy. The GLEI is a foundation for understanding the global liberal education phenomenon as well as a launchpad for future, more program-specific research. It provides an essential baseline for gauging growth and change in the global liberal education phenomenon as well as a means for programs and program leaders to connect with one another.

What is most important about this work, however, is the backdrop it creates for asking deeper and more critical questions about liberal education. What impact, for example, might the increased prevalence of liberal education worldwide have on traditional (specialized, professional, career-specific) education? What can institutions and higher education systems accustomed to liberal education—predominately the United States—learn from places implementing it for the first time? Who benefits from liberal education? Are there students, faculty, or populations who are marginalized by it? How might liberal education disrupt traditional approaches to learning and teaching, a central component of all higher education networks? How do various country contexts and political climates challenge or support liberal education ideals? In new cultural milieus, *what are the ideals of a liberal education*?

## Notes

1 Though the GLEI was comprehensive at the time of first analysis in 2013, the number of liberal education programs has grown to at least 200 since then. An updated inventory (version 2.0) and analysis are in progress. Data presented here is based on the 2013 study.

2 See Godwin (2013) and forthcoming publications for more detailed data including regional and country-centered analysis.

## References

Agarwal, P., & Srinivasan, R. (2012). "India: Structural roadblocks to academic reform. In Peterson, P. M. (Ed.) *Confronting Challenge to the Liberal Arts Curriculum: Perspectives of Developing and Transitional Countries*. New York, NY: Routledge, 48–74.

Altbach, P. G. (2002). "Centers and peripheries in the academic profession: The special challenges of developing countries." In Altbach, P. G. (Ed.) *The Decline of the Guru: The Academic Profession in Developing and Middle-Income Countries*. Rotterdam, Netherlands: Sense Publishers, 1–22.

Altbach, P. G., Reisberg, L., & Rumbley, L. E. (2009). *Trends in Global Higher Education: Tracking an Academic Revolution*. Boston, MA: Center for International Higher Education.

Association of American Colleges & Universities. (n.d.). "What is a 21st century liberal education?" Retreived from www.aacu.org/leap/what-is-a-liberal-education.

Banks, M., & Bhandari, R. (2012). "International student and scholar mobility." In Deardorff, D. K., de Wit, H., & Heyl, J. (Eds.) *The SAGE Handbook of International Higher Education*. Thousand Oaks, CA: SAGE Publications.

Becker, J. (2003). "What a liberal arts education is … and is not." Presented at the Open Society Institute's UEP Alumni Conference, Budapest, Hungary.

Bhandari, R., & Blumenthal, P. (2011). *International Students and Global Mobility in Higher Education: National Trends and New Directions*. New York, NY: Palgrave Macmillan.

Bradley, K. (2000). "The Incorporation of women into higher education: Paradoxical outcomes?" *Sociology of Education*, 73(1): 1–18.

Carnegie Foundation for the Advancement of Teaching. (2010). "Carnegie classifications of institutions of higher education." Retrieved from http://carnegieclassifications.iu.edu/.

Centre for the Study of Higher Education. (2008). *Participation and Equity: A Review of the Participation in Higher Education of People from Low Socioeconomic Backgrounds and Indigenous People*. Melbourne, Australia: University of Melbourne.

Dassin, J. (2011, December 1). "Opening opportunities in international higher education." *The Chronicle of Higher Education*. Retrieved June 27, 2013, from http://chronicle.com/article/Opening-Opportunities-in/129984/

Duczmal, W. (2006). "Poland." In Forest, J. J. F. & Altbach, P. G. (Eds.) *International Handbook of Higher Education*. Amsterdam, Netherlands: Springer, 935–49.

Godwin, K. A. (2013). *The Global Emergence of Liberal Education: A Comparative and Exploratory Study* (Doctoral dissertation). Boston College Center for International Higher Education.

Godwin, K. A. & Altbach, P. G. (2016, in press). "A historical and global perspective on liberal arts education: What was, what is, and what will be." *International Journal of Chinese Education*.

Gürüz, K. (2012). Turkey: Obstacles to and examples of curriculum reform. In Peterson, P. M. (Ed.) *Confronting Challenge to the Liberal Arts Curriculum: Perspectives of Developing and Transitional Countries*. New York, NY: Routledge, 201–25.

Knight, J., & de Wit, H. (1997). *Internationalisation of Higher Education in Asia Pacific Countries*. Amsterdam, Netherlands: European Association for International Education.

Marginson, S. (2016). "Higher participation systems of higher education." *Journal of Higher Education*, 87(2): 243–71.

Nussbaum, M. C. (1997). *Cultivating Humanity: A Classical Defense of Reform in Liberal Education*. Cambridge, MA: Harvard University Press.

Nussbaum, M. C. (2004). "Liberal education & global community." *Liberal Education, 90*(1): 42–7.

Peterson, P. M. (Ed.). (2012a). *Confronting Challenge to the Liberal Arts Curriculum: Perspectives of Developing and Transitional Countries*. New York, NY: Routledge.

Peterson, P. M. (2012b, June 18). "Liberal-arts education: Has the global migration stalled?" *The Chronicle of Higher Education*. Retrieved from http://chronicle.com/article/ Liberal-Arts-Education-Has/132327/.

Rothblatt, S. (2003). *The Living Arts: Comparative and Historical Reflections on Liberal Education. The Academy in Transition*. Washington, DC: Association of American Colleges and Universities.

Sadlak, J., & Liu, N. C. (2007). *The World-Class University and Ranking: Aiming beyond Status*. Bucharest, Romania: UNESCO European Centre for Higher Education.

Task Force on Higher Education and Society. (2000). *Higher education in developing countries: Peril and promise*. Washington, DC: World Bank.

Trow, M. (2006). Reflections on the transition from elite to mass to universal access: Forms and phases of higher education in modern societies since WWII. In J. J. F. Forest & D. P. G. Altbach (Eds.), *International Handbook of Higher Education*. Dordrecht, Netherlands: Springer, 243–80.

Tymowski, A. W. (2011). "Liberal education and the intercultural classroom." In O'Connor, M. & Wilczek, P. (Eds.) *Collegium / College / Kolegium*. Boston, MA and Warsaw, Poland: Boston College and University of Warsaw, 28–44.

Yang, X. (2010). "Access to higher education for rural-poor students in China." *Educational Research for Policy & Practice, 9*(3):193–209.

# 7

# THE EMERGENCE OF LIBERAL ARTS AND SCIENCES EDUCATION IN EUROPE[1,2]

## A Comparative Perspective

*Marijk van der Wende*

## Liberal Arts and the Origin of the European University

A 'liberal arts' institution can be defined as a 'college or university with a curriculum aimed at imparting general knowledge and developing general intellectual capacities, in contrast to a professional, vocational, or technical curriculum' (Encyclopedia Brittannica). In terms of institutional characterization, the Carnegie Classification (USA) identifies Baccalaureate Colleges — Liberal Arts as institutions that 'are primarily undergraduate colleges with major emphasis on baccalaureate programmes and which award at least half of their baccalaureate degrees in liberal arts fields' (Carnegie Foundation for the Advancement of Teaching website), The terms 'liberal arts' or 'liberal education' are often used as short hand for the more comprehensive term 'liberal arts and sciences education', although it is explicitly recognized that the sciences have their integral place in that concept. 'Despite its antiquity, liberal education is often assumed to be unique to the American Republic — perhaps with roots in other traditions' (Rothblatt, 2003, 1). Indeed, tracing back the history of this particular educational model leads to Europe, as the liberal arts tradition has its origins with the great Greek philosophers and constituted the basis of the medieval university in Europe (Nussbaum, 1997; Glyer and Weeks, 1998). The curriculum of the early European universities was organized around the seven liberal arts, which were divided into the *Trivium* (literary arts: grammar, logic, and rhetoric) and the *Quadrivium* (mathematical arts: arithmetic, geometry, music, and astronomy), all together focusing on the education of the 'whole' or 'well-rounded' person. This initial part of university education formed the basis for further, advanced level training in the main professions of that time, such as medicine, law, and theology. This is also how the *Athenaeum Illustre*, the predecessor of the University of Amsterdam, which was established in 1632, was structured. The collegiate model, that is the smaller-scale college context preferred for the liberal arts experience, also has clear historical roots in the early European universities, for example Oxford and Cambridge.

Rothblatt recognizes the European origins of the model, but also notes that, 'While liberal education has never exactly vanished from the European educational agenda, it has been decidedly low on the scale of priorities' (2003, 5). Furthermore, he writes, 'Liberal education is something of an educational industry in the USA as nowhere else' (2003, 1). This does of course not imply that it is free of critique, as witnessed by a flow of recent publications (see for instance AAC&U, 2005, 2007; Bok, 2006; Levine, 2006; Lewis, 2006), which will be discussed in more detail later in this article.

In order to answer the question of why liberal arts and sciences education is currently (re-)emerging in Europe, we first need to look into the question of why liberal education lost the scope that it continued to have in the USA. As 'Europe' is a complex concept, and in particular when it comes to its higher education histories and models, it seems to be difficult to present a single explanation for the fact that liberal arts did not make it to the mainstream of higher education in Europe. Rather, there is a range of factors that likely influenced the relatively weak role that the model has played during long periods in Europe.

## Explanations for the Sharp Decline of the Liberal Arts Model in Europe

The history of the European university is rich and characterized by distinct periods. Medieval concepts were followed by renaissance humanism and enlightenment with evolving emphases on what knowledge means and how it should be pursued and studied (de Ridder-Symoens, 1996). Major changes, with clear traces remaining in today's higher education institutions, occurred, and particularly so during the 19th century. On the one hand, the importance of liberal education and of teaching as the unique *raison d'être* of a university was defended fiercely by university founders and leaders of the time, notably by Cardinal Newman, who held that academic institutions should focus on training responsible citizens whose intellectual and emotional background would contribute to the smooth evolution of society as a whole and should (thus) *not* engage in research: 'That it is a place of teaching universal knowledge, this implies that its object is the diffusion and extension of knowledge rather than the advancement of it. If its object were scientific and philosophic discovery, I do not see why a university should have students'. Likewise, Mill emphasized the universal nature of learning and wrote on how it should take place within a university: 'It is not a place of professional education. Universities are not intended to teach the knowledge required to fit men for some special mode of gaining their livelihood. Their object is not to make skilful lawyers, or physicians, or engineers, but capable and cultivated human beings'. On the other hand, new models were emerging on the continent. For example, in

France there was the establishment of the elite part of French higher education, the *grandes écoles*, by Napoleon, who put great emphasis on their role in training for the professions crucial in serving the state, such as administration, engineering, and the military. Most importantly, the research university was established in Berlin by Wilhelm von Humboldt, who subscribed to the liberal education value of '*Bildung*', but who defined the teaching role of the university solidly in relation to its research mission (Nybom, 2003).

While these new influences helped to shape the European higher education system, with different combinations of professional training and/or research functions being integrated into various types of institutions, this does not in essence distinguish the situation very much from that in the USA, where von Humboldt's concept of the research university was also influential. Many American scholars attended German universities and in the late 19th century, the Ph.D. became established along the lines of the Humboldtian model, which in fact was the model after which the American research university has been shaped. The professions have also gained their place in the American university, although more explicitly at the graduate level (and in professional schools), rather than is the case in European universities, where training for the professions usually begins at the undergraduate level. This is still evident in, for instance, medical, engineering and law programmes in Europe, which start as specialized tracks upon entrance in the university system. For a long time, the division between undergraduate and graduate cycles was not very explicit or even absent in Europe, which has been (re-)adjusted by the Bologna initiative. This explains why these influences (the utilitarian-professional and the research-dominated model) have lead to a greater degree of early specialization here than in the USA. The dominance of professions and disciplines in undergraduate programmes in Europe may not only be held responsible for early or even over-specialization and professional bias, but also for a loss of the particular humanistic educational values such as preparation for citizenship and the universal nature and purpose of learning as such (exceptions in Europe are probably some of the Scottish and Irish colleges in which Newman's and Mill's ideas were more or less sustained). In American curricula, this has, through the traditions of general education and the definition of the academic core as part of the university undergraduate curriculum to some extent, always been preserved. Yet the focus and purpose of general education should be viewed in relation to the nature and length of secondary education in Europe, where part of the general education that is conveyed in American colleges and universities is typically offered in higher level secondary schools. The liberal arts model sustained an even more explicit focus on the important aim to educate the 'whole person' including the moral implications thereof.

Although, the impact of utilitarian and more research-led university models can be observed in both Europe and the USA, this seems to have led to a greater degree of early specialization in European undergraduate education, where this was not or only weakly defined as an educational phase (degree cycle) in its own right. This divergence, however, only developed throughout the 20th century and even more so after the World War II, when higher education entered a new phase during which other major trends emerged. These 20th century trends seem to add substantially to the explanation of why the liberal arts model survived better in the USA than in Europe.

The post-World War II period was characterized by the massification and democratization of higher education, although this emerged later in Europe (the 1970s) than in the USA (the 1950s) because of the recovery from World War II. More importantly, this took place in models that were less differentiated than in the USA, where the growth of the student body was paralleled by the emergence of more differentiated systems, for which the Californian Master plan became a major reference model (Rothblatt, 1992). In large countries such as Germany and France, most of the growth has been accommodated within the research universities (accommodating at present a large majority of the total student population). In smaller countries, such as the Netherlands and Belgium, the growth was mainly accommodated in the non-university or polytechnic sector (which currently hosts approximately two-thirds of the students). By and large the European systems are of a binary nature, with the undergraduate phase in universities being dominated by the disciplines and non-university undergraduate institutions mainly specializing in professional training.

Massification took place in combination with an increasingly stronger and ultimately almost complete dominance of public government, in most cases by the nation state (with exceptions in federal states such as Germany), in the steering of higher education. Here I subscribe to Rothblatt's main explanation for the fact that 'liberal arts education has been decidedly low on the scale of priorities in Europe', namely that, 'With only few exceptions, governments, ministries, politicians, and bureaucrats establish the parameters of educational discussion in Europe. Until about 1990, the agenda largely followed from the fact that higher education was almost wholly dependent upon public taxation' (2003, 5). He states that although the governmental agenda in the USA has also been concerned with questions of resource allocation and competitiveness, there is at the same time 'a large and important private sector committed to liberal education which guarantees that its interests are widely voiced and represented' (2003, 6).

Private initiative and associated funding to sustain the particular values and the mission of liberal arts education have by and large been missing in Europe. Instead, 'public' is the norm for both the governance and funding of higher education. The limitations of such a budgetary basis, which is almost by definition more restricted than that in countries such as the USA, Canada, Japan, and South Korea, where more substantial private contributions to higher education are common (OECD, 2008a), are recognized by many policy makers. Yet, the virtues of publicly funded higher education are strongly recognized by various stakeholders, notably the students who usually wish to preserve low or no tuition fees and open access without selective admission policies. This idea of 'free access for all' is strongly associated with the value of 'higher education as a public good'. Although there are notable exceptions to this model (like in England, where universities charge tuition fees and apply selective admission, and France in the case of the *Grandes Ecoles*), it is generally perceived as the core of the European egalitarian tradition and strongly defended by students, as expressed, for instance, in the emphasis they put in the Bologna Process on the 'social dimension' of higher education. At the same time, the model has been criticized repeatedly by international organizations for its (inherent) contradictions. The OECD commented that, despite strong social values, as regards access and equity, the EU is performing poorly as compared with the USA. The European Commission (EC) also admitted that, 'While most of Europe sees higher education as a "public good", tertiary enrolments have been stronger and faster in other parts of the world, mainly thanks to much higher private funding' (EC, 2005). The Commission also criticized the apparent uniformity in provision as being due to a tendency to egalitarianism and a lack of differentiation, as well as to over-regulation and the strong dependence on the state inhibiting reform, modernization, and efficiency (EC, 2005). These observations regarding the lack of differentiation (including the aforementioned relatively early specialization in undergraduate education) and the strong egalitarian tradition framed in a predominantly public (funding) model in Europe largely explain why liberal arts education has not developed in Europe to the extent that it has in the USA. Yet, as the conditions for European higher education are changing, the reappraisal of these factors may as a consequence also reveal why liberal arts is actually (re-)emerging in Europe. Before pursuing the second part of the analysis, a brief mapping of the emergence of liberal arts in Europe is presented.

## Mapping the (Re-)Emergence of Liberal Arts Education in Europe

It should be noted that the overview, as presented in Table 7.1, does not pretend to be a wholly up-to-date and comprehensive summary, since new developments may be underway but not yet announced publicly. The list includes established and formally announced initiatives, with reference to their age, origin, and legal status.

The chronology shows that all early initiatives were American by origin. This is shown by the institution names and by the fact that they are funded, accredited or otherwise governed by American bodies. And by their affiliation to associations as AMICAL, which is an international consortium of American-model, liberal arts institutions of higher learning or the Association of American International Colleges and Universities, although the membership of the latter is wider than liberal arts only. These initiatives usually have a private (not-for-profit) legal status.

**TABLE 7.1** Trends in the (Re-)Emergence of Liberal Arts Education in Europe

| Year of Establishment | Institution | USA Affiliated | Europe Affiliated | Private |
|---|---|---|---|---|
| 1886 | American College of Thessaloniki | X | | X |
| 1923 | American College of Greece | X | | X |
| 1962 | American University of Paris | X | | X |
| 1969 | American University of Rome | X | | X |
| 1969 | Franklin College, Switzerland | X | | X |
| 1972 | Richmond, The American International University in London | X | | X |
| 1972 | John Cabot University. An American university in Rome | X | X | X |
| 1988 | Vesalius College (Vrije Universiteit Brussel) (Belgium) | | | X |
| 1991 | American University in Bulgaria | X | | X |
| 1991 | Central European University | X | | X |
| 1992 | Collegium Artes Liberales (Interdisciplinary Studies Institute at the University of Warsaw) (Poland) | | X | |
| 1998 | Gotland University (Visby, Sweden) | | X | |
| 1998 | University College Utrecht (Utrecht University, the Netherlands) | | X | |
| 1999 | Smolny College (St. Petersburg) (Joint degree programme of Bard College (USA) and Saint Petersburg State University) (Russia) | X | | |
| 1999 | European College of Liberal Arts (Berlin) | X | X | X |
| 1999 | Jacobs University Bremen (Germany) | X | X | X |

(continued)

**TABLE 7.1** Trends in the (Re-)Emergence of Liberal Arts Education in Europe (*continued*)

| Year of Establishment | Institution | USA Affiliated | Europe Affiliated | Private |
|---|---|---|---|---|
| 2000 | Liberal arts degree at St Mary's University College, Belfast (UK) | | X | |
| 2002 | University College Maastricht (Maastricht University, the Netherlands) | | X | |
| 2004 | Roosevelt Academy (Utrecht University, the Netherlands) | | X | |
| 2004–2006 | Liberal arts programmes at the University of Amsterdam, Tilburg University and Utrecht University's main campus (the Netherlands) | | X | |
| 2006 | BISLA, Bratislava (Slovakia) | X | X | X |
| | Faculty of Liberal Arts, Charles University (Prague, Czech Republic) | | X | |
| 2007 | Academia Vitae, Deventer (the Netherlands) | | | X |
| 2009 | Amsterdam University College (joint degree programme of VU University Amsterdam & University of Amsterdam, the Netherlands) | | X | |
| 2010 | Leiden University College (Leiden University, the Hague Campus, the Netherlands) | | | |
| 2010 | Liberal arts programme at Winchester University (UK) | | | |
| 2011 | Liberal arts programme at University College London (UK) | | | |
| 2011/12 | Liberal arts programme at Freiburg University | | | |

More recent initiatives (started around 1990) are more genuinely European. They are typically initiated by a European university and became (later on) affiliated to the consortium of European Colleges of Liberal Arts and Sciences (ECOLAS www.ecolas.eu). There is some interesting overlap between these groups, since some of these later initiatives were still established with the help of American institutions or organizations, for example through joint degrees, US accreditation, and/or funding from American foundations. These colleges or programmes have both an American and a European affiliation, such as John Cabot University (established as an American university which recently joined ECOLAS) Jacobs University (co-established by Rice University in the USA), Smolny College in Russia and ECLA in Germany (both associated with Bard College in the USA). At the same time, institutions, which are listed as USA affiliated only (typically no ECOLAS membership), may of course well have European partners. It should also be noted that the ECOLAS membership is larger than the institutions listed in Table 7.1 only. It also includes institutions that are not (yet) recognized as having a liberal arts programme or college, or that may be interested in establishing one in the future (e.g. Bucerius Law School (Hamburg, Germany), Catherine's College of Tallinn University (Estonia), Catholic University Leuven (Campus Kortrijk, Belgium), Ghent University (Belgium), Liverpool Hope University (UK).

Although this article does not aim to make a detailed analysis of the character- istics of the various liberal arts colleges and programmes as presented in the table, some more general observations and comparisons between the USA and Europe can be made (Table 7.2).

The overview and comparative analysis clearly show that the re-emergence of liberal arts is not only a relatively recent, but especially also (still) a very small-scale feature of European higher education. A comparison of size is not easy to make, since European data frameworks, such as provided for the USA by the Carnegie Classification, are still under development (see www.u-map.eu/). According to the Carnegie website, there are 287 bachelor colleges providing programmes in the liberal arts and sciences (6.5 percent of all institutions), enroling together some 527,533 students (3 percent of total enrolment), an average enrolment of 1,838 students per institution (data for 2005). In Europe, the definition of liberal arts colleges and programmes is still by and large left to self-characterization and although the current provision will certainly exceed the approximately 30 insti- tutions listed above, the total size of the sector will still be much smaller than in the USA, as the European liberal arts colleges typically enrol <1,000 students each. Taken as a percentage of the total size of European higher education, which is comparable with that of the USA in terms of total student enrolment, that is 17.5 million vs 17.7 million (OECD data for 2007), it may not even exceed one percent.

**TABLE 7.2** Comparison of Similarities and Differences between Liberal Arts Programmes in the USA and Europe

| Similarities | Differences |
| --- | --- |
| • As is the case in the USA, there is a range of profiles, with a rather frequent focus on the humanities (e.g. ECLA and Warsaw) and the social sciences, but also some with an emphasis on the sciences (Amsterdam University College, Gotland University) or even an exclusive science and engineering profile (Jacobs University)<br>• As is the case in the USA, the majority focuses exclusively on undergraduate education<br>• As is the case in the USA, both the models of a separate, usually residential college (although these are in many cases associated with a larger university) and that of a college or degree programme integrated within a larger university can be found in Europe<br>• As is the case in the USA, liberal arts education in Europe is taught in English | • Unlike in the USA, where a college degree takes 4 years, the European liberal arts degree usually takes 3 years (although the American (accredited) colleges and universities in Europe also offer 4 years bachelor degrees)<br>• Unlike in the USA, liberal arts colleges and programmes in Europe are usually not accredited under a specific framework (although ECOLAS aims to develop this over time) and are not compared with each other in any sort of league table, such as the Liberal Arts Colleges Rankings in the USA (US World and News Report, 2010)<br>• Unlike in the USA, where private liberal arts colleges outnumber public institutions, in Europe (as could be expected on the basis of the contextual analysis above) the majority of European liberal arts colleges are public<br>• Although it is clearly growing, the liberal arts 'sector' is (still) significantly smaller in Europe than in the USA<br>• Uneven geographical spread: the majority of initiatives seem to be concentrated in the north-western part of Europe (notably in the Netherlands and the UK) and in Central and Eastern Europe |

## Explaining the (Re-)Emergence of Liberal Arts Education in Europe

The main factors explaining why liberal arts education did not evolve into a significant model in Europe have been discussed. As suggested, the explanation behind its more or less recent and small scale (re-)emergence is likely related to the revaluation of these same factors due to changing conditions in the European higher education landscape. Indeed, as was stated by Rothblatt, 'Revolutionary educational conditions in Europe have diverted some subsidiary attention to liberal education. Many European countries are now experiencing American-style problems in maintaining the type of advanced and specialized undergraduate education once deemed solely appropriate for universities. An increase in the number of students leaving high school with university qualifications and an expansion in the number and types of places offering higher education — an expansion that has accelerated since the end of the Second World War — have forced university leaders and academics, as well as government and civil service planners, to reconsider alternative forms of undergraduate education' (2003, 6). That is, the (re-)emergence of liberal education in Europe is a response to the need to differentiate the massified European systems, which are characterized by insufficient diversity and flexibility in terms of the types of institutions and programmes offered to an increasingly large and diversified body of students (Huisman and Van Vught, 2009). Specifically, this is related to two main dimensions of differentiation.

The first is the quest for broader bachelor programmes in order to overcome the disadvantages of too early and over-specialization at the undergraduate level. This pursuit has been made explicit by leaders and policy makers for more than a decade, for instance in the Dearing Report on 'Higher Education in the Learning Society' (UK, 1997), which pleaded for broad, multidisciplinary degrees and a stronger focus on skills development for employability. The report is now seen as one of the front-runners in suggesting new avenues for liberal arts programmes that 'might soon become a part of the UK higher education mainstream' (The Guardian, 19 January 2010). The President and Provost of University College London recently endorsed these rationales for establishing liberal arts programmes (to be started in 2011) by stating that he wanted to move away from producing students with a narrow view of the world by ones who are global citizens. This was, in his own words, a response to employers who demand 'students who are literate and numerate and broadly based'. He went so far as to say that, 'We are worried about the traditional model of higher education in the UK, which progressively focuses our students on narrower and narrower areas of study', while at the same time suggesting that, 'It may be particularly attractive to international undergraduate students' (Grant, 2009), which is a market of great importance to UK institutions.

The call for broader bachelor programmes has also been launched repeatedly by the European commission, which has criticized the monodisciplinary and rigid nature of most university programmes in Europe. With a view to enhancing the employability of university graduates, the commission proposes a stronger focus on more generic skills, flexibility, and interdisciplinarity. This message was mostly launched in the context of the Lisbon Strategy, under which the Commission developed its 'Agenda for the Modernization of Universities' (EC, 2005). However, in the parallel Bologna Process, which focused directly on degree structures and the reform of curricula, relatively little attention was paid to these issues (see below).

In the Netherlands, the rationale behind widening the approach to undergraduate education and to re-establishing the balance between breadth and depth of study has also been an important driver for change in this area. This is not only related to the many problems at undergraduate level, which are associated with early specialization (e.g. mistaken choice for study programmes, high dropout rates, deterioration in general academic skills in areas such as writing, speech and analysis, etc.), but also to the deeper need for generic skills, flexibility and interdisciplinarity required for innovation, a key factor for the success of a knowledge economy.

Clearly, this demand for broader bachelor programmes is framed by, on the one hand, the aim of improving learning effectiveness and, on the other hand, a knowledge economy discourse related to innovation and employability. In particular, the latter refers to the type of utilitarian rationale that belongs to the neo-classical economic paradigm positioning higher education as a producer of human capital for economic growth. The question of how this type of utilitarian rationale relates to the inherent humanistic values of the liberal arts tradition presents itself and will be addressed later in this article.

The second dimension of differentiation is the search for elite education in massified and overly egalitarian and democratic systems. One can speak of an almost total decline of elite or top tier higher education in continental Europe. 'Almost total' as there are certainly exceptions. These would include the aforementioned *Grandes Ecoles* in France and the UK with a selective system of university admission within stratified levels and Oxbridge as global brand name elite institutions (Palfreyman and Tapper, 2009). Other selective branches of higher education include schools of fine and performing arts, hotel schools, business schools, some military academies, etc. A turning point for Germany seems to have been reached recently with the launch of its 'excellence initiative', although this is mostly focusing on research (Kehm and Pasternack, 2009). As the OECD's Secretary General (Gurria, 2007) phrased it: 'Europe has no shortage of brilliant minds, but they are locked away in low-performing institutions'. European university leaders have, in fact, admitted that, 'It is evident that the European university system needs to broaden access on a more equitable basis, that it has to reach out to increased excellence and that it must allow for more diversification within the system. The American university system is "elitist at the top, and democratic at the base"; the European university system seems to be neither' (Winckler, 2006). Furthermore, the EC underlined that one of the main challenges of European higher education is not only to widen access but also to enhance excellence. The messages on excellence and 'top', however, are rather distant from the culture, tradition, and thus expectations in large parts of continental Europe, where widely accessible and free higher education is strongly associated with the value of 'higher education as a public good' (as discussed above; see also van der Wende, 2009). Introducing more elite and thus selective types of higher education will therefore require very deliberate strategies. The example of the Netherlands as a country with strong egalitarian traditions, which yet managed to introduce a range of liberal arts initiatives, demonstrates that change in this respect is feasible. This will be discussed in more detail in the next section of this article.

Two dimensions of the need to differentiate have been analysed: (1) the need to develop broader bachelor programmes with the aim of enhancing learning effectiveness and to generate graduates with the skills relevant for the knowledge economy, and (2) the need to establish more selective branches of higher education focusing explicitly on excellence. As these developments coincided in time largely with the implementation of the Bologna Process, it is relevant to ask what the role of this Europe-wide initiative has been in relation to the development of liberal arts in Europe.

It seems that Bologna has played an important role, yet mostly as a factor facilitating the development of new types of undergraduate education, such as liberal arts programmes, as an opportunity enabling the (re-)emergence of this type of education in Europe. In previous sections of this article, it was stated that the weak division between undergraduate and graduate education in Europe seems to have reinforced the influence of disciplinary and professional paradigms regarding undergraduate education, leading to a great degree of early specialization. Bologna has adjusted this division by (re-)introducing undergraduate education, that is the bachelor level, as an educational phase in its own right. At the same time, however, we noted that the Bologna Process held very few substantial messages regarding the importance of widening the scope of undergraduate curricula. There was general concern with flexibility of curricula, but this has mostly been worked out around the concepts of modularization and student-centred learning. Themes such as the development of generic skills, deeper understanding of knowledge, critical thinking, and interdisciplinarity were, however, less central in implementation of the process. In a recent evaluation report it was admitted that 'The lack of discussion has probably led to some confusion between the broad, humanistic objectives and the technocratic aspects of some Bologna action lines' (Sursock and Smidt, 2010, 31). Indeed, the liberal arts advocates in Europe are not impressed as yet. They believe that the introduction of the bachelor/master structure across Europe has not led to a significant improvement so far, and that in most countries, the attention seems to have been focused more on improving master's programmes, while the bachelor phase has remained largely undervalued. As they believe that it is during the undergraduate phase that a strong academic basis should be laid, their primary mission remains to promote undergraduate liberal arts and sciences programmes across Europe (www.ecolas.eu). Also, some American observers are sceptical about the Bologna Process, as for instance Gaston (2008), who stresses that the Bologna Process, despite its great accomplishments, has from the start concentrated more or less exclusively on the economic advantages of tertiary education, with a strong vocational and even utilitarian thrust, whereas the strength of the American liberal arts tradition emphasizes a broader set of competencies, that is growth in 'critical thinking, quantitative literacy, communication skills, ethical reasoning, and civic engagement'. Rothblatt is more optimistic and observes that the transnational dialogue on liberal education has become more meaningful as 'Europeans dissolve parts of a particular type of elite higher education system and acquaint themselves with the challenging traits of a system more highly differentiated as to kinds of institutions, academic expectations, degree and diploma awards, part-time and continuing education, and types of students' (Rothblatt, 2003, 8). At the same time, however, he notes that the understanding of the term 'liberal arts' differs quite substantially and that the emerging concern for this type of education may in some places be not for liberal education so much as for better student services, which, as he admits, may be an unavoidable outcome in a state of mass enrolment. Indeed, the small scale and intensive teaching model that characterizes liberal arts colleges is most popular with European students who feel lost in the large-scale institutions of mass higher education. Other reasons may be that it allows them to avoid (or delay) making the difficult choice for a disciplinary study programme. Foreign, especially US students may be attracted for yet another reason, that is the relatively low price of liberal arts programmes in Europe. In their turn, policy makers and administrators may convert into proponents of the liberal arts and sciences model supported by research findings, which indicate that the intensive teaching model leads to higher learning effectiveness, however, without necessarily recognizing or adhering to the deeper meaning and values of it.

The main factors behind the emergence of liberal arts education in Europe are related to a need to differentiate massified higher education systems, both in terms of alternative — broader or more interdisciplinary — programme offerings and more selective admission procedures for undergraduate education. The Bologna Process facilitated these developments as it (re-)instituted undergraduate education as an educational phase in its own right. As has been emphasized before, it is impossible to generalize the trends for Europe as a whole. The need for more selective admission may for instance be more strongly felt in certain countries than in others, as will be discussed in more detail in the context of the development of liberal arts in the Netherlands (below). Another particular case is the development of liberal arts in Central and Eastern Europe, where the fall of the Berlin wall (i.e. the disintegration of the Soviet empire) allowed a range of countries to re-integrate into Europe, to break away from imposed educational models and to benefit from economic and educational reforms associated with democratic societies.

## The Development of Liberal Arts in the Netherlands

Compared with other European countries, the Netherlands has produced the greatest number of new liberal arts initiatives in one single country (nine out of 19 between 1990 and 2010; see Table 7.1). Almost half (six) of the Dutch research universities have established a liberal arts college or programme and some even two. This remarkable fact requires further analysis: How and why has the liberal arts model emerged here so successfully? What were the reasons and conditions for this?

The Netherlands has a binary higher education system composed of 14 universities that cater for roughly one-third (231,823 in 2009) of the students and some 40 universities of applied science (*hogescholen*) that accommodate roughly the other two-thirds (403,212 in 2009) of the students. Both types of higher education institutions exist under the same legislation and have a relatively high degree of autonomy, although new programmes can only be established after *ex ante* accreditation by the national accreditation council, tuition fees are determined by the government, and admissions criteria are set by law. The establishment of new institutions is particularly difficult due to the fact that their formal recognition (necessary for governmental funding) requires a change of the Higher Education Act in which they are all listed. Despite these restrictions, it has proven possible to develop a range of liberal arts colleges and programmes across the country.

Although the liberal arts model was considered in the Netherlands in the mid-1980s as part of an intended national higher education reform plan, which was never implemented (see Rupp, 1997), it developed some 10 years later in a bottom-up fashion, that is emerging from initially personal and then institutional initiatives. In the mid-1990s, a former dean of Utrecht University initiated the establishment of University College Utrecht, which opened in 1998. It started as a small scale, residential college in the vicinity of Utrecht University's main campus. It quickly attracted a great deal of attention in the higher education community and gained a strong reputation. As a result of a lack of adequate frameworks, for instance for accreditation as a liberal arts programme, it initially drew on provisional arrangements in order to regularize its functioning as an independent programme, which was by and large inspired by an American liberal arts curriculum. The fact that it provided evidence for enhanced learning outcomes and higher learning effectiveness in combination with strong features of internationalization stimulated other institutions to follow the new model. Maastricht University opened its college in 2002 and Utrecht University opened a second college in Middelburg (the Roosevelt Academy) in 2004. In addition, programmes labelled as liberal arts were opened on Utrecht's main campus, in the University of Amsterdam and in Tilburg University in the same period. These can be considered as broader or less straightforward interpretations of the liberal arts college model, are not all taught in English, and are not necessarily residential. Another major initiative emerged in 2009, when the University of Amsterdam and the VU University Amsterdam jointly established Amsterdam University College (AUC). Finally, Leiden University opened its university college in September 2010. At present, at least three more liberal arts initiatives are being planned by other Dutch universities.

These liberal arts colleges and programmes were all initiated by established and reputable Dutch research universities and obtained national accreditation and public funding. The only private project, that is the Academia Vitae in Deventer, which was established without any institutional affiliation to an existing university, did not. This proved to substantially hinder its functioning and it was forced to declare bankruptcy in early 2010.

Although the new initiatives required substantial advocacy and energy to be accepted, the impression is such that the overall higher education framework in the Netherlands provides sufficient scope for this type of innovation, which did not only entail a more open and flexible curriculum model, but also alternative, that is more selective, approaches to admission, a collegiate (usually residential) campus model, and a strong internationalization component. In fact, the new model was gradually embraced by new policy frameworks, such as designed by an advisory committee on opportunity for talent. This 'Commissie Ruim Baan voor Talent, 2007' advised the government on creating opportunities for talented students (2007), which resulted among other things in national experiments with selective admission that enabled the university colleges to implement those. And consequently by the Sirius Programme for excellence in higher education, which subsidized from 2008 on some 50 million Euros for initiatives to develop excellence, from which the various university colleges benefitted to a great extent, as well regular programmes for instance for the development of honours tracks. The Association of Universities in the Netherlands (VSNU) developed an agenda to increase the study success of bachelor students, that is to reduce dropout rates and increase on-time completion of the bachelor degree (www.vsnu.nl/Focusareas/Key-objectives/Study-success.htm), which was by and large inspired by the success demonstrated by the university colleges. This illustrates that not only the founding universities but also the university sector at large expect the university colleges, with their liberal arts models, to be lighthouses of good practice which should, through dissemination of best practices, become beneficial to the mainstream of undergraduate programmes. In other words, the university colleges are accepted as a new branch of excellence in Dutch university education. One could say that they became gradually 'embedded' by the various policy frameworks. Ultimately also the regulatory framework was adapted. First with the development of a tailored accreditation framework for liberal arts programmes and second by a proposed change in the Higher Education Act which will grant university colleges an exceptional status by allowing them structurally to select their students and to set differential tuition fees. This proposal is currently (after the elections of June 2010) pending upon approval from Parliament.

This particular bottom-up course of institution-driven innovation, paralleled in the first instance by 'soft' (i.e. advisory committees and temporary subsidies) policy measures at national level and weak governmental involvement, leading ultimately to structural change in the higher education system and regulation, is typical for the Netherlands. This was asserted in Witte's (2006) study on the implementation of the Bologna Process in the country.

The main reasons for the emergence and steady acceptance of liberal arts in the Netherlands are largely identical to those presented above for Europe in general. It was felt that there was insufficient differentiation in the massified and strongly egalitarian system. This was underlined by the OECD, which stated that Dutch higher education demonstrates an insufficient level of differentiation, excellence is underrepresented, the international dimension should be enhanced, and too-early specialization should be avoided (OECD, 2008b). The liberal arts model, with a broader curriculum approach and small-scale collegiate setting, seemed to provide an effective response to the inefficiencies of the undergraduate phase. This was in 2010 confirmed by an international committee (the 'Veerman Committee') established by the Dutch minister of Education, Culture and Sciences that advised on how to further differentiate Dutch higher education. Also in this report, the university colleges were set as an example of good practice (Commissie Toekomstbestendig Hoger Onderwijs Stelsel, 2010). Selective admission and higher learning standards responded to the complaint expressed by not only academics but also one-third of the students: Regular programmes are not sufficiently challenging. In the Netherlands, the Bologna Process was a facilitating factor, although the first initiatives preceded and inspired its implementation and the internationalization ambition was more comprehensive. University colleges in the Netherlands have very high (30–60 percent) proportions of international students and genuinely internationalized curricula. Furthermore, they provide a response to the increasing internationalization trends in Dutch secondary education, with substantial growth in bilingual education (English — Dutch) and in International and European Baccalaureates. This growing demand has been analysed as a type of social mobility of 'new global elites' (Weenink, 2007, 2008).

The foundation of AUC confirmed the significance of the new liberal arts model in Dutch higher education, as it was established jointly by the capital city's two major research universities and with substantial up-front support from the Ministry of Education, the City of Amsterdam, and corporate sponsors. They established AUC based on the belief that the leaders of the future will have to be successful in working together across the boundaries of nationalities, cultures and disciplines, that they will have to perform on an international competitive level in scientific, corporate and public service sectors. Furthermore, it was felt that the global city of Amsterdam, with its two major research universities, was the perfect context where excellence and diversity could naturally meet. The underlying considerations reflect the factors (described above) that led to the development of liberal arts in the Dutch university sector:

- The globalization of our society and the need, in a globally competitive environment, to nurture talent, develop it and attract it internationally.
- The need to widen choice in Dutch higher education and to create more avenues for excellence.
- The increasing demand for study programmes that are intellectually challenging and call for broad academic, cultural and social interests.
- The need for more opportunities for students to major in science and science-related fields in a liberal arts and sciences context.

- Developments in bilingual and international education at Dutch secondary schools.
- The multicultural character of Amsterdam and the presence of so many international companies and institutions, offering the perfect environment for connecting excellence and diversity in an academic context (AUC Faculty Handbook).

AUC capitalized on the previous initiatives, mainly introduced by the Universities of Utrecht and Maastricht. It also capitalized on the American experience, but not without a critical stance. In considering its profile, it drew on recent accounts of liberal arts education in the United States including strong pleas to reinvent liberal education in the view of especially new pedagogies (Levine, 2006) and sharp critiques of how even great universities such as Harvard failed to fulfil their basic mission in undergraduate education, that is to educate students to become responsible citizens (Lewis, 2006) and, in particular, on the serious reflections on undergraduate education in the USA, as expressed by Bok (2006), who admitted that basic levels in academic skills such as mathematics, writing, speaking, and critical thinking were not achieved by the majority of students. Furthermore, it was acknowledge that global knowledge, such as foreign languages, international understanding and intercultural awareness was virtually lacking in most programmes, including those run by top-level institutions. The critical AAC&U (2007) report on College Learning in the Global Century, which presented an interesting review of liberal arts education underlining the importance of a global perspective by stating that recent world events have brought into the foreground the importance of linking academic education to issues of democratic citizenship, pluralism, and interculturalism, was also considered. An earlier (2005) AAC&U report on essential learning outcomes in liberal arts demonstrated that intercultural knowledge received low ratings from both faculty and students. Low scores on learning outcomes from liberal arts programmes in quantitative literacy were also quite striking.

AUC benefited from these lessons learned and demonstrates that European initiatives are not necessarily a simple copy of American liberal arts models. Its motto, 'Excellence and Diversity in a Global City' reflects the belief that both excellence and diversity matter, as both competition and cooperation are key to success in a globalized world. Leadership does not only require excellence, but also the understanding and valuing of diversity (AUC, 2009). Diversity is reflected in its student and staff body. Global issues, multilingualism and intercultural skills are integral to the curriculum. Another profiling choice was made to emphasize the sciences (AUC aims for 50 percent science majors) and the training of quantitative skills (numeracy) for all students. This was, on the one hand, a strategic choice since the country and especially the city produced insufficient numbers of science graduates and it was clear that potential science candidates were attracted more by broader programmes than by the traditional monodisciplinary science studies. On the other hand, it was based on the belief that the sciences need to be an integral part of an all-round education and that they can be successfully taught in a liberal arts context (see, for instance, the evidence provided in favour of teaching the sciences in a liberal arts context by Nobel Laureate T. Cech, 1999). Moreover, that the bridging of the sciences and the humanities and social sciences is essential to solving the world's greatest problems, as expressed by the president of the Royal Netherlands Academy of Sciences and Arts in his address at AUC's opening, referring to C.P. Snow's famous lecture on 'The Two Cultures and the Scientific Revolution' (1961): 'We are increasingly dependent on and driven by science and technology, the silent forces of history, and ignorance of the working and ideas of science is dangerous'. These considerations inspired the development of a new curriculum, drawing on imminent scholars in all disciplines from the two founding universities. The bare question of what should be taught in order to equip graduates for success in the 21st century led them to outline an engaging curriculum that reaches across disciplinary boundaries, focusing on the 'the big questions in science and society' (www.auc.nl/acadprog).

## Conclusions and Reflection

Recent European developments urged higher education systems to adapt in order to better prepare college graduates for the complex realities of this new global world, in which Europe wants to play a role as a leading knowledge economy. However, the realization of the Humboldtian tradition, with its blessed link between research and education and its strong emphasis on the disciplines, had led to overly narrow areas of study. The Bologna Process, underlining the importance of undergraduate education as an educational cycle in its own right, has not yet achieved its potential for broadening undergraduate education. European higher education needs to differentiate more in order to generate excellence and, as such, has pushed the search for new avenues and solutions. Also, in the USA, it was realized that the traditional modular and disciplinary curriculum had become dysfunctional, as it results in a fragmented and incoherent educational experience, whereas the frontiers of knowledge call for cross-disciplinary enquiry, analysis, and application and the major issues and problems of our time — from ensuring global sustainability to negotiating international markets to expanding human freedom — transcend individual disciplines (AAC&U, 2007). In both Europe and in the USA, the requirements resulting from globalization and the innovative character of the knowledge economy are leading to a revival and revaluing of the liberal arts and sciences tradition. The question was raised before, however, how the utilitarian rationales of the knowledge economy are to be related to the inherent humanistic values of the liberal arts tradition. The (provisional) answer is that they need to be combined, as the 21st century requires graduates to be broadly educated, global citizens, both literate and numerate. Thus, they should ideally pursue an educational approach that bridges the humanities and the sciences, as defended by Snow (1961). The liberal arts and sciences model is qualified to pave the way and the fact that it is developing in Europe creates promising opportunities for cross-Atlantic learning, inspiration, and cooperation. At the same time, it should be noted that this development in Europe is only nascent and far from having the scope, size, and elite status that it has in the USA. Despite its European origins and re-emerging popularity, substantial advocacy is required by and within the European higher education community in order to deepen the understanding of the liberal arts model of education in order to truly benefit from its potential for the 21st century.

## Note

1   A version of this article was previously published under the same title in the journal *Higher Education Policy*.
2   This article is based on a key note address delivered at the International Symposium 'Liberal Arts Education: Global Perspectives & Developments', co-organized by the Center for International Higher Education, Boston College, USA and Amsterdam University College, the Netherlands, on 14 April, 2010, in Boston, MA.

## References

Amsterdam University College. (2009). 'Impressions of the grand opening.' Retrieved from www.auc.nl/aucnews/home.cfm/933925A3-1321-B0BE-A45F0D08931C38D7

Association of American Colleges and Universities. (2005). *Liberal Education Outcomes. A Preliminary Report on Student Achievement in College*. Washington, DC: AAC&U.

Association of American Colleges and Universities. (2007). *College Learning for the New Global Century. A Report from the National Leadership Council for Liberal Education and America's Promise (LEAP)*. Washington, DC: AAC&U.

Bok, D. (2006). *Our Underachieving Colleges. A Candid Look at How Much Students Learn and Why They Should be Learning More*. Princeton, NJ: Princeton University Press.

Cech, T. R. (1999). "Science at liberal arts colleges: A better education?" *Daedalus* 128(1): 195–216.

Commissie Ruim Baan voor Talent. (2007). "Wegen voor Talent." Retrieved from www.leroweb.nl/docs/lero/wegen_voor_talent.pdf

Commissie Toekomstbestendig Hoger Onderwijs Stelsel. (2010). *Differentiëren in drievoud. Omville van kwaliteit en verscheidenheid in het hoger onderwijs*. Den Haag, the Netherlands: OCW.

Dearing, R. (1997). *Higher Education in the Learning Society*. Leeds, UK: National Committee of Inquiry into Higher Education.

De Ridder-Symoens, H. (Ed.). (1996). *A History of the University in Europe*. Cambridge, UK: Cambridge University Press.

European Commission (EC). (2005). "Mobilising the brainpower of Europe: Enabling universities to make their full contribution to the Lisbon strategy." Retrieved from http://ec.europa.eu/education/policies/2010/ doc/comuniv2005_en.pdf

Gaston, P. L. (2008). *Bologna: A Challenge for Liberal Education and an Exceptional Opportunity*. Washington, DC: AAC&U.

Glyer, D. and Weeks, D. L. (Eds.). (1998). *The Liberal Arts in Higher Education. Challenging Assumptions Exploring Possibilities*. Lanham, MD: University Press of America.

Grant, M. (2009). "US-style liberal arts degree at UCL." *Financial Times*. 30 October.

Gurria, A. (2007). "Human capital: Europe's next frontier". Schuman Lecture 2007, for the Lisbon Council, Brussels, 27 February.

Huisman, J. and Van Vught, F. A. (2009). "Diversity in European higher education: Historical trends and current policies." In F. A. van Vught (Ed.) *Mapping the Higher Education Landscape. Towards a European Classification of Higher Education*. Dordrecht, Germany: Springer, 17–39.

Kehm, B. and Pasternack, P. (2009). "The German 'Excellence Initiative' and its role in restructuring the national higher education landscape." In D. Palfreyman and T. Tapper (Eds.). *Structuring Mass Higher Education. The Role of Elite Institutions*. London: Routledge, 113–28.

Levine, D. N. (2006). *Powers of the Mind. The Reinvention of Liberal Learning in America*. Chicago, IL: The University of Chicago Press.

Lewis, H. R. (2006). *Excellence Without a Soul. Does Liberal Education have a Future?* New York: PublicAffairs.

Nussbaum, M. (1997). *Cultivating Humanity: A Classical Defense of Reform in Liberal Education*. Cambridge, MA: Harvard University Press.

Nybom, T. (2003). "The Humboldt legacy: Reflections on the past, present and future of the European university." *Higher Education Policy* 16(2): 141–60.

OECD. (2008a). *Tertiary Education for the Knowledge Society*, Vol. 1. Paris: OECD.

OECD. (2008b). *Reviews of Tertiary Education — The Netherlands*. Paris: OECD.

Palfreyman, D. and Tapper, T. (2009). "Oxbridge: Sustaining the international reputation." in D. Palfreyman and T. Tapper (Eds.). *Structuring Mass Higher Education. The Role of Elite Institutions*. London: Routledge, 303–320.

Rothblatt, S. (Ed.). (1992). *The OECD, the Master Plan and the California Dream: A Berkeley Conversation*. Berkeley, CA: Center for Studies in Higher Education University of California.

Rothblatt, S. (2003). *The Living Arts: Comparative and Historical Reflections on Liberal Education*. Washington, DC: Association of American Colleges and Universities.

Rupp, J. C. C. (1997). *Van oude en nieuwe universiteiten. De verdringing van Duitse door Amerikaanse invloeden op de wetenschapsbeoefening en het hoger onderwijs in Nederland 1045–1995*. Den Haag, Netherlands: SDU Uitgevers.

Snow, C. P. (1961). *The Two Cultures and the Scientific Revolution. The Rede Lecture 1959*. Cambridge, UK: Cambridge University Press.

Sursock, A. and Smidt, H. (2010). *Trends 2010: A Decade of Change in European Higher Education*. Brussels, Belgium: EUA.

The Guardian. (2010). *Liberal Arts Offer Something Completely Different* Retrieved from http://www.guardian.co.uk/education/2010/jan/19/liberal-arts-degrees.

US World & News Report. (2010). "National liberal arts rankings." http://colleges.usnews.rankingsandreviews.com/best-colleges/liberal-arts.

van der Wende, M. C. (2009). "European Responses to Global Competitiveness in Higher Education." In J. Douglass, J. King, and I. Feller (Eds.) *Globalization's Muse: Universities and Higher Education Systems in a Changing World*. Berkeley, CA: Berkeley Public Policy Press, 317–41.

Weenink, D. (2007). "Cosmopolitan and established resources of power in the education arena." *International Sociology* 22: 492–516.

Weenink, D. (2008). "Cosmopolitanism as a form of capital: Parents preparing their children for a globalizing world." *Sociology* 42(6): 1089–1106.

Winckler, G. (2006). "The contribution of universities to Europe's competitiveness." speech given to the Conference of the European Ministers of Education; 16–17 March 2006; Vienna, Austria. Retrieved from www.eua.be/eua/jsp/en/upload/EUA_Winckler_Speech_160306.1142503291615.pdf

Witte, J. (2006). "Change of degrees and degrees of change." *Comparing Adaptations of European Higher Education Systems in the Context of the Bologna Process*, Ph.D. dissertation. Enschede: Centre for Higher Education Policy Studies, University of Twente.

# 8

# THINKING CRITICALLY ABOUT LIBERAL ARTS EDUCATION

## Yale-NUS College in Singapore

*Charlene Tan*

## Introduction

Liberal arts education has gained traction in many countries as government leaders seek to borrow new educational models to prepare their graduates for a competive and globalised world. With its accent on broad-based learning, discursive reasoning and higher-order thinking, the liberal arts approach is increasingly embraced as a means to promote 21st century competencies in learners. A case in point is the establishment of a joint liberal arts college (NUS-Yale College) between Yale University and the National University of Singapore. Since its inception in 2011, the College in Singapore has attracted many students from the region and beyond who are keen to have a taste of liberal arts education. Its first three application cycles witnessed more than 30,000 highly qualified applications from around the world, with an admission rate of less than five per cent (Salovey & Chuan, 2016).

Among the thinking skills, critical thinking is closely associated with liberal arts education; Barnett (1997) describes it as "one of the defining concepts of the Western University" (p. 3, cited in Moore, 2013, p. 506). Robinson (2011) observes that the "perceived significance of critical thinking skills is reflected in the requirement of many North American Liberal Arts Colleges and universities that students complete at least one course in critical thinking prior to graduation" (p. 276). Despite its prevalent use, there is no commonly agreed definition of critical thinking (Johnson, 1992; Capossela, 1998; Bailin et al, 1999; Baidon & Sim, 2009; Tian & Low, 2011). In his literature review, Walters (1994) identifies two dominant conceptions of critical thinking: an adversarial nature of logicistic thinking versus an empathic, interpersonal, and connected style of thinking. The former is a confrontational type of thinking that values and showcases one's skilful application of logical analysis and argumentation. This type of critical thinking is analogous to fighting a battle where one attacks and defends one's position, and where 'the winner takes it all' (Bailin, 1995). Antipodal to adversarial critical thinking is cooperative critical thinking that seeks to reconcile one's own position and that of the other party (Waller, 2012; Durkin, 2008). Elaborating on the latter, what he calls 'dialogical thinking', Paul (1987) advocates approaching an issue from more than one frame of reference. This involves entering "empathically into more or less alien belief systems" and bringing "our implicit ideas and reasonings into open dialogical conflict with opposing ones to decide rationally, as best we can, upon their merit as candidates for mindful belief" (p. 284). Paul (1981) models this self-reflection by giving an example from his own teaching: "Since I teach in the United States and since the media here as everywhere reflects, and the students have typically internalised, a profoundly 'nationalistic' bias, I focus on issues that, to be approached dialectically, require the student to discover that 'American' reasoning and the 'American' point of view on world issues is not the only dialectical possibility" (p. 5). It should be pointed out that the two traditions only represent two extreme forms of critical thinking; there exists other types of critical thinking along a spectrum across space and time.

It is evident that an understanding of critical thinking at a particular locality needs to take into consideration the influences of local conditions and cultures (e.g., Paul, 1981; Fishman, 1988; Norris, 1995; Bailin, 1995; Atkinson, 1997; Ennis; 1998; Vandermensbrugghe, 2004; Peters, 2007; McGuire, 2007; Durkin, 2008). Far from being neutral, apolitical and independent of the contexts, critical thinking comprises "culturally and historically situated critical social practices" (Baidon & Sim, 2009, p. 411). How then is critical thinking defined and appropriated in a non-Western context such as Singapore? Focussing on the controversies surrounding NUS-Yale College in Singapore, this chapter explores the different notions, presuppositions and expression of critical thinking by various educational stakeholders. The first part of this chapter gives an introduction to NUS-Yale College, followed by a discussion of two controversies related to the College. The next section examines the different conceptions and presuppositions of critical thinking held by various parties who are involved in the controversies. The last section proposes a form of critical thinking that is contextually appropriate for the flourishing of liberal arts education in Singapore.

## Yale-NUS College in Singapore

Yale-NUS College, established in 2011, is the first liberal arts college in Singapore. A partnership between Yale University in the U.S. and the National University of Singapore (NUS) in Singapore, it started with 150 students in August 2013. The numbers has since grown to over 500 students who hail from 38 countries (Yale-NUS College, 2016). The 2015 enrolment for the Class of 2019 saw more than 8,500 applicants from around the world vying for 198 places (Yale-NUS College, 2016). In alignment with the tradition of a liberal arts college, critical thinking is a cornerstone of Yale-NUS College's educational philosophy, curriculum and pedagogy.

Yale-NUS College describes itself as a "liberal arts college" dedicated to "building a community in which living and learning are intertwined and habits of creativity, curiosity, and *critical thinking* are encouraged" (ibid., italics added). The curriculum has been designed to drive "*critical*, creative and active thinking" (ibid., italics added) so that its graduates possess "the capacity to think critically" (National University of Singapore, 2012). At its official opening in 2014, the Prime Minister of Singapore Lee Hsien Loong affirmed that the College "offers broad-based, multidisciplinary undergraduate curriculum, one which we hope will develop *critical thinking*, appreciation for complexity, communications and leadership skills" (cited in Government of Singapore, 2014, italics added). In a recent article jointly written by the Presidents of Yale University and the National University of Singapore (Peter Salovey and Tan Chorh Chuan respectively), both of them reiterate the goal of Yale-NUS College to empower its students to "reflect critically" (Salovey & Chuan, 2016).

An interesting feature of Yale-NUS College that sets it apart from typical liberal arts colleges in the U.S. is its aspiration to "redefine" (Yale-NUS College, 2016) or "re-imagine" liberal arts and science education (Salovey & Chuan, 2016). This desire signifies that the College is not a mere carbon copy or offshoot of Yale University, what the Human Rights Watch (2012) erroneously describes as "Yale's Singapore campus". As clarified by the Prime Minister of Singapore, "It is not a replica of Yale, but a bold effort to create something new and different" where the College "takes the best of US liberal arts education from Yale, New Haven, adds NUS' distinctive Asian and global strengths, adapts this mix to our different social and cultural contexts, and creates an experience which is more relevant to students" (cited in Government of Singapore, 2014). Positioning itself as "a community of learning, founded by two great universities", the College hopes to draw on "the resources and traditions of two great universities" and "introduce our students to the diverse intellectual traditions and cultures of Asia and the world" (Yale-NUS College, 2016). Highlighting the unique East-West hybridised framework, the president of Yale-NUS College Pericles Lewis claims, "Here you get a chance to study major works of Western and Asian civilisations in conversation with one another so in that sense it's a truly global curriculum" (cited in Goochaug, 2012).

The task of redefining liberal arts education at Yale-NUS College involves introducing corresponding policies, curriculum, teaching methods and assessment systems that combine the traditions and practices of both Yale University and NUS. This requires a process of selection and (re)construction, as noted by the dean of faculty Charles Bailyn: "NUS and Yale both did things differently, so we pretty much had to start everything from first principles" (cited in Grove, 2015). Examples of judicous adaptation of practices from both institutions include the introduction of a common curriculum for all first-year students (an NUS practice) and not grading the students' work in the first semester (a Yale practice). As for the recommended pedagogy at Yale-NUS College, critical thinking naturally takes centre place, as indicated in the college's website (Yale-NUS College, 2016). But it is unclear what is meant by critical thinking and how it should be applied by the staff and students. Is it conceived as an adversarial nature of logicistic thinking or as an empathic, interpersonal, and connected style of thinking? To what extent do the local culture and socio-politial constraints influence the notion and practice of critical thinking at Yale-NUS College? To answer these questions, the rest of the essay focuses on the controversies related to Yale-NUS College.

## Controversies Surrounding Yale-NUS College

Since its genesis in 2011, Yale-NUS College has attracted international attention not just for its success in recruiting high-performing students from around the world, but also for a few contentious issues associated with it. This essay discusses two such issues.

### Controversy over Freedom of Expression

The first controversy originated from the concerns and opposition from the Yale faculty and other stakeholders in the U.S. regarding freedom of expression in Singapore. A central question is how the perceived restriction on the free speech, assembly and association in Singapore may affect the exercise of freedom of thought and critical thinking at Yale-NUS College. In April 2012, the faculty members of Yale University passed a resolution to express their "concern regarding the lack of respect for civil and political rights in the state of Singapore" and argued for the need to "respect, protect, and further those rights" which "lie at the heart of liberal arts education" (cited in Sleeper, 2014). The American Association of University Professors (AAUP) also sent an open letter to the Yale community to "express the AAUP's growing concern about the character and impact" of the collaboration (AAUP, n.d.). Citing an earlier 2009 joint statement by the AAUP and the Canadian Association of University Teachers, AAUP cautioned, "In a host environment where free speech is constrained, if not proscribed, faculty will censor themselves, and the cause of authentic liberal education, to the extent it can exist in such situations, will suffer" (ibid.). Stronger words came from the deputy Asia director of Human Rights Watch, Phil Robertson, who charged that "Yale is betraying the spirit of the university as a centre of open debate and protest by giving away the rights of its students at its new Singapore campus" (cited in Human Rights Watch, 2012). He drew attention to Yale's 1975 University Policy on Freedom of Expression that states:

> The primary function of a university is to discover and disseminate knowledge....To fulfill this function a free exchange of ideas is necessary not only within its walls but with the world beyond as well....The history of intellectual growth and discovery demonstrates the need for *unfettered freedom, the right to think the unthinkable, discuss the unmentionable, and challenge the unchallengeable* (cited in Human Rights Watch, 2012, italics added).

Urging the Yale faculty to protest, he contends, "If it [Yale University] truly values those freedoms, and expects its students to, it will need to fight for them" (cited in Human Rights Watch, 2012).

In response, both the president of Yale-NUS College (Pericles Lewis) and president of Yale University at that time (Richard C. Levin) issued statements on July 19, 2012. Giving the assurance that "Yale-NUS's policy specifically protects academic freedom for research, teaching, and discussion on campus and for publication of the resulting scholarship", Lewis asserts, "I believe without reservation in the mission of the new College, and my Yale-NUS colleagues and I are working to create an intellectual community where open debate and critical inquiry will thrive" (cited in Yale University, 2016). He points out that the College has obtained guarantees from the Ministry of Education in Singapore that the staff and students are free to conduct research, publish, teach and discuss issues on campus, and that there will be no discrimination based on sexual orientation at the campus (Goochuang, 2012). The reference to discrimination arising from sexual orientation is due to the unhappiness from some international observers such as the Human Rights Watch that Singapore law, under Section 377A of the Penal Code, makes sex between men a crime. Lewis' statement was reinforced by the then president of Yale University who stated, "We negotiated language protecting academic freedom and open inquiry on the Yale-NUS campus, as well as the freedom to publish the results of scholarly inquiry in the academic literature" (ibid.). Allying the fear that critical thinking may be curtailed, he added that Yale-NUS College is on the way to advance "both the development of liberal arts curriculum and pedagogy encouraging critical inquiry" (ibid.).

But even as both Lewis and Levin attempt to assuage critics of Yale-NUS College that academic freedom is maintained, they stress, in the same statements, that the College should respect the laws of the country where it is located. Lewis averred that "[a]ny college or university must obey the laws of the countries where it operates" and that "[w]e are aware that there are restrictions on speech and public demonstrations in Singapore" (Yale University, 2016). In the same vein, Lewin posited that "freedom of assembly was constrained in Singapore, and that students and faculty would have to observe national laws, as do students and faculty in Yale programmes from London to Beijing" (ibid.). What is instructive about their statements is not just their take on the question of freedoms in Singapore, but also their views on the right approach to resolve differences among the parties and across cultures. Both advocate the primacy of cross-cultural awareness, and learning through open-mindedness and dialogue. Quoting the liberal philosopher J. S. Mill, Lewis highlighted continued engagement and exchange as the means for progress:

> When I was appointed President of Yale-NUS College, I invoked John Stuart Mill's statement from 1848, "It is hardly possible to overstate the value of placing human beings in contact with persons dissimilar to themselves,

and with modes of thought and action unlike those with which they are familiar. Such communication has always been one of the primary sources of progress." I think this remains as relevant today as when Mill wrote it. In my view, progress depends on continued engagement and dialogue rather than retreat or insularity (ibid.).

Concurring with Lewis, Levin objected to the "sense of [Western] moral superiority" implied in the Yale faculty resolution (cited in Sleeper, 2014). Underscoring the need for humility, cross-cultural understanding and open-mindedness, he elaborated:

> We have approached our engagement in Singapore in the spirit that has characterised Yale's many other engagements around the globe: that *we have much to learn.* Social norms, practices, and values differ widely across nations and cultures. We (our students and faculty) seek to embrace these differences and seek to understand them, as the first step toward building the *cross-cultural understanding* that must be the foundation of global citizenship and cooperation in the face of the great challenges confronting our planet. We believe that engagement with difference, and the education that inevitably flows from it, is a far more effective instrument for advancing the human spirit than either isolation or *insistence that ours is the only true way* (ibid., italics added).

It is noteworthy that the appeal by Lewis and Lewin for a culturally-embedded and cooperative form of critical thinking is in tandem with the position of the Ministry of Education in Singapore. The former Education Minister of Singapore, Heng Swee Keat, stated that Yale-NUS College should exercise "academic freedom and open inquiry … in a manner sensitive to the Singapore context." (cited in Human Rights Watch, 2012). Observing that "countries are not converging on a single universal social or political model that will best deal with these challenges under all circumstances", the Prime Minister of Singapore believes that what Yale-NUS needs is "a curriculum and a college ethos that respond to this regional context" (cited in Khamid, 2015).

## Controversy over a Speech Made by a Governing Board Member

The second controversy occurred in early 2016. It began when Singapore's Ambassador-at-Large, Chan Heng Chee, who is also a governing board member of Yale-NUS College, spoke at the 24th session of the United Nations Human Rights Council's Universal Periodic Review in Geneva in January 2016. At the meeting, she defended the Singapore Government's Section 377A of the Penal Code that criminalises sex between men by noting that "Singapore is basically a conservative society" (Heng, 2016). But she added that the law would not be proactively enforced and that "[w]e firmly oppose discrimination and harassment and we have laws to protect our citizens from such acts" (ibid.).

Chan's action prompted a Yale-NUS student Nicholas Carverhill to criticise her speech in a Yale-NUS publication, *The Octant* (Caverhill, 2016). He challenged Chan to repudiate the Singapore government's stance on Section 377A or resign from the college's governing board. This is based on his argument that it is unacceptable for Yale-NUS College to retain Ambassador Chan as a member of its governing board so long as she advocates for the preservation of Section 377A. In his words, "Barring a willingness to defend the rights of LGBTQI+ [Lesbian, Gay, Bisexual, Transgender, Queer or Questioning, and Intersex+] students—including a stand against official discriminatory government policies— Ambassador Chan must be asked to relinquish her position on the Governing Board" (ibid.). Rallying support for his stand, he contended that not demanding for Chan's resignation from the governing board (unless she recants) is to "sacrifice our LGBTQI+ peers at the altar of political expediency" (ibid.).

Besides Caverhill, a student group of the College also issued a 'Statement of Concern' and requested a closed-door meeting with Chan on the matter (Xu, 2016). While it is unclear how many students and staff were supportive of Caverhill's stance, what is interesting was the response given by the President of Yale-NUS College on this matter. While noting that the College's leadership "has been in close dialogue with our students and we've heard their views", Lewis stated that the College does not support the call for Chan to give up her position in the governing board. Instead, "we advised our students to be open to a range of views and to engage broadly, rather than to be intolerant of perspectives that are different from theirs" (cited in Heng, 2016). Such an appraoch, he adds, is in line with the vision for the College to be a "community of learning, where all viewpoints are heard and a respectful understanding of different opinions and beliefs is tolerated and understood" (cited in ibid.). Lewis' statement implies that Caverhill as well as his supporters, in criticising and issuing the ultimatum to Chan, are not accepting of opposing views. A more critical response came from Singapore's Ambassador-at-large Bilahari Kausikan, who claims that the attitude of Caverhill and his supporters "fundamentally contradicts the supposedly liberal tolerance for different views" and demonstrates "the illiberalism of liberals" (cited in Tan, 2016b).

## Discussion

A shared theme in both the controversies is a debate on the socio-cultural condition needed for the flourishing of liberal arts education in general and critical thinking in particular. How much freedom of expression is needed and how critical should one be in Singapore? With respect to critical thinking, a fundamental question is whether the freedoms and rights given to the staff and students of Yale-NUS College are sufficient for them to engage in robust critical inquiry and open debate. The answer to this question depends, among other things, on one's interpretation of 'freedom' and 'critical thinking'. We can identify at least two contrasting viewpoints arising from the Yale-NUS College controversies.

On the one hand is an interpretation of freedom as unfettered and critical thinking as challenging the status quo and adversarial. This position is encapsulated in Yale's 1975 University Policy on Freedom of Expression, cited earlier, that propagates "unfettered freedom, the right to think the unthinkable, discuss the unmentionable, and challenge the unchallengeable" (cited in Human Rights Watch, 2012). This view is exemplified by the deputy Asia director at Human Rights Watch Phil Robertson who cited the above policy in his critique of freedoms in Singapore. Using battlefield language where there is a clear winner and loser, he challenges the Yale faculty to "fight" for the freedoms or risk "giving away" their rights and "betray[ing] the spirit of Yale University" (Human Rights Watch, 2012). The same combative, 'we versus them' approach was adopted by Caverhill who champions the freedom and right of LGBTQI+ community by insisting that Ambassador Chan must either recant her views or relinquish her position on the governing board of Yale-NUS College. Like Robertson, who warns that a failure to fight is an act of betrayal, Caverhill posits that not removing Chan from the board is to "sacrifice our LGBTQI+ peers at the altar of political expediency" (Caverhill, 2016). Assuming an adversarial style of critical thinking, the goal of Robertson and Caverhill is to win the argument or battle by attacking the opponent's argument and showing that one's argument is superior to the opponent's.

Contrasting with the above-mentioned view of freedom and critical thinking is the position exemplified by Lewis (president of Yal-NUS College) and Levin (then president of Yale University). They generally understand freedoms not as unfettered but as situated within historical, political and socio-cultural realities and constraints. Rather than espousing adversarial critical thinking, they stress a culturally embedded and cooperative model of critical thinking that foregrounds empathy, engagement and cooperation. As noted earlier, Lewis maintains that "progress depends on continued engagement and dialogue" (cited in Yale University, 2016) where "all viewpoints are heard and a respectful understanding of different opinions and beliefs is tolerated and understood" (cited in Heng, 2016). Lewin stresses that "we [Yale University] have much to learn" and propounds "cross-cultural understanding" and "engagement with difference" without the "insistence that ours is the only true way" (cited in Yale University, 2016).

Returning to the vision of Yale-NUS College to redefine or re-imagine liberal arts education, it would appear that part of the redefinition/re-imagination involves an approach towards critical thinking that differs from the one promoted in the Yale's 1975 University Policy on Freedom of Expression and demonstrated by Robertson and Caverhill. The conception of critical thinking advocated for Yale-NUS College rejects the adversarial form of critical thinking that is common in Western universities and liberal arts colleges. Vandermensbrugghe (2004) highlights the trend of Western academics presenting "Anglo-Saxon university practices" as being natural and often assume that the conventions surrounding these practices are either universally known, or that they should be universally applied" (p. 418). In the same vein, Fox (1994) observes that the practice of critical thinking as well as the dominant communication style and world view of the U.S. university are derived from "western—or more specifically U.S.—culture" (p. xxi, cited in Atkinson, 1999, p. 75). Underpinning the different conceptions of critical thinking in the controversies surrounding Yale-NUS College are different cultural worldviews and assumptions. An example is the definition and scope of 'freedom'. As Yale-NUS's inaugural dean Charles Bailyn puts it, "What we [Americans] think of as freedom, they think of as an affront to public order" (cited in Sleeper, 2014). The Singapore experience illustrates Paul's (1981) claim that the American reasoning and point of view "is not the only dialectical possibility" (p. 5). Insisting that one's view is *the* right one or that others' views have no place in the discussion, is to evince egocentric and sociocentric bias (Paul, 1981). Arguably this is what Levin has in mind when he asserts that the Yale faculty resolution implies a "sense of [Western] moral superiority" (cited in Sleeper, 2014). Commenting on Caverhill's militant stance, a Singaporean undergraduate at Yale-NUS College opines that it "demonstrates a lack of understanding of local politics" and that "extreme and confrontational means" will not work in Singapore (cited in Xu, 2016).

Instead of adversarial critical thinking, cooperative critical thinking is recommended for Yale-NUS College that allows ample space for diversity of opinions, conciliation and relationship-building. A number of scholars have argued that a form of critical thinking that underlines collaboration, dialogue and empathy is more suitable for the Asian contexts. Drawing upon her empirical research with students from Confucian Heritage Culture societies, Durkin (2008) concludes that these students reject "the confrontational, battlefield approach" where one has to "battle between two polarised positions, as in the western adversarial approach to debate" (p. 23). Instead they prefer a "more conciliatory approach which allows ample space for diversity of opinions" so as to preserve harmony and not embarrass anyone publicly (also see Hofstede & Hofstede 2005; Nguyen, Terlouw & Pilot, 2006; Tan, 2006). I have also argued elsewhere that it is culturally difficult for Asians to handle disagreements, as the person's cultural background prompts him/her to perceive a difference of opinion as an attack on both himself/herself and the group of which he/she is a part (Tan, 2006, 2016a; also see Osterloh, 1986; Kwok et al., 1993; Kinney, 1995; Ho, 2001). That Asian students are generally uncomfortable with adversarial critical thinking has also been observed in the classrooms of Yale-NUS College. It has been reported that Yale-NUS administrators observed that many Singaporean students hesitated to speak up in class, and that the lively exchanges and loud debates often found in American seminars are absent in the classrooms in Singapore (Kofman & Stephenson, 2012). The same report noted that "students in Singapore often feel dissuaded from speaking out in class at the risk of looking foolish in front of their peers. Instead, students may choose to remain quiet and 'save face'—a tendency NUS administrators said is more common in Asian cultures" (ibid.).

However, a form of critical thinking that over-emphasises consensus-building and acceptance of local political and socio-cultural conditions is inadequate in developing confident and mature critical thinkers. This is because this model of critical thinking may inhibit the participants from asking tough and unpopular questions for fear of disrupting the social harmony and challenging the status quo. Consequently, the participants are not encouraged to self-reflect and critique their own egocentric and sociocentric tendencies. To guard against this development, it is recommended that the staff, students and other educational stakeholders understand and interrogate different worldviews, including their own, that shape different formulations and applications of critical thinking. Against a backdrop of multiple voices, perspectives, worldviews and conceptions of the good, it is essential for learners to question the construction, presuppositions and application of knowledge as well as related issues of power, justice, identity and the ways texts and practices are shaped by ideology (Baidon & Sim, 2009). An example would be to explore and compare the historical and political roots of liberal arts education and critical thinking in Yale University and NUS. Related issues for reflection and debate include examining how ideologies such as liberal individualism, communitarianism and Confucianism play a part in shaping one's views of critical thinking; how to strike a balance between respecting another country's laws and cultures and avoiding any form of critical inquiry and judgement altogether; the pros and cons of adversarial and cooperative thinking; the sufficiency, strengths and weaknesses of freedoms in Singapore; and the political and socio-cultural changes needed for liberal arts education to flourish in Singapore and the region. This process of inquiry requires active and constant engagement with oneself and others that will result in the re-construction of critical thinking and the redefinition/re-imagination of liberal arts education in Singapore

## Conclusion

This chapter explored the concept and application of critical thinking using the establishment of a joint liberal arts college (NUS-Yale College) between Yale University and the National University of Singapore as an example. By examining the debate surrounding the joint project, this essay identified and discussed the different views and assumptions of critical thinking held by various educational stakeholders. It was argued that critics of Yale-NUS College generally subscribe to a context-free and adversarial form of critical thinking while supporters of the College hold to a culturally embedded and cooperative conception. It was further proposed that participants seek to understand diferent perspectives empathetically, acknowlege one's own biases, and engage in cross-cultural dialogue. Our case study highlights critical thinking not only as having multiple meanings, but also as being a contested notion (Moore, 2013). For Yale-NUS College to succeed, it is essential for the educators and other educational stakeholders to co-construct not only the contents of liberal arts, but also the notion of critical thinking itself that facilitates such studies. As Moore (2011) rightly points out, "the ways in which key attributes like critical thinking are understood and conceptualised in our institutions are likely to have a major bearing on the shaping of university curricula and of higher education policy as a whole" (p. 262).

It is interesting to note that proponents of the respective conceptions of critical thinking (adversarial versus cooperative) do not fall neatly into the West/U.S./ Yale University camp vis-à-vis the East/Singapore/Yale-NUS College camp. On the contrary, the supporters of cooperative critical thinking include the presidents of Yale University and Yale-NUS College who are both Americans and faculty members of Yale University. Likewise, among the supporters of Robertson and Caverhill are Singaporeans, including members of the student group of the College who issued a Statement of Concern over Ambassador Chan's comments and those who support the repeal of Section 377A of the Penal Code. By the same argument, the varied and incompatible interpretations of freedoms is not simply a 'East versus West' issue. Even among the American academics, they do not always agree on the nature and extent of freedom of expression needed to support liberal arts education. We have seen how the presidents of Yale University and Yale-NUS College believe that the degree of freedom allowed by the Singapore government is sufficient for Yale-NUS College to succeed. This view, however, is challenged by the Yale faculty, AAUP and Human Rights Watch, among others. What the Yale-NUS College case study has demonstrated is that different interpretations and practices of critical thinking are not the result of a simplistic clash of cultures. Rather, the differences reflect the reality of historically situated critical social practices constructed by various agents and conditions. Far from being context-free, universal and neutral, critical thinking and by implication, liberal arts education, takes its shape and evolves by interacting with local worldviews and presuppositions.

## References

AAUP (n.d.). "An open letter from the AAUP to the Yale community." *American Association of University Professors*. Retrieved from www.aaup.org/news/2012/open-letter-aaup-yale-community (accessed 2 Feb 2016).

Atkinson, D. (1997). "A critical approach to critical thinking in TESOL." *TESOL Quarterly*, 31(1): 71–94.

Baidon, M. C., & Sim, J. B.-Y. (2009). "Notions of criticality: Singaporean teachers' perspectives of critical thinking in social studies." *Cambridge Journal of Education*, 39(4): 407–22.

Bailin, S., Case, R., Coombs, J. R., & Daniels, L. B. (1999). "Conceptualising critical thinking." *Journal of Curriculum Studies*, 31(3): 285–302.

Barnett, R. (1997). *Higher Education: A Critical Business*. Milton Keynes: Open University Press.

Capossela, T. (1998). What is critical writing? In Capossela, T. (Ed.) *The Critical Writing Workshop: Designing Writing Assignments to Foster Critical Thinking.* Portsmouth, NH: Heinemann, 1–10.

Caverhill, N. (2016). "On the Yale-NUS governing board, tolerance is not enough." *The Octant,* Feb 3. Retrieved from http://theoctant.org/edition/issue/uncategorized/on-the-yale-nus-governing-board-tolerance-is-not-enough/ (accessed 2 Feb 2016).

Durkin, K. (2008). "The adaptation of East Asian masters students to western norms of critical thinking and argumentation in the UK." *Intercultural Education, 19*(1): 15–27.

Ennis, R. H. (1998). "Is critical thinking culturally biased?" *Teaching Philosophy, 21*(1): 15–33.

Fishman, A. (1988). *Amish Literacy.* Portsmouth, NH: Heinemann.

Fox, H. (1994). *Listening to the World: Cultural Issues in Academic Writing.* Urbana, IL: National Council of Teachers of English.

Goochaug, L. (2012). "With opening near, Yale defends Singapore venture." *The New York Times,* Aug 27. Retrieved from www.nytimes.com/2012/08/27/world/asia/27iht-educlede27.html?_r=0 (accessed 2 Feb 2016).

Government of Singapore (2014). Speech by Prime Minister Lee Hsien Loong at Yale-NUS college groundbreaking ceremony. Retrieved from www.pmo.gov.sg/mediacentre/speech-prime-minister-lee-hsien-loong-yale-nus-college-groundbreaking-ceremony (accessed 2 Feb 2016).

Grove, J. (2015). "Yale-NUS College extends reach of liberal arts' 'forbidden fruits'" *Times Higher Education,* Oct 22. Retrieved May 15, 2016, from www.timeshighereducation.com/news/yale-nus-college-extends-reach-liberal-arts-forbidden-fruits.

Heng, J. (2016). "Yale-NUS rejects call on envoy to quit post." *The Straits Times,* Feb 7. Retrieved from www.straitstimes.com/singapore/yale-nus-rejects-call-on-envoy-to-quit-post (accessed 2 Feb 2016).

Ho, C. L. (2001). "The cultural grounding of Singapore English." In Ooi, V. B. Y. (Ed.), *Evolving Identities: The English Language in Singapore and Malaysia.* Singapore: Times Academic Press, 102–11.

Hofstede, G., & Hofstede, J. (2005). *Cultures and Organization – Software of the Mind.* 2nd ed. New York: McGraw-Hill.

Human Rights Watch (2012). "Singapore: Yale to curtail rights on new campus." Retrieved from www.hrw.org/news/2012/07/19/singapore-yale-curtail-rights-new-campus (accessed son 2 Feb 2016).

Johnson, R. H. (1992). "The problem of defining critical thinking." In Norris, S. P. (Ed.) *The Generalisability of Critical Thinking: Multiple Perspectives on an Educational Ideal.* New York: Teacher College Press, 38–53.

Khamid, H. M. A. (2015). "Yale-NUS should not be carbon copy of US college to succeed: PM Lee." *Channel NewsAsia,* Oct 12. Retrieved from www.channelnewsasia.com/news/singapore/yale-nus-should-notbe/2186918.html (accessed 2 Feb 2016).

Kinney, B. A. (1995). *Chinese Views of Childhood.* Honolulu, HI: University of Hawaii Press.

Kofman, A., & Stephenson, T. (2012). "Liberal arts – Different in Yale and NUS?" *Yale Daily News,* May 20. Retrieved from https://generalpaperpress.wordpress.com/2012/05/20/liberal-arts-different-in-yale-and-nus/ (accessed 2 Feb 2016).

Kwok, K. W., Chang, C. T., & Ko, Y. C. (1993). The use of the 'ideal type' approach in the comparative study of Chinese childhood socialisation. Paper presented at the Conference on Chinese Childhood Socialisation, Honolulu, HI, East–West Centre.

McGuire, J. M. (2007). "Why has the critical thinking movement not come to Korea?" *Asia Pacific Education Review*, *8*(2): 224–32.

Moore, T. J. (2011). "Critical thinking and disciplinary thinking: A continuing debate." *Higher Education Research & Development*, *30*(3): 261–74.

Moore, T. (2013). "Critical thinking: seven definitions in search of a concept." *Studies in Higher Education*, *38*(4): 506–22.

National University of Singapore (2012). "The Yale-NUS College and liberal arts education." Retrieved from www.nus.edu.sg/registrar/nusbulletin/yale-nus-college/yale-nus-college-and-liberal-arts-education (accessed 2 Feb 2016).

Nguyen, P. -M., Terlouw, C., & Pilot, A. (2006). "Culturally appropriate pedagogy: The case of group learning in a Confucian Heritage Culture context." *Intercultural Education*, *17*(1): 1–19.

Norris, S. P. (1995). "Sustaining and responding to charges of bias in critical thinking." *Educational Theory*, *45*(2): 199–211.

Osterloh, K. (1986). "Intercultural differences and communicative approaches to foreign-language teaching in the third world." In Valdes, J. M. (Ed.) *Culture Bound: Bridging the Cultural Gap in Language Teaching*. Cambridge, UK: Cambridge University Press, 77–84.

Paul, R. (1981). "Teaching critical thinking in the 'strong sense': A focus on self-deception, world views, and a dialectical mode of analysis." *Informal Logic*, *4*(2): 2–7.

Paul, R. (1987). "Dialogical thinking: Critical thought essential to the acquisition of rational knowledge and passions." In Baron, J. & Sternberg, R. (Eds.) *Teaching Thinking Skills: Theory and Practice*. New York: W. H. Freeman and Company, 127–48.

Peters, M. A. (2007). "Kinds of thinking, styles of reasoning." *Educational Philosophy and Theory*, *39*(4): 350–63.

Robinson, S. R. (2011). "Teaching logic and teaching critical thinking: Revisiting McPeck." *Higher Education Research & Development*, *30*(3): 275–87.

Salovey, P. & Chuan, T. C. (2016, March 16). "Thinking deep and broad." *The Straits Times*, A25.

Sleeper, J. (2014, Sept. 26). "For Yale in Singapore, it's deja-vu all over again." *Huffpost Education*,. Retrieved from www.huffingtonpost.com/jim-sleeper/for-yale-in-singapore-its_b_5887258.html (accessed 2 Feb 2016).

Tan, C. (2006). "Creating thinking schools through 'Knowledge and Inquiry': The curriculum challenges for Singapore." *The Curriculum Journal*, *17*(1): 89–105.

Tan, C. (2016a). The cultural challenges for critical thinking: Perceptions of educators in Singapore. Unpublished manuscript.

Tan, J. (2016b). "Some Yale-NUS students want Ambassador-at-Large Chan Heng Chee removed from the school's board." *Mothership.Sg*. Retrieved from http://mothership.sg/2016/02/some-yale-nus-students-want-ambassador-at-large-chan-heng-chee-removed-from-the-schools-board/ (accessed 2 Feb 2016).

Tian, J., & Low, G. D. (2011). "Critical thinking and Chinese university students: A review of the evidence." *Language, Culture and Curriculum*, *24*(1): 61–76.

Vandermensbrugghe. J. (2004). "The unbearable vagueness of critical thinking in the context of the Anglo-Saxonisation of education." *International Education Journal*, *5*(3): 417–22.

Waller, B. N. (2012). *Critical Thinking: Consider the Verdict*. 6th ed. Upper Saddle River, NJ: Pearson.

Walters, K. (1994). "Introduction: Beyond logicism in critical thinking." In Walters, K. (Ed.) *Re-Thinking Reason: New Perspectives in Critical Thinking*. Albany, NY: SUNY Press, 33–42.

Xu, Q. (2016). "Yale-NUS admin speech sparks debate." *Yale Daily News*. Retrieved from http://yaledailynews.com/blog/2016/02/05/yale-nus-admin-speech-sparks-debate/ (accessed 2 Feb 2016).

Yale University (2016). "Presidential statements regarding Yale-NUS College." *YaleNews*. Retrieved from http://news.yale.edu/2012/07/19/presidential-statements-regarding-yale-nus-college (accessed 2 Feb 2016).

Yale-NUS College (2016). "Vision and mission." Retrieved from www.yale-nus.edu.sg/ (accessed 2 Feb 2016).

# 9

# ACADEMIC FREEDOM AND THE LIBERAL ARTS IN THE MIDDLE EAST

## Can the US Model Be Replicated?

*Neema Noori*

Advocates for expanding university branch campuses across the Middle East argue that by broadening the public sphere, Western institutions will serve as bastions of civil society in an otherwise authoritarian political landscape. However, there is considerable evidence that even Western branch universities in the region cannot openly speak on regionally contentious issues. To be sure, from 2011 to 2015, a series of high profile events have called into question the ability of Western branch campuses to safeguard academic freedom, arguably the cornerstone of the liberal arts model of higher education. Indeed, in 2011, one year into the Arab Spring, the UAE arrested Nasser bin Ghaith, a part-time lecturer at the Paris-Sorbonne-Abu Dhabi. On February 24, 2013, the London School of Economics (LSE)—citing concerns about academic freedom—cancelled a conference on the Arab Spring to be held at the American University of Sharjah in the United Arab Emirates (UAE). And, finally, in 2015 NYU professor Andrew Ross, a vocal critic of the UAE's labor policies and NYU's expansion to Abu Dhabi, was prevented from entering the country.

This chapter concerns the question of whether the expansion of Western universities to the Middle East can reproduce the liberal arts model of higher education and protect academic freedom. In other words, does academic freedom globalize? I argue that the limited curricular offerings, scarcity of tenure, and the absence of organizations to advocate on behalf of faculty restrict academic freedom in unacknowledged ways. Also, branch campuses such as New York University (NYU) Abu Dhabi cater to a slim pool of applicants who can afford the exorbitant tuition. These prestigious branch campuses—which do serve as oases of free speech—are more akin to the high-end Western resort hotels in Dubai and Abu Dhabi, where the sale and consumption of alcohol is legal despite strict bans everywhere else. It turns out that academic freedom, much like alcohol, is restricted to only a small group of regional elites and to the increasing number of academic tourists who seek a Western education outside of the West.

There is a growing body of literature on globalization and higher education that documents the degree to which universities around the world conform to the same organizational blueprints (Lindblad and Lindblad 2009). World-society theorists, in particular, provide a compelling account of the global spread of tertiary education and its strong isomorphic tendencies, recognizing that "The same subjects are … taught with the same perspectives leading to very similar degrees and to credentials that take on world-wide meaning" (Schofer and Meyer 2005, 917). Due to a theoretical emphasis that privileges the external organizational characteristics of universities and colleges around the world, these studies are unable to account for what transpires inside particular institutions. In other words, for our purposes, how accurately do universities that purport to embody the attributes of the liberal arts model translate themselves in the Middle East?

Schofer and Meyer assert that universities, much like international nongovernmental organizations (INGOs), need to be acknowledged as instruments for the dissemination of world culture because "they produce individuals who study neoclassical economics and wish to work for the [World Trade Organization] WTO, just as they produce sociologists who decry the WTO's evils. Yet, such people are linked by a (mostly) common cultural freedom" (Schofer and Meyer 2005, 917). My own research on Western universities in the Middle East, particularly in the Cooperation Council for Arab States of the Gulf (GCC) states, questions the assumption that these institutions are largely linked by what Schofer and Meyer call a "common culture of freedom" (Schofer and Meyer 2005). Furthermore, as I argue in this chapter, critical differences that pertain to protections of academic freedom may not be readily apparent to outside observers. Perhaps more important, academic freedom as practiced by American universities is a particularly American institution that does not easily lend itself to export.

## Academic Freedom: From Internalization to Academic Outposts

In the height of the Cold War, noted intellectual and historian Henry Steele Commager argued that the United States was uniquely suited to the task of promoting the global expansion of tertiary education. "We have to do for the new countries," he argued, "what New England and Virginia did for the American frontier in the earlier period; what Harvard, Yale, and Princeton did to build up colleges and universities in Ohio, Michigan, and Illinois in the early nineteenth century" (Commager 1963, 369). He further stated:

> We have a responsibility to transmit to the new institutions which we create or develop not merely the physical facilities but the moral and intellectual

characteristics of the university. That means that the American academic community ... must represent to the rest of the world the habits of freedom. It must show by all of its activities and by all of its commitments what can be done to solve problems under a system of freedom. It must show that problems can be solved only if those who work at them are free from improper pressures of politics, religion, ideology. (Commager 1963, 369)

Commager foreshadowed both the expansion of prestigious branch campuses in the Middle East and the call for these institutions to promote democratization by inculcating the "habits of freedom." The Cold War university, however, was not expansionist—as Commager called for—but rather internalizing, attracting international students to American universities to spread liberal norms and American influence.

The Global War on Terror—and the growing difficulty of attracting students to the United States due to visa and other restrictions—has resulted in a renewed interest in the creation of American branch campuses in the Middle East. Branch university campuses have even been included in American geopolitical strategy, as evinced by the United States Agency for International Development (USAID) support for the American University of Kabul in Afghanistan and the American University of Sulaimani in Iraq. Clearly, even more than during the Cold War, externalist education initiatives have become a critical component of US strategy in the Global War on Terror. The US–Middle East Partnership Initiative oversees a budget devoted primarily to education in a variety of forms and designed for students and working professionals (Salime 2010). Despite the robust military presence of the United States in the Middle East, popular demand for American-style education is the primary driving force for the regional diffusion of American higher education institutions (HEIs). From Kyrgyzstan to Qatar, American military installations are located in each country that now hosts an American-affiliated HEI. Furthermore, most of these institutions are private entities that do not receive financial support from USAID or any other US government agency.

## Overview of Higher Education in the Middle East

Although American universities in the Middle East have been in operation for more than a century, the recent expansion of branch campuses in the Persian Gulf is unprecedented. As Romani points out, "One important pattern characterizing the current academic boom is a dual process of privatization amidst globalization. Two-thirds (around 70%) of the new universities founded in the Arab Middle East since 1993 are private, and more and more (at least 50) of them are branches of Western, mostly American universities" (Romani 2009, 4). No other region in the world comes close to matching the Persian Gulf with respect to the diffusion of American universities.

The institutions that comprise this "academic boom" fall into three categories: branch campuses, hybrid universities, and independent standalone universities. Branch campuses of institutions based in the United States are the most common. With a student population of over 1000, NYU Abu Dhabi is a good example of this model (NYU Abu Dhabi 2016). Other than NYU Abu Dhabi, many branch campuses are clustered in compounds; as such, they are relatively small and cater to students who desire specialized academic or vocational training. Education City in Qatar hosts the following branch-campus programs: a fine-arts program administered by Virginia Commonwealth University, a medical school administered by Cornell University, engineering programs administered by Texas A&M, and a division of Georgetown University's School of Foreign Service.

The second category consists of international universities that partner with an HEI in the Middle East. For example, in 2008, the University of Texas at Austin announced that it had signed a contract to collaborate with King Abdullah University of Science and Technology in the development of new graduate programs in engineering and earth sciences.

The third category consists of independent standalone universities—locally rooted and locally financed—that offer an American-style education. With approximately 4,800 students, the American University of Sharjah (AUS) and Zayed University in Dubai provide examples of this type. Because of their comparative size and the English-language support services that they offer, American-style universities historically have drawn more students from both the host country and the Middle East region. By comparison, NYU Abu Dhabi—which is required to adhere to the more stringent admissions standards of its New York affiliate— attracts a global student body. American-style universities typically adhere to American curricular standards, embrace the liberal-arts model, use textbooks published in the United States, employ faculty members trained in the United States, and encourage faculty to use American pedagogical techniques: a style of teaching described as student-centered, relying less on traditional lectures and more on classroom activities that promote active learning and facilitate discussion.

## The American Model of Academic Freedom

Academic freedom in the United States owes its distinctive character to its particular historical context. Thus, this element of the American model of education is understandably more difficult to reproduce than a set of textbooks or course offerings. Academic freedom and the institutional safeguards designed to nurture and protect were only formalized within the last century. Many of the early debates on academic freedom took place during the Cold War. In 1940, the American Association of University Professors (AAUP) and the Association of American Colleges and Universities (AACU) agreed to principles supporting academic freedom in teaching and research; the cornerstone for academic freedom was to be tenure (AAUP 2006, 3). For the leftist wing of the AAUP, which largely favored unionization and a more robust set of measures that protect academic freedom, the agreement on tenure represented a weak compromise (Barrow 1990; Kamola and Meyerhoff 2009). Freedom in the classroom was circumscribed by the stipulation that faculty not stray beyond their expertise and "introduce into their teaching controversial matter which has no relation to their subject" (AAUP 2006, 3). The basis for academic freedom, as opposed to free-speech laws, was argued to derive from the professional knowledge, qualifications, and credentials of the university professor (Gerber 2010). Principles including peer review supported the belief that only equally trained and knowledgeable professionals, rather than laymen, were qualified to judge research publications and deliver lectures (Gerber 2010, 8). Notably for this chapter, religious institutions were given some flexibility to limit freedom in the classroom, as long as the university's employees were made aware of these limitations when they were hired. In the United States, tenure allowed HEIs to compete more successfully with the private sector for talented faculty who were willing to forgo higher salaries for employment security and intellectual freedom (Kolodny 2008, 3).

American-style universities in the Middle East, in contrast, offer high salaries but limited guarantees of continuous employment in the future, in the hope that financial incentives will be enough to lure established American scholars from the relative safety of tenure. The Kafala system, which binds all foreign workers to a citizen sponsor, limits *all* expatriates to a renewable three-year term of employment (Ali 2010). This system, designed to undercut the bargaining power of low-wage workers by carefully controlling where and how long they work, also provides a convenient justification for not extending tenure to the Middle East region's growing academic labor force. Branch campuses circumvent these restrictions by drawing tenured faculty from their main campus in the United States. However, standalone private universities (e.g., Zayed University in Dubai and AUS) do not have this luxury. Therefore, they hope that tax-free salaries, supplemented by free or subsidized housing as well as other benefits, are enough to lure expatriate academics from domestic labor markets.

Other than tenure, there are a number of additional safeguards in the United States to protect academic freedom. Chief among them are accreditation agencies, disciplinary associations such as the American Political Science Association, advocacy organizations such as the AAUP, and a normative and legal framework supporting free-speech rights. Although most branch and standalone campuses in the Middle East region are accredited, the institutional phalanx that supports academic freedom in the United States is mostly absent in the Persian Gulf. Clearly, many of these institutional safeguards do not transfer as readily as other elements of the American model of education. Also, as discussed in the next section, even accreditation agencies have demonstrated a reluctance to act transnationally in defense of academic freedom.

Although they lack protections afforded by tenure, standalone American-style universities (e.g., AUS) offer a wider spectrum of classes, are more engaged in their communities, and are more likely to teach citizens of the host country. Furthermore, the absence of tenure at standalone campuses does not mean that academic freedom is nonexistent. What is restricted, however, is the ability for academics at American universities to engage with a wider public *off campus*. When I was conducting research for this chapter, many of the untenured faculty members that I interviewed admitted surprise at the level of freedom they experience in the classroom. However, several also admitted to self-policing, a finding that is supported by a recent survey of university professors in the Middle East region (Romanowski and Nasser 2010). Many instructors expressed concerns about being sensitive to cultural differences and not wanting to offend students who have different worldviews. The instructors that I interviewed developed strategies to broach sensitive topics in the classroom, including "case-obfuscation," wherein the instructor critically describes human-rights violations in a neighboring country while entertaining the hope that students realize that similar violations are taking place locally. However, the university campus marks the outer boundary beyond which faculty members cannot cross when debating politically, socially, or even environmentally sensitive matters. Thus, there are limits to the argument that American universities can act reliably as INGOs or that they can inculcate, as Commager suggested, "the habits of freedom."

## Academic Freedom and the Arab Spring

As alluded to in the introduction, the Arab Spring has had a particularly chilling effect on the public sphere in the Persian Gulf. In 2012, the UAE closed the offices of the Abu Dhabi Gallup Center (i.e., a polling and research firm) and the German-affiliated Konrad-Adenauer-Stiftung organization. In 2011, the Gulf Research Center, an independent think tank, was shut down by the UAE. Curiously, most INGOs with branches in the region had originally moved to oil-rich Persian Gulf states for fund-raising purposes. They operate with a skeleton staff and use their presence in the region as a staging ground for humanitarian interventions in neighboring countries. Like so many of the universities that opened branch campuses in the Persian Gulf, their presence in the region is driven more by access to wealthy donors and publicity than advocacy. As such, they pose no direct challenge to the regional governments.

The Arab Spring also engendered a more repressive atmosphere for college campuses in the region. In 2012, a journalism professor at Zayed University—an accredited American-style university in Dubai—had his contract terminated for "unspecified reasons." This faculty member had regularly written columns in local papers calling for greater journalistic freedom. In response to public queries, Zayed University's provost, Larry Wilson, cited the university's statement on academic freedom, which calls for an environment "characterized by the free flow of information and ideas, in which students can be exposed to a wide range of unfettered points of view … and the need to be respectful of the principles of Islam and the values of the United Arab Emirates" (Nelson 2012). By citing the need to be sensitive to Islam, the university's position is formally consistent with the principles laid out by the joint 1940 AAUP and AACU declaration on academic freedom, which controversially included a loophole that restricted academic freedom at religious institutions. As I have argued elsewhere, university administrators in the region frequently justify punitive measures taken against faculty "who cross the line" as an attempt to prevent Western cultural imperialism. In so doing, they are implicitly making the claim that academic freedom is a culturally contingent value (Noori 2016). Though I take a critical stance in this chapter towards these efforts to stifle intellectual inquiry, I recognize the challenge of creating a vibrant environment for debate that is nonetheless sensitive to cultural difference and is self-conscious of the ways in which Western universities are vehicles for a very real form of cultural imperialism. From their reliance on English as the language of instruction to their dependence on academics trained in the US, American-style universities and branch campuses harbor both implicit and explicit political and cultural biases.

When contacted by *Inside Higher Ed* about the incident at Zayed University, a representative of the Middle States Accreditation Agency noted that "If there's evidence that this was not the university's doing, but rather the government's doing, that probably would not impact their accreditation" (Nelson 2012). This case demonstrates the importance of the extra-institutional forces and constraints under which American universities in the Middle East operate. However, the case also suggests that accreditation agencies—the only transnational regulatory bodies with the authority to enforce academic freedom—lack the power to effectively protect this key component of the American model of education (Noori 2013). The Zayed University case similarly reflects the limits of the argument that universities can act as civil-society agents in an otherwise politically repressive environment. American-style universities such as Zayed provide some protections for academic freedom; however, when faculty members try to make their voice heard outside the confines of campus, they risk severe sanctions. Expulsions such as the one referenced previously are not a frequent occurrence, but they happen often enough to create a climate of wariness for untenured faculty members.

The high profile challenges to academic freedom that receive international media scrutiny mask the many day-to-day occurrences that impinge on academic freedom. To assess academic freedom in a way that extends beyond surface-level organizational structures requires a theory of power that is sensitive to what Steven Lukes (2004) refers to as non-decisions. Stated otherwise, a less apparent effect of the exercise of power is that alternative or contrarian views never get voiced. Because of this lack of public contestation, the exercise of power goes unnoticed. Less visible evidence of the exercise of power is reflected in the faculty who are not hired because of fears over what they might say in public or in class; courses that are not offered out of concern that they will offend those who wield power; and topics for discussion that are never considered because they are of a sensitive or controversial nature.

The narrow spectrum of classes offered by most branch campuses and some standalone institutions offers an equally insidious threat to academic freedom. When these institutions offer a stripped-down version of the liberal arts model and neglect courses in the humanities and the social sciences, their academic communities are not diverse enough to foster a robust exchange of ideas. Curricular diversity is a necessary precondition for academic freedom. In its absence, there is limited need for prophylactic measures to ensure that free speech is protected. If sensitive subjects are not taught, then controversial topics are less likely to be broached and universities will be less likely to hire faculty who research tendentious issues. Under these conditions students are limited with respect to the coursework that they can take. Curricular diversity is a neglected dimension of liberal arts education and academic freedom. However, it is important to point out that neoliberal prescriptions for higher education reform have also reduced curricular diversity in North American and European universities as unpopular or costly academic programs are shut down.

In conclusion, academic freedom in the Middle East exists but within quite profound limits. Clearly, academic freedom does not globalize as readily as other elements of the liberal arts model of education. Because the international desire for American-style and branch campuses remains strong, it is important to question the taken-for-granted belief that these institutions can reliably safeguard academic freedom—whether inside or outside of the classroom.

From Kyrgyzstan to Qatar, American military installations are located in each of the countries that now hosts an American-affiliated HEI. Most of these institutions are private revenue-seeking entrepreneurial agents that are not acting at the behest of the US Department of State. Their inability to authentically replicate the liberal arts model of education does not mean that substantial academic freedoms are not available to the faculty who teach at these universities. What is restricted, however, is the ability for academics at American universities to engage with a wider public off campus.

## References

Ali, Syed. (2010). *Dubai: Gilded Cage*. New Haven, CT: Yale University Press.

American Association of University Professors (AAUP). (2006). *1940 Statement of Principles for Academic Freedom and Tenure: With 1970 Interpretive Comments*. Washington, DC: American Association of University Professors. Retrieved from www.aaup.org/file/principles-academic-freedom-tenure.pdf (accessed January 21, 2014).

Barrow, Clyde W. (1990). *Universities and the Capitalist State: Corporate Liberalism and the Reconstruction of American Higher Education, 1894–1928*. Madison, WI: University of Wisconsin Press.

Commager, Henry Steele. (1963). "The university and freedom: 'Lehrfreiheit' and 'Lernfreiheit.'" *Journal of Higher Education* 34(7): 361–70.

Gerber, Larry G. (2010). "Professionalization as the basis for academic freedom and faculty governance." *Journal of Academic Freedom* 1: 1–26.

Kamola, Isaac, and Eli Meyerhoff. (2009). "Creating commons: Divided governance, participatory management, and struggles against enclosure in the university." *Polygraph* 2 1: 15–37.

Kolodny, Annette. (2008). "Academic freedom, and the career I once loved." *Academe* 94(5): 22–6.

Lindblad, Sverker, and Rita Foss Lindblad. (2009). "Transnational governance of higher education: On globalization and international university ranking lists." *Yearbook of the National Society for the Study of Education* 108(2): 180–202.

Lukes, Steven. (2004). *Power: A Radical View*. New York: Palgrave Macmillan.

Nelson, Libby A. (2012). "Kicked out of the UAE." Insidehighered.com, August 31. Retrieved from www.insidehighered.com/news/2012/08/31/american-professor-suddenly-fired-zayed-university (accessed March 29, 2014).

Noori, Neema. (2013). "Globalization, governance, and the diffusion of the American model of education: Accreditation agencies and American-style universities in the Middle East." *International Journal of Politics, Culture, and Society* 26(2): 159–72.

Noori, Neema. (2016). "The political economy of transnational higher education and academic labor in the Persian Gulf." In Meng-Hsuan Chou, Isaac Kamola, and Tamson Pietsch (Eds.) *The Transnational Politics of Higher Education*, (pp. 63–84). New York: Routledge.

NYU Abu Dhabi. (2016). "Over 320 students representing 76 nationalities join NYU Abu Dhabi in this year's Class of 2020." Retrieved from http://nyuad.nyu.edu/en/news/press-room/press-releases/over-students-representing-nationalities-join-nyu-abu-dhabi.html.

Romani, Vincent. (2009). "The politics of higher education in the Middle East: Problems and prospects." *Middle East Brief* 36(May): 1–8.

Romanowski, Michael H., and Ramzi Nasser. (2010). "Faculty perceptions of academic freedom at a GCC University." *Prospects* 40: 481–97.

Salime, Zakia. (2010). "Securing the market, pacifying civil society, empowering women: The Middle East Partnership Initiative." *Sociological Forum* 25(4): 725–45.

Schofer, Evan, and John W. Meyer. (2005). "The worldwide expansion of higher education in the twentieth century." *American Sociological Review* 70(6): 898–920.

# 10

# THE AFRICAN LIBERAL ARTS

## Heritage, Challenges and Prospects[1]

*Grant Lilford*

## Introduction

The liberal arts have a central place in the history of African education and African scholars and institutions played key roles in the development of the "western" tradition. Specialized higher education is the product of the attempt to impose a limited version of the English university model in the immediate aftermath of the Second World War. This model does not accommodate the global knowledge economy, or the need for African responses to actual social and cultural needs and practices, and to rediscover traditional wisdom in culture, society and the sciences. Specialized higher learning treats education as a rare privilege for a talented and industrious minority. It creates intense competition, separating the successful from their peers, their parents, their communities, and their home languages, while teaching them to scorn indigenous knowledge systems. Engaged and committed African academics and professionals reveal the power of kinship and community, and the pervasiveness of traditional values. While African universities reflect, and contribute to, many of the challenges facing the continent, a new generation of thinkers and institutions offers solutions. These initiatives draw upon a comprehensive vision which adapts the liberal arts to African insights and requirements.

## The Liberal Arts in Pre-Colonial Africa

African traditional knowledge systems blur the disciplinary boundaries which have defined European education since Aristotle. Cultural knowledge and literature were inseparable; oral praise poetry served throughout the continent as the repository for history and genealogy. Al-Sa'di (1999:1–2) refers to the oral recounting of history as a popular pastime among his ancestors in Songhai.

AC Jordan notes the prevalence of poetic skills in Xhosa society. Most children could recite their own praises, as well as praises of family and of cattle. A few select talented praise poets then went on to praise larger groups, and different levels of chiefs (Jordan 1973:71–2, 51–2, cited in Opland 1983:42–3). While social, political, economic, legal, linguistic, and education systems in pre-colonial Africa were extremely diverse, most developed general technical and cultural knowledge, while developing specialist skills in metallurgy, medicine, poetry, music and the arts and crafts. Advanced skills developed from a generally-known baseline.

For example, a broad, general medical education was available to most individuals, through the oral tradition. Specialists emerged in areas such as midwifery and divination. In traditional Zulu homesteads, the family provided the initial triage for illness or injury, and people knew where to find herbs and how to prepare them (Ngubane 1977:100–1). The family referred more serious matters to diviners, specialized herbalists, and other traditional doctors. The specialist identified and treated the root cause: an underlying medical problem, sorcery, or ancestral anger because of impurity or negligence. Healers also educated the patient in both curative and prophylactic methods. More holistic approaches to treatment and care in western medicine suggest the need to investigate the practices, as well as the medicines, used in African traditional medicine. Law similarly requires a shared baseline of knowledge. Traditional Tswana justice and governance occurs at the *kgotla*, a gathering which resembles the Athenian assembly. The *kgotla* is a court, judging cases according to precedent (Schapera 1970:40) and a legislature, debating any decision taken by the chief (41). Participation thus requires knowledge of both precedents and the responsibilities of citizenship. African traditional politics represent a diversity of systems which provide fertile grounds for both specialized academic study and a broader education in the rights and duties of citizenship.

## Africa's Place in the Liberal Arts

The universities of Europe owe their origins largely to two scholars, Augustine and Aquinas. Through his *City of God*, Augustine brought the then rapidly expanding Christian faith into contact with Platonic philosophy and set the stage for Christian higher education. Augustine lived most of his life in Africa. He was a Berber by ethnicity and, after a brief visit to Italy, whose educational institutions fell short of his expectations, established a school in his native Carthage. After Augustine's death, ignorance and anarchy extended into Italy and Greece. A thousand years later, Europe rediscovered classical education. The *Tarikh-al-Sudan* reveals that Arab scholars introduced the trivium into sub-Saharan Africa, at the University of Sankoré, in Timbuktu (Diop 1987:178). These Islamic African scholars used the Koran as their central text and Arabic as the language of instruction and discourse, just as later European scholars focused upon the Bible and deliberated in Latin (Diop 1987: 177; see also de Villiers and Hirtle 2007; Al-Sa'di 1999).

The Islamic madrasah system included primary, secondary and tertiary instruction. It covered all of knowledge, placing theological knowledge at the pinnacle. The basic education aimed to teach all Muslims a fundamental understanding of the Koran and the Arabic language. The madrasah made provision for talented scholars to continue with their studies, to the equivalent of post-graduate level:

> The curriculum of the madrasahs was typically made up of three categories: the first dealt with the fundamental Islamic sciences: Qur'anic exegesis (*tafsir*); the traditions of Prophet Muhammed, namely behavioural precedents (*sunnah*) and public utterances (*hadith*); and Islamic law (*Shari'ah*), which itself was made up of two components: Islamic law proper (*al-fiqh*) and the sources of this law (jurisprudence—termed *usul al-fiqh*). The second comprised elements of language, namely: the Qur'anic language (*al lughah*)—which in this case of course it was classical Arabic; grammar (*al nahw wa'l-sarf*); literary style and rhetoric (*al balaghah*); literature (*al-adab*), and the art of Qur'anic recitation (*al qira'at*). The third category, which was usually considered to be of slightly lower level of importance included subjects such as astronomy, history, medicine, and mathematics. (Lulat 2005:65–6)

This system anticipates the medieval European liberal arts by incorporating theology, grammar, law and science. Like orally-based traditional African education, literate Islamic education provides common knowledge for every individual, allowing for further study by those with the necessary ambition and talent. Al-Sa'di praises his teacher, Baghayogho, not only for his extensive knowledge but also for his infinite patience in dealing with the "dull-witted" (1999:62–4). Individual teachers received licenses to teach specific texts since universities could not achieve corporate status; Islamic law does not recognize corporations (Hunwick 1999:lix). This model resembles both traditional African skilled training, where students would travel great distances to seek out teachers, as well as early European higher education.

Ashby and Anderson (1966) assert that "higher education is not new to the continent of Africa, but the modern universities in Africa owe nothing to this ancient tradition of scholarship" (148). The early African universities influenced European institutions, which in turn provided models for the later generation. Thomas Aquinas brought the Catholic Church and its universities into dialogue with classical philosophy, preserved by Islamic Scholars in Arabia and Persia as well as northern and eastern Africa, and Spain. Catholic universities thus rediscovered the Aristotelian system, which incorporated everything we now think of as Arts and Sciences. They also encountered Arabian mathematics, including Algebra and our current numeral system, which includes the Indian concept of zero. Pagan, Muslim, Jewish and Christian interaction across Europe, Africa and Asia paved the way for the renaissance and the enlightenment.

## Higher Education in British Imperial Africa

British colonial governments in Africa initially left education to missionaries. Course offerings could be restricted, or surprisingly broad, since the missionaries also worked as engineers, medical doctors, builders, dentists and teachers. Missionary education did not offer a planned and coherent system. Similarly, education in North America, particularly in the United States, arose from hundreds of local and disparate efforts.

In the 1940s, the Crown convened the Asquith commission to unify and standardize higher education in the colonies. The Commission's 1948 report notes the existence of four universities in the British Empire, outside the Dominions and India. These were: Malta (1769), Jerusalem (1918), Ceylon (medical college 1870, UC 1921, university status 1942) and Hong Kong (1911) (Colonial Office 1945:7–8). The African colonies had no universities and few facilities for higher education (6). Three institutions offered university-level courses in West Africa. The Church Mission Society founded Fourah Bay in Sierra Leone in 1827 as a theological college. It had 16 students in 1944. The higher college at Yaba, Nigeria, originally an agricultural training college, had about 100 students. Achimota, the Ghanaian secondary school had 98 students, including 2 women. Ashby identifies "... the remarkable Achimota College near Accra, which covered education from kindergarten to first-year university courses; for a short time, in engineering, its students were even eligible to take the examinations for the external degrees of London University.(Ashby 1964:14). Apart from Gordon Memorial College, Khartoum, Makerere served all of East Africa. Since 1937, it had offered courses as a university college and, by 1943, it had 114 resident students. Fort Hare had 220 students in 1942, and receives a favourable mention in the report, even though South Africa, as a Dominion, fell outside the report's terms of reference (Colonial Office 1945:9).

## Fort Hare

The South African Collegiate School, later the University of Cape Town, founded in 1829, did not admit black South African students until the 1920s. Even these were a tiny minority until the 1980s. Fort Hare, founded by churches in 1915, by contrast, was non-racial from the outset, including two white students in its first class. Fort Hare offered both BA and BSc degrees, following the curriculum and examinations of the University of South Africa, with little variation from the courses offered at the white university colleges:

> The general direction of the major studies was towards the standard of the matriculation examination of the South African universities, for the conduct of which at the time there was a common board for all the nine or ten European colleges. From the list of subjects recognized for this external examination we selected six—English, a Bantu language, South African and European History, Latin, Mathematics and Physical Science. (Kerr 1968:39)

While the college lacked the staff and facilities for a full BSc, it offered a very successful pre-medical programme (Kerr 1968:109–10). From 1920 to 1925, at least 84 graduates completed their medical studies in "Edinburgh, Birmingham, Durham, Liverpool and even Frankfurt-am-Main" (81). After 1925, the university expanded its range of offerings to allow for both general and specialized education. Fort Hare achieved a breadth and depth of study, emphasizing African language and culture, without excluding the western liberal arts and sciences (156–7). As in many current African secondary schools, a student's preparation depended on the subjects the schools had the staff and facilities to offer, so many Fort Hare matriculants had little grounding in mathematics and the sciences. Fort Hare, with basic laboratories and limited funding, provided science and mathematics to BA candidates, whereas contemporary universities, in spite of extensive laboratories and foreign, national and international funding, restrict their courses to students with high passes in science subjects. ZK Matthews asserts that effective and passionate teaching, not expensive facilities or well-prepared students, is the key to mastery of mathematics: "…it had been regarded as a fluke, if not a miracle, to do well in mathematics. But when Murdock took over, the subject ceased to hold any terrors for us" (Matthews 1981:64). Fort Hare also required philosophy because it met University of South Africa requirements and did not require that a student had completed it in secondary school (Kerr 1968:157). The college instituted the Wednesday Assembly, a 45-minute College Meeting where visitors or members of staff could address the entire student body on any topic (43).

Fort Hare appealed to various funding sources. The Union Education Department pledged £600; the Native Affairs Department earmarked £250 for Agricultural studies; and the United Free Church offered another £250. As General Louis Botha, then Union Prime Minister, acknowledged at the opening of the college: "The Natives of certain districts of the Transkeian Territories were in a position to take united action, and through the Transkeian Territories General Council contributed the substantial sum of £10,000" (Kerr 1968:25–6).[2] Few black South Africans were in wage employment in 1915, and wages were low, so the sum is indeed substantial. The contributions of state and church are parsimonious compared to that of the community. This generosity recalls Casely Hayford's 1911 vision for the Mfantsipim National University in his novel *Ethiopia Unbound* (Hayford 1969:16). Hayford's vision seems naïve in an age of state and corporate university funding, but the formula of community support for liberal arts colleges continues in North America and is not unknown in Africa. In 1977, when the government of Lesotho decided to convert a multinational university to a national one, students from Botswana and Swaziland returned home. The government of Botswana launched an appeal, entitled "Motho le motho kgomo" (one man one cow) towards the building of the University of Botswana. The proceeds of this campaign are commemorated with the statue of a man leading a cow towards the University of Botswana library. The students themselves contributed financially to their education like their counterparts at American labor colleges. ZK Matthews recalls: "We were called to the high task of launching the college academically. We were also called to the no less useful task of laying some its physical foundations" (1981:51). Students completed specific tasks, in assigned work groups, under the supervision of their instructors. Fort Hare students did not experience the dichotomy between Booker T. Washington's emphasis on physical labour and technical skills and WEB Du Bois' insistence on the development of the mind.

From 1951, the National Party government in South Africa brought all education for black South Africans under the direct control of the Department of Bantu Administration and Development, specifically targeting missionary institutions. By 1960, the government held hearings on the future of Fort Hare, in spite of submissions by both Kerr and ZK Matthews. Kerr, in particular, was cross-examined over whether "Europeans" and "non-Europeans" could work amicably and effectively as part of a common governing council. He replied that his experience on the Fort Hare Council had been a model of effective interracial co-operation. The Government dissolved the council, replacing it with two councils divided on racial lines (Kerr 1968:280–3). Fort Hare was a community-funded institution, providing a high-quality education at minimal cost, and engaging in extensive outreach and development programmes. It contributed economically and intellectually to its rural community. While proclaiming community self-determination, rural values, Christianity, and anti-communism the apartheid government nationalized an independent, rural college, founded on Christian principles and supported by an African community.

In 2002, The National Working Group, charged with rationalizing South African Universities, provides a near post-mortem for Fort Hare:

> The University of Fort Hare has had a proud history in South African higher education. However, in recent times a number of factors have had a detrimental effect on the institution. As a rural institution in a small and remote town, it is not as attractive for staff and students as other institutions based in larger towns and cities. In recent years there has been a sharp fall in the university's intake of first-time entering undergraduates, which has affected its enrolment stability. It has been able to maintain a total head count enrolment of about 4 200 only by registering large numbers of teachers for in-service programmes in education. Its graduation rates and its research outputs have been low. In 2000 Fort Hare produced a total of only 536 graduates; of whom only 12 obtained masters or doctoral degrees. Its research publication total has been below 50 units for a number of years. (National Working Group 2002:16)

The Group reveals its bias in favour of large, urban research institutions. Fort Hare's size, location and emphasis on undergraduate instruction are the hallmarks of an effective liberal arts college. The report condemns Fort Hare for its low research outputs and small numbers of graduate students, as well as its low degree completion rate. The latter is a cause for concern, but it reflects the appalling legacy of Bantu Education. The criteria of research outputs and number of graduate students would not apply to the most selective of American liberal arts colleges, which offer a superior undergraduate education to the selective research universities. Instructors at liberal arts colleges conduct quality research, and encourage undergraduate participation, but are not judged solely on their research output. Its distance from large cities allowed Fort Hare to form a cohesive community. Similarly, liberal arts institutions in North America use their relative cultural isolation to bridge cultural, economic or ethnic division; Berea and Oberlin Colleges, with their abolitionist, anti-racist heritage, are small campuses within small communities and, like Fort Hare, offer unique perspectives on rural development.

While teaching at the University of Zululand, I surveyed the state of the liberal arts in South African universities (Lilford 2013). The Zululand BA Dual Major admits students to a faculty, rather than a specific course of studies, and allows students to select major and minor subjects. Students may even choose from a limited range of science subjects, provided that their matriculation results meet the minimum admission requirements for those subjects. Students choose four subjects in the first year, may change a subject in the second, and then restrict themselves to two modules of two major subjects in the third year. A subject taken for three years is classified as a major, for two years as a minor, and for one year as an elective. A consultant had challenged the program, due to timetabling and financial constraints, suggesting that the Faculty of Arts replace the current level of flexibility with specific allowable subject combinations. Like Zululand, other South African universities provide both for "named degrees" such as development studies and flexible BA or BSc programs. The one exception was the University of the Northwest at Potchefstroom, which requires students to apply to one of 59 different named degree combinations, some of which are either not offered or being phased out. The greatest flexibility was at the prestigious, historically white liberal institutions, such as the University of Cape Town, which allowed students to choose from 20 arts subjects, 11 social sciences, and 23 sciences and other subjects from outside the faculty. Historically black universities, such as Venda and Limpopo, were more restrictive in their course offerings, with Limpopo moving to phase out any choice in selection of subject combinations. Fort Hare remains true to its liberal arts roots in offering a range of choices comparable to Cape Town. St Augustine College in Johannesburg, a new Roman Catholic institution, promotes integration of disciplines through flexible, though limited, course offerings and an interdisciplinary "capstone seminar" which emphasizes research and problem-solving.

Under the leadership of Jonathan Jansen, the University of the Free State requires core liberal art classes, including critical reasoning, of all students, and offers a BA with management, responding to the need for culturally-astute critical thinkers in South African enterprises. Like some other South African institutions, UFS offers an additional year for promising students who do not meet the entrance requirements. Jansen has been a compelling advocate for the liberal arts, particularly in an editorial piece: "Don't Kid Yourself about BAs" in *The Times* (Jansen 2010). Jansen identifies the core skills and attributes that make a BA graduate successful, and developments under his leadership at the UFS clearly reflect his commitment.

## Makerere

Initially a technical school, Makerere upgraded to the status of a junior college as recommended by a Ugandan Government committee in 1924 (Ashby and Anderson 1966:192). In 1933, the Curry report recommended a further upgrade towards university status (194). Makerere's progress reflected a difference between colonial officials in East and West Africa. During and before the 1920s, West Africans, notably Horton, Blyden and Hayford, proposed various schemes for higher education. The Governors of Nigeria and the Gold Coast rejected these proposals because each believed that primary and secondary education should receive priority. Both governors were liberal proponents of the Africanization of the civil service, but each rejected university education as a means of achieving that objective. They ignored the historical record: "universities flourished in Europe before there was a comprehensive system of secondary education" (Ashby and Anderson 1966:182). They anticipated the World Bank, whose "... studies claimed to show that the rate of return on investment in higher education was much lower than that in secondary or primary education, and that the benefit was mainly private" (Mamdani 2007:261). The 1937 De la Warr Report promoted higher education in East Africa. Its Commission included ZK Matthews as its only African member, and Alexander Kerr as the only other member with experience of African higher education (Matthews 1981:105). It offered a comprehensive vision of a rigorous liberal education, which specifically incorporated African culture and thought, striving towards a "synthesis of both African and European elements" (cited in Ashby and Anderson 1966:198).

Between 1945 and 1972, Makerere became the most prestigious institution on the continent. It set very high admissions standards, admitting the most qualified students from East and Central Africa, who passed the external examinations with distinction. It also introduced creative and dynamic programmes of study. In 1955, a group of Makerere social scientists published an article in *Universities Quarterly* on an interdisciplinary social science course which emphasized East African examples of politics, sociology and economics (Ehrlich et al. 1955: 56–63). This course did not survive the "special relationship":

> The course was a brave experiment destined to extinction because it was not "examinable" by London, yet its underlying premise—that enquiry into local topics should be the bedrock of East African higher education—grew stronger and, as research accelerated exponentially in the 1960s, resulted in curricular change. (Sicherman 2005:29)

From 1964, the University College of Dar es Salaam applied Makerere's social science course in the establishment of "a locally focused, broad-based three-year Common Course" (Sicherman 2005:52). But in 1955, it was ahead of its time as University of London "standards" clashed with the intelligence and creativity needed to respond directly to African curricular needs. A few programmes, such as the Medical School and Music, Dance and Drama remained outside London's influence, offering excellence and innovation, but the highly specialized "Honours Degree" remained the norm. By the 1960s, British universities questioned the value of over-specialized degrees. Ashby correctly anticipated "a broadening of the curriculum," as British universities offer more interdisciplinary programmes and the former polytechnics introduce new types of degrees. However, Ashby concludes "at the time when Britain was exporting universities to tropical Africa, the fashion of specialization was at its height" (Ashby 1964:9).

Ashby contrasts the highly selective British system with the more accessible US one. Britain had limited university places and assigned them purely on the basis of exam results. Students had already effectively specialized in choosing subjects for their A-level exams; university merely confirmed that specialization. American students took a more general secondary school course and did not specialize until the second year of university. As Ashby observes: "The statistical chance that a Boston boy or girl born in 1945 is now receiving full-time higher education is about 1 in 3; the equivalent chance for a London boy or girl born in 1945 is about 1 in 12" (Ashby 1964:10). Because such a small proportion of the population would attend university, specialization made sense. Even as it served all of East Africa, Makerere's enrolment numbered in the hundreds until 1960, and in the thousands until the mid-1990s.

The history of Makerere reveals a series of articulate warnings about specialization. In the 1990s, the AIDS pandemic showed the danger of overspecialization, as the unexpected deaths of colleagues left survivors unprepared for new duties (Sicherman 2005:51). In 1963, a committee planning the expanded University of East Africa advocated a general degree structure. Makerere allowed more combinations within the honours degree while continuing to separate Arts and Sciences (61). Even though Makerere's staff, students and facilities suffered appalling abuses under Idi Amin and in the subsequent period of anarchy, Makerere's reputation for excellence remained intact until the 1980s, despite crumbling buildings, looted libraries and murdered or exiled scholars. Mahmood Mamdani (2007:9) explores market-driven reforms at Makerere at the instigation of the World Bank. From Makerere's inception, government provided each student with comprehensive support, including a living allowance. In 1990–1991, with the rapid depreciation of the Ugandan Shilling, the government proposed "cost sharing," in which students would lose some allowances (19). The result was an immediate and protracted student strike. The government retreated, proposing instead that faculties and departments could become "income generating units" by admitting entirely self-funded private students. The Faculty of Arts was unexpectedly successful in offering programs that combined traditional humanities subjects with marketable commercial subjects, such as "Religious Studies and Conflict Resolution, Geography and Tourism, Linguistics and Secretarial Studies, History and Development, Philosophy and Public Management" (53). These offerings overwhelmed the university with private students. They also continued the trend towards greater specialization, since departments competing for funds and students ceased any interdisciplinary collaboration. In 2005, a reporter for the *Sunday Vision* in Kampala wrote Makerere examinations without a student ID and claimed that he could buy undergraduate coursework and post-graduate dissertations from Makerere departments. His report correlates Mamdani's thesis, that commercialization undermined academic quality and integrity. The University responded by immediately denying the allegations. The scandal represented a severe blow to Makerere's reputation.

Growing demand during the 1990s led to a proliferation of private, usually faith-based universities in Uganda, including the Anglican Uganda Christian University (UCU), the Roman Catholic Uganda Martyrs University (UMU), and The Islamic University in Uganda (IUIU), Each of these institutions draws upon a more holistic model of education associated with its religious tradition. UCU, for example, requires general education courses in academic writing, computer literacy, ethics, comparative world views and Old and New Testament of all students. These institutions have expanded access while maintaining comparable fees to state institutions. Private and public options, and the resulting competition, encourage greater accountability and integrity in all Ugandan universities.

## Beyond Asquith

The University of Nigeria, Nsukka and the University of Zambia, as the first post-independence universities, looked to the American land grant university as a model, given its development role, its expansion of access, and its extension programs. From the late 18th century, American municipalities and states provided land for educational initiatives. The 1862 Morrill Land Grant Act provided land for campuses and in lieu of an endowment. The states applied their land grants to the ongoing support of universities and colleges, including many "A&M" colleges, dedicated to the "useful arts" (Thelin 2004:76). Both Kwame Nkrumah and Nnamdi Azikiwe attended American universities, developing a critical perspective on the British higher education (Ashby and Anderson 1966:263). Azikiwe founded the University of Nigeria-Nsukka, the first post-independence institution in Nigeria, on the American Model. Nsukka combined liberal and useful arts, and offered students a choice of courses:

> In place of the specialization already to be found in the sixth form courses at secondary schools, the University of Nigeria offers a year's course in general studies, including English language and literature, social science, natural science, and the humanities. Thereafter follow in the prospectus—in true

American style—literally hundreds of courses covering subjects as esoteric as The Rise and Fall of the Ottoman Empire (3 credits), Igbo Phonology and Morphology (2 credits), Advanced Tectonics (4 credits), Vector Analysis (9 credits), and Ethnomusicology—including Eskimo Music (2 credits); to subjects as down-to-earth as Seed Testing (4 credits), Insurance (3 credits), Woodwork (9 credits), Household Sanitation (2 credits), Planning and Serving of Meals (4 credits); Shorthand (9 credits); and Techniques of Dancing (3 credits). The conservatives—African graduates of British universities—shake their heads reproachfully at this exuberance. They cannot conceive how the serious business of a university can be conducted in such a supermarket of education.... (Ashby 1964:66–7)

The land endowments furthered the independence of American colleges and universities, established by the 1819 Supreme Court Decision in *Dartmouth College v. Woodward*, where the United States Supreme Court overturned a lower court decision, and agreed that Dartmouth was accountable to its governing board, not to the State of New Hampshire (Thelin 2004:70–3). Nsukka implemented American course flexibility without the autonomy of a land grant. As the first President of Nigeria, Azikiwe became University Chancellor for Life, loading the council with political appointments (Ashby 1964:83). The founding presidents of American Universities showed similar determination (Thelin 2004:33–4), and Thomas Jefferson's influence on the University of Virginia (51) offers a parallel. However, Azikiwe was deposed in a 1966 coup and thereafter associated with the Biafran secession. His political legacy has tainted his academic legacy, and so the Nsukka model has not received wide analysis and propagation.

The dissolution of the Federation of Rhodesia and Nyasaland, whose Asquith College was located in Salisbury, Rhodesia, led to the foundation of the University of Zambia, which, like Nsukka, had no "Special Relationship" with any British University. Tembo comments on the range of choices available to the first generation of University of Zambia students, and applauds the university's resistance to "over-specialization" through its rejection of the single honours model (Tembo 1973:240–1). In 1964, Zambia abolished A levels, so that university admission was based on a general secondary examination. Once admitted, students could choose a major (229–30). Lulat highlights the flexibility of the curriculum, but calls for still greater flexibility (Lulat 2005:258–9). President Kaunda stated, "The University is not a government department, and the government has no intention of creating it as one ... we appreciate that the University cannot meet its heavy responsibilities to the nation unless it is able to grow and prosper within an atmosphere of freedom" (Tembo 1973:234). The University Council had not more than three government representatives, as opposed to six members drawn from the academic staff, and three international representatives. However, in 1971, demonstrations on campus led to the government to close the university, expel student leaders and deport expatriate staff, all without consulting the University Senate (Tembo 1973:235).

In 2002, former Microsoft project manager Patrick Awuah returned to Ghana to found Ashesi University. A Swarthmore College alumnus, Awuah recognized the need for comprehensive, ethical education in creating the next generation of African leaders. Awuah attributes the corruption plaguing the continent, in some part, to the higher education its leaders endure:

> When I asked my peers what should be done, they shrugged. Their reaction led me to explore the educational system, which looked grim. Africa's universities are overcrowded and underfunded. Students line up hours before class, hoping for a seat. Students learn a narrow subject matter, and are tested on recall. Academic dishonesty is too common. How can Africa's future leaders possibly learn to think and behave differently if we don't educate them in a different way? (Awuah 2012:17)

Ashesi University emphasizes science and technology while maintaining a liberal arts core, and offers generous scholarships for needy students. This model directly tackles both the technological and ethical challenges facing the continent. It offers the opportunity for students from a variety of educational backgrounds to acquire STEM knowledge and skills.

## Prospects

Pluralism in higher education, particularly the re-emergence of a vigorous non-profit sector, can promote a comprehensive and independent higher education network. Community colleges, research universities, faith-based colleges, other private institutions, and state-funded institutions each have a role. Articulation agreements should allow for movement within and across national educational networks. The liberal arts have a critical role. Programmes within larger institutions, distribution requirements and small colleges can each help to provide the breadth of thought which has been present in every proposal for higher education on the African continent. The liberal arts can take us deeply into African traditions and languages and break down the barriers between science and humanities which are a feature of western, not African, thought. The liberal arts also provide a means for Africans, secure in the firm understanding of African history and society, to engage globally not as aid recipients or cheap labour, but as equals in the transmission and creation of knowledge and wisdom.

## Notes

1 An earlier variation of this paper was published as "The Liberal Arts in Anglophone Africa" in *Journal of General Education*, Vol. 61, No. 3 (2012). University Park, PA: The Pennsylvania State University Press, pp. 189–210. An initial draft was presented at *Looking Back & Moving Forward: The Next 100 Years of Liberal Arts: Confronting the Challenges.*

International Conference on the Liberal Arts. St Thomas University, Fredericton, New Brunswick, Canada. I am grateful to the organizers of this conference and to the Faculty of Humanities and the Office of the Deputy Vice Chancellor, Academic Affairs, University of Botswana, for funding my attendance at the conference.

2 According to www.measuringworth.com, this is equivalent to £597,000.00 using the retail price index or £3,220,000.00 using average earnings in 2008 pounds. Using oanda.com to convert to 2008 South African Rands, the Transkei contribution is equal to between R8 597 710 and R46 372 900.

## References

Al-Sa'di, Abd. (1999). "Ta'rikh al-Sudan (History of the lands of the Blacks)." In Hunwick, John O. (Trans. and Ed.). *Timbuktu and the Songhay Empire: Al-Sadis Tarikh al-Sudan down to 1613 and Other Contemporary Documents*. Leiden: Brill, 1–270.

Ashby, Eric. (1964). *African Universities and the Western Tradition: The Godkin Lectures at Harvard University*. Cambridge, MA: Harvard University Press.

Ashby, Eric, in association with Anderson, Mary. (1966). *Universities: British, Indian, African: A Study in the Ecology of Higher Education*. London: Wiedenfeld and Nicolson.

Awuah, Patrick. (2012). "Path to a new Africa." *Stanford Social Innovation Review*, Summer, 17–8. Retrieved December 20, 2016, from http://ashesi.org/wp-content/uploads/2013/06/Path-to-a-New-Africa.pdf.

Colonial Office. (1945). *Report of the Commission on Higher Education in the Colonies: Presented by the Secretary of State for the Colonies to Parliament by Command of His Majesty, June 1945* ("The Asquith Report"). London: His Majesty's Stationery Office.

De Villiers, Marq and Sheila Hirtle. (2007). *Timbuktu: The Sahara's Fabled City of Gold*. New York: Walker & Co.

Diop, Cheikh Anta. (1987). *Pre-Colonial Black Africa*. Translated from the French by Harold Salemson. Trenton, NJ: Africa World Press.

Ehrlich, G., Engholm, G. F., Goldthorpe, J. E., and Powesland, P. G. (1955). "Social studies at an African university college." *Universities Quarterly* (now *Higher Education* Quarterly), 10(1), 56–63.

Hayford, J. E. Casely. (1969). *Ethiopia Unbound: Studies in Race Emancipation*. London: Frank Cass.

Hunwick, John O. (Trans. and Ed.). (1999). *Timbuktu and the Songhay Empire: Al-Sadi's Tarikh al-Sudan down to 1613 and Other Contemporary Documents*. Leiden, Netherlands: Brill.

Jansen, Jonathan. (2010). "Don't kid yourself about Bas." *The Times* (Johannesburg), December 8. Retrieved from www.timeslive.co.za/opinion/columnists/2010/12/08/don-t-kid-yourself-about-bas

Jordan, A. C. (1973). *Towards an African Literature: The Emergence of Literary Form in Xhosa*. Berkeley, CA: University of California Press.

Kerr, Alexander. (1968). *Fort Hare 1915–48: The Evolution of an African College*. London: Shuter and Shooter.

Lilford, Grant. (2012). "The liberal arts in Anglophone Africa." *Journal of General Education* 61(3), 189–210. University Park, PA: The Pennsylvania State University Press.

Lilford, Grant. (2013). "Comparison of general BA offerings at South African universities." Unpublished Report to the Faculty of Arts, University of Zululand, July.

Lulat, Y. G. -M. (2005). *A History of African Higher Education from Antiquity to the Present: A Critical Synthesis.* Westport, CT: Praeger Publishers.

Mamdani, Mahmood. (2007). *Scholars in the Marketplace: The Dilemmas of Neo-Liberal Reform at Makerere University, 1989–2005.* Dakar, Senegal: Council for the Development of Social Science Research in Africa.

Matthews, Z. K. (1981). *Freedom for My People: The Autobiography of Z. K. Matthews, Southern Africa 1901 to 1968.* Cape Town: David Philip.

National Working Group. (2002). *The Restructuring of the Higher Education System in South Africa.* Pretoria, South Africa: Government Printer.

Ngubane, Harriet. (1977). *Body and Mind in Zulu Medicine: An Ethnography of Health and Disease in Zulu Thought and Practice.* London: Academic Press.

Opland, Jeff. (1983). *Xhosa Oral Poetry: Aspects of a Black South African Tradition.* Cambridge Studies in Literature and Culture 7. Cambridge, UK: Cambridge University Press.

Schapera, Isaac. (1970). *A Handbook of Tswana Law and Custom* (2nd Ed.). London: Frank Cass & Co.

Sicherman, Carol. (2005). *Becoming an African University: Makerere, 1922–2000.* Trenton, NJ: Africa World Press.

Tembo, Lyson P. (1973). "University of Zambia: An analysis of some major issues." In Yesufu, T. M. (Ed.) *Creating the African University: Emerging Issues in the 1970's.* Ibadan, Nigeria: Oxford University Press, 226–43.

Thelin, John R. (2004). *A History of American Higher Education.* Baltimore, MD: The Johns Hopkins University Press.

Vision Reporter. (2005). "I illegally sat for Makerere exams." *New Vision,* July 10. Retrieved from www.newvision.co.ug/new_vision/news/1121604/illegally-sat-makerere-exams.

# PART III

# Evolutions and Revolutions in the Global Age

# 11

## IS "DESIGN THINKING" THE NEW LIBERAL ARTS?

*Peter N. Miller*

The "d.school," or Hasso Plattner Institute of Design at Stanford University, to use the formal name that no one at Stanford ever does, sits in a newish building just behind the main Quad, inconspicuously nestled among the other buildings of the School of Engineering to which it belongs. The engineering school has divisions of aeronautical engineering and mechanical engineering, an earthquake center, and also a division of product design. But the d.school is something very different.

It sees itself as a training ground for problem solving for graduate students by fostering creative confidence and pushing them beyond the boundaries of traditional academic disciplines. Whereas design schools elsewhere emphasize the design of products, Stanford's uses what the local culture calls "design thinking": to equip their students with a methodology for producing reliably innovative results in any field.

What is design thinking? It's an approach to problem solving based on a few easy-to-grasp principles that sound obvious: "Show Don't Tell," "Focus on Human Values," "Craft Clarity," "Embrace Experimentation," "Mindful of Process," "Bias Toward Action," and "Radical Collaboration." These seven points reduce to five modes—empathize, define, ideate, prototype, test—and three headings: hear, create, deliver. That may sound corporate and even simplistic, but design thinking has been used to tackle issues like improving access to economic resources in Mongolia, water storage and transportation in India, and elementary and secondary education and community building in low-income neighborhoods in the United States.

John L. Hennessy, president of the university, and David Kelley, head of the d.school, have been having a conversation about what the d.school and design thinking mean for Stanford. Hennessy sees them as the core of a new model of education for undergraduates. Two such classes on design thinking have already been created: "Designing Your Life," which aims to help upperclassmen think about the decisions that will shape their lives after graduating, and "Designing Your Stanford," which applies design thinking to helping first- and second-year students make the best choices about courses, majors, and extracurricular activities. Both are popular. Kelley argues for incorporating design thinking into existing courses across the humanities and sciences.

Hennessy and Kelley see design thinking as something valuable for all undergraduates, not only those interested in design or engineering. When we are talking about a way of thinking that all students should be exposed to because it enhances their understanding of everything else they do, learning and living, then we're actually on familiar terrain. Because what's happening in Palo Alto right now is really about the future of the liberal arts.

Is design thinking the new liberal arts?

Last semester I taught simultaneous video-linked seminars with my friend and colleague Michael Shanks. I'm a historian working in New York City at the Bard Graduate Center. He's a classical archaeologist teaching at Stanford. The course focused on the practices developed by early modern antiquarians to study artifacts from the past that lived on into the present, and argued that those same methods could be used today by designers interested in the experiences people have with objects. Michael teaches in the d.school in Stanford and brought design thinking into our classroom in New York. By the end of the semester I was fascinated enough to head out to Palo Alto to immerse myself in the ways of the d.school. What I discovered got me thinking about more than design thinking. A very important experiment in humanities higher education is going on.

Last year the d.school offered more than 80 courses, enrolling 1,250 students. Some courses are for a full 10 weeks and others, "pop-up" courses, for four weeks or sometimes only for a weekend. The "pop-up" courses don't give grades and don't count toward a professor's teaching load. As a rule, d.school classes are team-taught by up to six instructors from different disciplinary and professional backgrounds, but the school itself has no dedicated faculty of its own. Students come from all over the university, and the courses are oversubscribed; there is also real pressure from undergraduates wanting to take the two graduate-level offerings. These enrollment figures suggest that whatever it is the d.school is doing, it's working.

Walking around the d.school, one encounters the full range of courses: some lectures, some bench work, some sitting around tables. But all of them buzz with energy, all of them feature teams of students working collaboratively, all of them involve coursework based on problem solving. It's like the famous business-school case method made practical, opened up from the challenges facing businesses to the challenges facing all people.

Design at Stanford began in the engineering school and grew out of the product-design program, itself born of the union of art and mechanical engineering. Launched in the mid-1960s, the master's degree program was open to students in art and engineering, and included what were then new types of courses like "How to Ask a Question" and new materials-based projects like constructing a wooden ship and racing it on the campus lake.

A second crucial influence came from outside Palo Alto, from Esalen. Founded by two Stanford graduates in 1962, Esalen became an "antihumanities" institute, with lectures, seminars, retreats (and Eastern philosophy, music, and more), but no grades or credits. Bernie Roth, a young Stanford faculty member in the design division, attended a faculty retreat at Esalen in the mid-1960s and brought what he had learned there into courses and programs that focused on creativity and empathy. Today Roth is the academic director of the d.school.

A third important influence came from the world of commerce. Kelley, who was a master's-degree student in mechanical engineering in 1977, and who taught at Stanford off and on afterward, brought the emphases on creativity and empathy to a company he helped found in 1978, which eventually became IDEO—and created Apple's first mouse. At IDEO, empathy became "human-centered design," shifting the focus from designing products to designing the experience of using the products. IDEO brought in psychologists, behavioral economists, and anthropologists to work alongside product designers, and together they tried to think their way into the mind of the consumer.

Self-conscious reflection on the design process puts thinking about how to design on the same level as the thing designed. The success of the approach is reflected in the way IDEO the design company became, little by little, IDEO the design-thinking company, and its subsequent move into areas increasingly remote from traditional product design. IDEO showed how the process of designing, say, a car could be abstracted from the specific product and used to develop "toolkits" to tackle more complex design problems, like building clean-water systems in Africa, a neighborhood association, or a school. With the formalization of the abstract notion of process as "design thinking," IDEO became a consulting group.

In 2005, Kelley turned to an IDEO client, Hasso Plattner, co-founder and later chief executive of the software giant SAP AG, with the idea of creating a home for design thinking at Stanford. A gift of $35 million from Plattner launched the d.school; Kelley is credited with leading its founding.

Larry Leifer, professor of mechanical engineering and director of the university's Center for Design Research, calls the half of the d.school building that isn't occupied by mechanical engineering "IDEO.edu." Standing next to a poster of the animated character Bob the Builder, Leiffer explains that at the d.school, "We build people first, then things." Indeed, the emphasis has shifted from traditional product design to the process of designing, and now to the process of designing producers, and even people—all with the aim of "social innovation." And that, in turn, gets at the core of what is significant about the d.school's work for the rest of academe, and for the humanities in particular: human-centered design redescribes the classical aim of education as the care and tending of the soul; its focus on empathy follows directly from Rousseau's stress on compassion as a social virtue.

That's why Hennessy's discussions with Kelley aren't just about Stanford's future, but about all of ours. Harry J. Elam Jr., vice provost for undergraduate education, elaborated on Hennessy's thinking: "The d.school is not unlike a center for teaching and learning on steroids: Pedagogy and design thinking inform how to portray content and learning goals." In other words, Stanford's administration put two and two together: if the d.school already represented a kind of insurgent consultancy, why not focus that consulting work on Stanford itself? If collaborative project-based learning, real-world challenges, and multidisciplinary research architectures were already being taught in the d.school, why not leverage that experience for Stanford as a whole?

Asked whether the administration was aware that the d.school was furnishing the university with nothing less than a new educational model, Elam answers, "Yes. The simple answer is yes." One vision of what that might mean is the Stanford2025 exhibition project, an attempt to reimagine undergraduate experience. Instead of a four-year-and-out program with a progressive narrowing of focus, students have a "mission" instead of a major, and "loop" in and out of the university throughout their work careers, with punctuated periods of different kinds of learning, and with fact-based expertise giving way to skills-based expertise.

For Leifer, the d.school is a kind of anti-university. Universities and their academic disciplines, he says, provide "context-independent knowledge." The world and its problems are not, however, organized by discipline. Even if humanists still tend to look down on "applied" learning, Leifer argues, knowledge has to fit the shape of the problem, not the other way around. The d.school's learning is all "context-dependent," pulling whatever it needs from any discipline in order to solve specific problems. The "d in d.school," he says, refers "not to design but to demilitarized." He gestures to one side of the atrium: "Mechanical engineering: a body of knowledge that is extended and defended." Pointing to the other side: "This is the anti-establishment, no journal, no research, no labs, no students, no degrees, no faculty." In between, where he stood, was an agora-like open space in which students milled about, and where, equally, they can stage exhibitions, gather for events, or sit drinking coffee.

Could it be that every university needs a "d.school"? Do disciplines, in order to evolve and advance, need some place in which to play and from which to be provoked?

That is the role institutes can play within the current ecology of higher education. With independent identities, budgets, staff, and, most important, vision, they can offer a space for play and for focus. Native to Europe, they are still relatively rare in the United States. Anyone who has come across the arcane two-volume survey *Forschungsinstitute: Ihre Geschichte, Organisation, und Ziele* (Research Institutes: Their History, Organization and Goals) and leafed through its 782-page second volume, an A to Z listing of institutes in Germany in 1930, when the book was published, can glimpse a world that could have been ours, but never was.

That same year, the Institute for Advanced Study was being founded in Princeton, New Jersey, in explicit imitation of what existed in such number in Germany. Since then, the Warburg and Courtauld institutes have flourished in London, as have the various Max Planck institutes around the globe. In the humanities, in the United States, we can point to the relatively late creations of the Getty Research Institute, the research unit of the Sterling and Francine Clark Art Institute, and the many humanities centers that have sprouted on university campuses.

The institutes support fellowships, intellectual projects in specific fields, and collecting; the centers have opened up new kinds of cross-disciplinary questions. Both, however, remain places where scholars take refuge from teaching and administrative demands—to be left free to do creative work. But the real labor of shaping students and making careers is still in departments.

By standing outside the professional structure of the disciplines—graduate training and tenure and promotion—institutes remain free to ask questions and follow less-frequented tracks across the intellectual landscape. The d.school—officially, after all, the "Hasso Plattner Institute for Design"—embraces this extra-disciplinary position (they call it "multidisciplinary"). Research conducted at Stanford's Center for Design Research, for example, shows that the greater the degree of linguistic diversity in a project team, the greater the degree of linguistic invention over the course of the project. Diversity, in short, begets creativity.

We are far away from the old vision of humanities scholarship brilliantly captured in a casual aside by the French historian Fernand Braudel. Presented late in life with highly original works of scholarship, he asked if they were written in prison—the presumption being that conversation was generally inimical to creativity. The Stanford research seems to show the exact opposite: if one wants to promote original scholarship, one ought to bring together as many people as possible from as many different disciplines as possible. Almost by definition, that kind of creative interchange cannot happen in a university department precisely because there is simply too much that is held in common. Disciplines are about answers, or mastery, and therefore favor convergence. Institutes can be more open to questions, and therefore divergence, because they are freed from gatekeeping, whether intellectual or professional. By the same token, humanities centers may also be too much a part of existing university structures to stand outside.

The challenge is how to not be too departmental, but also not too cut off from department life. The answer may turn on rethinking the separation between "research" and "teaching." IDEO's many design-thinking tool kits always include an extended treatment of research. One of the d.school's basic courses, "Research as Design: Redesign Your Research Process," aims to improve "the research process to make us more innovative scholars or scientists."

Sounds good, right? But research in the d.school and research in the surrounding university's humanities departments is very different. In the latter, research is about finding answers to the discipline's questions. In the d.school, it is a process not of finding answers but of discovering questions, the questions that the subsequent design phase—in IDEO terms, "ideation" and "prototyping"—is supposed to answer.

Research-as-questioning is a much freer and more playful approach to discovery. It keeps us in closer contact with our natural disposition to curiosity and wonder. It is also much closer to pedagogy. Shaping classes to share the excitement and skills of doing research as opposed to communicating content could be another way of "flipping" the classroom, but one in which research centers could actually help rethink teaching.

On the other hand, as university-based readers of the IDEO toolkits would immediately see, research in the design world is very closely linked to action-oriented solutions, i.e., to client needs. In fact, close attention to the way "research" is described in IDEO's own publications shows that it is all conducted in the present tense, with no sense that the past matters to the present. Everything is ethnography. Libraries, archives, museums, the great repositories of the human past, are rarely called upon for help. That puts a contradiction at the heart of design thinking, given the premise of a human-centered design practice, and the fact that we humans are all sedimentary beings in whom the past lives on and helps shape our experience of the present.

A truly human-centered design, if it takes culture at all seriously, would have to take pastness seriously. As my colleague Michael Shanks, one of the very few tenured professors of humanities teaching regularly in the d.school, points out, design thinking needs to be seen as "necessarily archaeological and represents what prior generations called 'the liberal arts'—the belief that knowledge from and about the past is important for living well in the future." In our class, students studied antiquarians—the early modern scholars of the material world who are the ancestors of all those who now study material culture.

Looking at their historical scholarship, our students isolated a series of practices modeled on the "method cards" developed by IDEO to actually help designers work. These antiquarian cards are anything but. Turns out that the antiquarians whose very names used to breathe their distance from us, and their distaste for us, are speaking to us. Shanks and I plan to teach a pop-up course in the d.school in which these cards would be used by design students to tackle complex present problems—and test the presumption that the past is a foreign country.

The absence of serious consideration of "pastness" in design thinking is a blind spot. It's also symptomatic of the way in which the balance of basic versus applied research is generally evaluated outside university humanities departments. But aside from the obvious fact that without doing the basic research, we'll never have something we want to apply, the absence of "pastness"—and we can take that to be synonymous with "basic" research for the purpose of this argument—points toward a different sort of problem: "complexity."

If we think hard about what the liberal arts teach, we find that the study of the past achievements of humans, whether history, literature, philosophy, music, or art, provides us with a richly nuanced appreciation for the complexity of human existence. We may live in a city or a suburb, on a farm or in an industrial slum, born into a family of means or poverty, but on our own we have only our own experiences to go on. What the liberal arts—or humanities—give us are the experiences of those who have come before us to add to our own. These surrogate experiences help us to live well in the world.

Where the liberal arts are about problems—they take the familiar aspects of life and defamiliarize them in the interest of interpretation—design thinking is about solutions. It's about taking the complexities of life and simplifying them in the interest of problem solving.

So, is design thinking the new liberal arts?

Not yet.

Those 1,200 students a year taking courses and spending hours learning, some without any expectation of credit, seem almost like they are living out Cardinal Newman's idea of a university. It looks like liberal learning at its best. But without taking the measure of the way the past lives on in the present, and without acknowledging the educational value of defamiliarizing the familiar, if those courses were to replace the classical liberal arts, we would lose precisely the practical value of classical education: seeing ourselves as existing in time and managing a range of imperfect complexities.

Design thinking that took the past more seriously could provide a framework in which humanists and scientists could work together on problems that need to be understood and even solved, such as climate, food, poverty, health, transportation, or built environments. A colleague once told me of a complex research project of the sort beloved by design thinking. It aimed to help farmers in Africa reach some self-sufficiency. But because the project paid no attention to local traditions of food and its consumption, something that went beyond the ethnographically accessible, the farmers ended up refusing to eat the bounty they had succeeded in growing.

Institutes, like the Hasso Plattner at Stanford, can be places of real exploration and new forms of teaching and research, in the world of discipline but not of it. We in the university, at many different organizational levels, may all need our own "d.schools." But for them to really shape the future of university learning, they will have to do a better job of engaging with precisely what the university was designed to promote, and what design thinking, with its emphasis on innovation, has thus far completely ignored: the past.

# 12

# HONG KONG'S LIBERAL ARTS LABORATORY

## Design Thinking, Practical Wisdom, and the Common Core@HKU

*Gray Kochhar-Lindgren*

How might design thinking and the practical wisdom of the deliberative know-how that the Greeks named *phronēsis* contribute to the reconfiguration of Liberal Learning and General Education as such experiments are established in different parts of Asia? As colleges and universities in the United States continue to suffer from the devastation of the financial crisis and a retreat from the Liberal Arts tradition, different sites in Asia are making a very different set of decisions. These regions know that the contemporary knowledge-economy is one of invention, collaboration, prototyping, failure, iteration, and innovation, and that higher education, as one of its primary tasks, must reconfigure itself to prepare students to take up fluid and capable positions in this rapidly changing global economy.

As Kara Godwin (2015) has shown, using the Global Liberal Education Index (GLEI), Asia "accounts for 37 percent of liberal education programs outside the United States" (Godwin, 2015:2) and this number has rapidly increased since the year 2000. Examples of such a focus include, among others, the Underwood International College at Yonsei University, South Korea; the School of International Liberal Studies at Waseda University, Japan; Fudan University's General Education Program; Peking University's Yuanpei College; United International in Zhuhai; NYU-Shanghai; and, the most recent experiment, Yale-NUS (National University of Singapore). In Hong Kong, all eight publically funded universities were mandated by the government to shift from three- to four-year degrees in 2012 and to include in that curricular reform some type of General Education, designed in each case by the respective universities. There are, across the city, distribution models, Great Books models, and, at the University of Hong Kong (as well as at the Hong Kong University of Science and Technology), what is called the Common Core (which has no connection with the way this term is used in the US).

There is, then, a great deal of enthusiastic experimentation in this region around the Liberal Arts and cross-disciplinary undergraduate education. How might these multiple forms of experimentation with Liberal Learning intersect with the emergence of "design thinking" and the shift from an understanding of reason as primarily a force for abstract speculation toward—a word which moves both forward and backward in history—an understanding of reason as *phronēsis*, as a more practical knowing that deliberatively responds within particular situations to particular constellations of questions? In this tradition all knowledge is situated and involves questions of the responsive navigation of ethical conundrums rather than an abstract category called "knowledge" (and, much less, a list of "facts").

Liberal Learning and General Education—the latter perhaps the dullest and most misleading term ever invented—is in desperate need of a kind of philosophical blood transfusion, but such a metaphor requires that we have a healthy body and an efficient blood bank and transfer system somewhere nearby if we are to re-enliven the ailing body of Liberal Learning. We need to re-exercise our institutional and individual pedagogical imaginations and move beyond taken-for-granted reiterations of "whole person," "holistic," "general," and even, for the most part, "integrative." As Michel Serres reminds us in *Thumbelina* (2015) that "we are still teaching our young people in institutional frameworks that come from a time they no longer recognize. Buildings, playgrounds, classrooms, lecture halls, campuses, libraries, laboratories—even forms of knowledge—these frameworks date from a time and were adapted to an era when both the world and humans were something they are no longer" (Serres, 2015:10).

It is time for all of us to reconfigure the practices related to the meaningfulness of Liberal Learning. Gilles Deleuze (1994), in his reorientation of metaphysics, has argued that it is a "question of making movement itself a work … of inventing vibrations, rotations, whirlings, gravitations, dances or leaps which directly touch the mind" (Deleuze, 1994:8). Our goal here is far more modest: to re-envision not metaphysics, but, instead, Liberal Learning and General Education as a creative design process linked to the tradition of the practical wisdom of *phronēsis*. Perhaps this, too, might produce vibrations and whirlings?

We live, to write in shorthand, in a period of immensely rapid and contested globalization. Ours is a time of the neoliberal financialization of much of higher education; the destruction of large swathes of the planet's ecosystems; of an audit and fetishistic culture of fantasies of the quantification of quality using performance metrics; of major systemic advances in understanding genetics, digital electronics, and the nano- and cosmic limits of physics; personalized molecular medicine; and a humanities and social science trajectory that, for the most part, moves away from individuality and other social essences toward singularities and assemblages, subjectification rather than the subject, the precaricity inherent in capitalism, the micro- and macro- forms of biopower, disequilibriums and transversalities, actants, networks, and quasi-objects, and various forms of the cybernetic as its categories of research and understanding. The world is turbo-charged.

All of this turmoil creates a necessity and opportunity for a recalibration in order to (re)invent Liberal Learning in a multiplicity of contexts, many of which are in Asia. This never occurs, of course, on a blank slate, an empty screen, but it is also the case that historical accretions manifest themselves differently in different situations. Hong Kong, for example, was extraordinarily fortunate to be able to add an entire additional year to the undergraduate three-year curriculum. Two overlapping areas of current programmatic and pedagogical exploration, both of which are connected in different ways in the Common Core@HKU, are design thinking and *phronēsis*, and these, in turn, must always be thought under the sign of our contemporaneity with its chaos, hybridities, and complexities.

This revitalization will not dismiss the specialized expertise needed by the knowledge economy, but will, rather, require the most evocative fervor of philosophy, the arts, the sciences, and all the professional schools. But the time is now right for the slightest (dis)inclination of thought to occur that will reconfigure the tiredness of the debates about General Education—which are intertwined with the more encompassing goals of higher education—and enhance the movements of ontology (of all domains), ethics (as an abiding that questions), and of how best to prepare our students for the local, global and conflictive political-economies into which they will soon enter. This latter category will lead us toward *phronēsis* and design thinking.

In a wonderfully provocative essay, which originally appeared in *The Chronicle of Higher Education* and is now reprinted in this volume, Peter N. Miller has suggested that "design thinking" might provide an approach toward a "new liberal arts." Not surprisingly, it is Stanford's famous d.school, with its deep ties to IDEO, that serves as the model as a pedagogical, social, and creative force for design thinking, which is related to but distinctive from more traditional forms of product design programs that have been developed in engineering, arts, architecture, or graphic design programs.

The d.school articulates its basic principles—and how many academic units have actually made such an attempt?—as the following:

Show Don't Tell
Focus on Human Values
Craft Clarity
Embrace Experimentation
Mindful of Process
Bias Toward Action
Radical Collaboration

Although the many consultations and decisions around the structure of the Common Core at the University of Hong Kong did not explicitly use the language of design thinking, there is a great deal of relevance between the way such processes operate, their goals, and the teaching and assessment culture that is emerging in and beyond the Core. To try to capture the tone and intentions of this effort, I very often use the term "inspired pragmatism," by which I hope to evoke both the practical and the aspirational aspects of learning.

For the Common Core@HKU, design thinking provides a framework for helping us articulate engaged learning—the type of projects that lead beyond the classroom and beyond the grade-sheet of the professor—for students across all ten Faculties at the University. In the Core, each undergraduate must take a total of six courses across four Areas of Inquiry: Science and Technological Literacy, Global Issues, Humanities, and China. The more than 170 courses, all of which address "issues of fundamental importance," are designed specifically for the Core by full-time faculty, are interdisciplinary in scope, are taught as interactively as possible, include students of all levels from across the whole campus, are all taught by full-time faculty members, and engage students with multiple forms of assessment (the great majority of which are not traditional exams).

The classes tend to be large "lectures"—although we are working very hard on insuring that these are interactive as well—with accompanying small tutorials, although we are now also beginning to include courses with a greater emphasis on experiential learning and blended learning options (which we call SPOCs: Special Private Online Courses), and may well begin experimenting with a variety of internationally oriented classes as HKU begins to develop additional ways to insure options for such experiences for our students. Both the University as a whole, and the Common Core in particular, are interested in how "design think-ing" might enhance our capacity to teach, to create appropriately scaled responses to the dilemmas Hong Kong and the larger world are struggling with, and how such practices—in which imagination, conceptualization, practice, and feedback are not a linear process, but, instead, are inextricably linked in multidimensional loops—might reconfigure our experience of Liberal Learning and General Education.

In a sense, the so-called "practicality"—which can be traced back to Aristotle's interpretation of *phronēsis* and is always in need of a more resonant articulation— of the engineering workshop, the science labs, the studio practice in art and architecture, clinical training in the medical sciences, and the case studies of busi-ness are all making their way into the student experience of the Core. In such activities, there a utilitarian drive toward the practicality of the present that at times does, as Miller suggests in the final part of his essay, occlude the past, as well as, I would add, the complexities inherent in all acts of critical interpretation. This, to me, seems like the fundamental frictional field between various aspects of what are usually grouped under the "Liberal Arts" and how they "apply" to work, suc-cess, identity, and national and university reputations. What, in each instance, *counts* as important, as a valuable value? It is important, as we respond to this question, not to fall into the easy oppositions with their devaluation of one side of the binary, but to always be aware of an "understanding-in-motion," all the relational networks at work in the learning that occurs in situated—which is not to say rigidly bounded—forms of knowing.

Proponents of design thinking think that such principles and practice of know-how are valuable capacities for everyone to develop because they engender forms of learning—which are both new and very old—that are tied to both the deliberations and doability of actions. Thinking—which occurs within the collaborative space of speaking, experimenting, and the "hearsomeness" that Joyce refers to—is always necessary, but it is a thinking-in-motion in the context of a situation. "When we are talking about a way of things that all students should be exposed to because it enhances their understanding of everything else they do, learning and living, then we're actually on familiar terrain. Because what's happening in Palo Alto [at Stanford's d.school] right now is really about the future of the liberal arts" (Miller, 2015:7). Miller points to three primary influences on the current organization of the d.school: product engineering (always an alliance between arts and mechanics, though often not explicated as such), commerce (especially IDEO), and—the one that most surprised me—of the Esalen Institute in Big Sur, California. Human potential is built into the core process of design thinking. Who shall we become?

IDEO, in its own mission statement, articulates the process of design thinking in the following manner:

> Design thinking is a deeply human process that taps into abilities we all have but get overlooked by more conventional problem-solving practices. It relies on our ability to be intuitive, to recognize patterns, to construct ideas that are emotionally meaningful as well as functional, and to express ourselves through means beyond words or symbols. (www.ideo.com/about/)

It is a "recovery" and an expansion of the creativity we all engage with constantly but don't always know how to speak of and enhance; it acts out of the non-cognitive—affect and intuition—as well as the cognitive (and this is essential for universities to remember); and it uses methods beyond the traditional analytics of word and number (although these are of course quickly folded back into the design process). It has, in other words, an *expressive* element embedded within it and it requires multiplicity and singularity to play with, and off of, one another.

The description continues by noting that design thinking is "best thought of as a system of overlapping spaces rather than a sequence of orderly steps. There are three spaces to keep in mind: *inspiration, ideation*, and *implementation*. Inspiration is the problem or opportunity that motivates the search for solutions. Ideation is the process of generating, developing, and testing ideas. Implementation is the path that leads from the project stage into people's lives" (www.ideo.com/about/). These three overlapping spaces—which must be imagined as constantly dynamic— are *not* the abstract spaces of classical physics or Cartesian metaphysics, but the potential and produced spaces talked of by geography, topology, performance and cultural studies, new media, philosophy, theatre and dance, and the theoreticians of "everyday life" across multiple fields. These are the spaces of experience, all of which have contours, permeable boundaries, friction, and possibilities to be tried out.

Every undergraduate should feel as if s/he is deeply engaged with discovering the world of these lived spaces, that is, with a research process that is defined with different inflections and scales of precision depending on its context. It will not be linear (which is only a methodological fantasy, at times useful to be sure). In design thinking, "Research-as-questioning is a much freer and more playful approach to discovery. It keeps us closer contact with our natural disposition to curiosity and wonder. It is also much closer to pedagogy. Shaping classes to share the excitement and skills of doing research as opposed to communicating content could be another way of 'flipping' the classroom …" (Miller, 2015:9). It is through these two modalities of research and pedagogy—and the line very much blurs when the process is working well—that design thinking speaks to the goals of the Common Core@HKU. Intense curiosity, working together to pose questions and to make things, and a desire to have a modest impact on the larger world drive the momentum of the Core to be a sandbox, a laboratory, and a studio for university as a whole and for the undergraduates who are learning to learn, learning to connect the incessantly moving dots.

The Olin School of Engineering, for example, has explicitly adopted a design-stream for its majors and its students are not "just challenged to apply their area of expertise to 'design it right,' which is a narrow subset of these activities. They also take ownership of figuring out how to 'do the right thing,' to add value to people's lives in meaningful and appropriate ways" (Miller and Lindner, 2015:4). Meaning, action, and a "right fit" are all essential to the process. Design thinking is a very powerful set of tools—and a tool is always a complex operator of the sort that Deleuze and Guattari have called an "assemblage" (*agencement*)—for inspiring, prototyping, relooping, and taking viable projects and products beyond the post-it notes and collaborative inventiveness of the workshop. Such a process, however, is only one form of the contemporary move toward profound recuperations and re-visioning of *phronēsis*.

Throughout his work, Serres has gestured toward the turbulence of Hermes, invisibly connecting the living and the dead as he moves transversally across all domains of knowledge, as well as (more recently) the efficacious if ineffable voices of the angels, who do nothing all day and all night but send instant messages. We live immersed, as humans always have, in a sea of messages, of signals, of (potential) meanings, and if Liberal Learning is to maintain its significance for university education and its multiply-layered contexts—which now always includes the virtuality of the digital—we will all need to reflect on, and refract, this messaging-world and consider how best to accompany students and colleagues in the invention of new pathways that navigate the turbulence of our period of history.

This is not, for the most part, a navigation through a previously mapped domain, but, instead, learning to navigate as we navigate, in a process that creates its pathways as it unfolds. Professors know something of compasses, ship-building, tidal charts, and the wind and the waves, but they do not know the destination. How, if innovation is the goal, could they?

This reorientation includes the very simple observations that the so-called "content" of academic disciplines will not remain the same as they have been previously delimited and that the tenor and style of teaching will also change. We are all co-navigators mapping a dynamic, non-static new world of relations. What is it that we are all hoping—and already working within and toward—to concoct as the improvisational university of surfing and of the most precise forms of all the specializations from cosmology to the quantum idiosyncrasies of nano-technology, from protein foldings to a kingfisher's silent entry into the water, from the history of the concept to the future of the screen, the surface, and the support for new discursive platforms for learning? How can we create a form of learning that resonates, hums, vibrates?

As one of the primary sites for Liberal Learning, General Education—as we rethink it and work to rename it—can best be thought of as a cluster of skills of making, habits of collaborative and individual curiosity, and a capacity for invention that is contextualized by the strife and possibility offered by globalization, technocapital, local currencies, and the continuing need for an ethic of the social good. Such an approach, while not necessarily jettisoning the traditional organization of the liberal arts, does, however, revise the enterprise in light of emerging transitions of the "university," "disciplines," "the whole person," "critical thinking and communication," and "service to the community." And, as part of the endeavor, the new Liberal Learning will have to learn to do a better job of constructing looping and linking narratives between and beyond the individual courses. An unreflective and fragmented system of distribution requirements is not sufficient for the needs of the day.

Design thinking is design doing. Can creative problem solving across different sectors and disciplines be taught? Of course. And the students will be thoroughly engaged. Does this knowledge need to be complemented by other forms of practice, other epistemologies? Of course. The question for a university is how best to organize these forms of complementary practices and knowledges that are called the Liberal Arts. How to relate a General Education program to the majors? Undergraduate and graduate education? The campus to the city to the world? This are the set of questions that all Liberal Learning programs are incessantly, and inevitably, engaged with. They cannot be, and should not be, fully resolved into a "solution," but they do demand of us that along with the proverbial content of knowledge we are also always asking questions of ethics.

Ethics is not as a set of prescriptive moral rules, although these will inevitably be close at hand to stand in as a proxy for a more authentic ethics of questioning and response. Ethics is knowing how to live well, a capacity we are all trying to learn, to practice our way through our blind-spots, our awkward dance moves, and our pettiness. Jeffrey Sachs, in a speech given to the University of Columbia Medical Faculty, asks a penetrating question:

> Can the university, its faculty, students or administrators be indifferent to such problems as racial equality, demography, the world rule of law, the deteriorating relationship between science and the other humanities, the moral foundations of democracy, the true nature of communism, the understanding of non-Western cultures, the values and goals of our society…. These are real problems—of intellectual content, of urgent consequence, of frightening proportions. Where are they going to be studied in all of their dimensions, and where are truly ultimate solutions to be elaborated, if not in that one institution that is committed to the mind at work, sing all of the disciplines and intellectual skills available? (Sachs, 2015:4)

"Almost all of us," Sachs continues, "are out of practice in moral reasoning. Moral reasoning, like other kinds of specialized knowledge, is an undertaking that requires training, practice, and experience. Indeed Aristotle argued that only the older members of the *polis*, the community, could have *phronēsis*, often defined as practical wisdom, including moral wisdom" (Sachs, 2015:3). Again, the multiple resonances of "right" come into play, including the "right fit" between problem and solution; the "right direction" for activity; and the "right" to the rights of ethics.

Aristotle defined *phronēsis*, practical wisdom, as a "true and reasoned state of capacity to act with regard to the things that are good or bad for man [sic]…. Now what it preserves is a judgement of the kind we have described. For it is not any and every judgement that pleasant and painful objects destroy and pervert, e.g. the judgement that the triangle has or has not its angles equal to two right angles, but only judgements about what is to be done" (Aristotle, n.d.:VI, 5). *Phronēsis* is neither specialized nor general knowledge in a strictly logical sense; it does not organize itself into that type of schema. *It cannot be asserted, contained, or reproduced by a statement of fact*. It is understanding, which *makes* judgments, *plus* the doing of what is to be done; it is *deliberation-in-action*. Practical wisdom involves but is not synonymous with the understanding:

> For understanding is neither about things that are always and are unchangeable, nor about any and every one of the things that come into being, but about things which *may become subjects of questioning and deliberation*. Hence it is about the same objects as practical wisdom; but understanding and practical wisdom are not the same. For practical wisdom issues commands, since its end is what ought to be done or not to be done; but understanding only judges. (Aristotle, n.d.:VI, 10, my emphasis)

*Phronēsis* and design thinking are not "applied" theory, as if the rational cognition of theory comes first and then, secondarily and derivatively, is somehow or another *applied* to a situation like a bandage to a wound, an ointment to a sting, or a coat of paint to a wall.

Serres is correct when he insists that "application" is not simply a

> return of information onto the observation from which it comes. *It is the changing of things by the very presence and activity of knowledge … everything begins with the pure activity of observation or collection as such. The application is already there.* It drives a wedge into the system and makes it deviate…. Knowledge, yes, analyzes, paralyzes, catalyzes. And thus it is a parasitic activity that transforms milieu and society. (Serres, 2007:213, my emphasis)

In this context, the Serresian "parasite"—as guest, host, and a transformer of energy—is the conjunction between theory and practice, between understanding and judgment, between epistemology and ethics. It is the *para-situ*: that which is alongside; it is the between of relations, not the essence of a thing or a rational perspective as-if from above. It is transversal and changes the relations of all the terms that gather around General Education, Liberal Learning, and the University as an institution. We learn *alongside* one another, alongside our texts, our histories, our cities, our computers, our images, and our questions.

Miller is extremely impressed by the design thinking at Stanford's d.school and in other parts of the global institutional ecology. But he is not quite sold that this is the "new liberal arts," since the liberal arts—though as inflected toward the humanities but not the sciences as they are most often conveyed to students— teach the "study of the past achievements of humans, whether history, literature philosophy, music or art provides us with a richly nuanced appreciate for the complexity of human existence" (2015:9). This inclusion of "pastness," as Miller observes, is something that design thinking, emphasizing innovative solutions to current problematic problems (that are felt as urgent by someone or some group), has completely missed. Until this "blind spot" (9)—as well as other such as attention to the processes of interpretation and meaning-making—is supplemented, design thinking cannot become the "new liberal arts." What comes before, during, and after the stage of designing?

Whatever the new Liberal Learning and General Education do become, they will be structured by the "alongside," the "with," the "between," and the movements of the "through" characterized by the "*trans-.*" All Liberal Learning must move across, through, between, alongside and beyond all the structures of disciplinarity. Transdisciplinarity, as Hans Dieleman has put it, is "not so much about disciplines but about that what is 'between, across and beyond' those disciplines" (2013:68). While it is true that the binarism of classical logic needs to be resituated, it is also true that the "third space" is included only as a space-between, a region or force—I am not sure which—that acts to both conjoin and separate. As Serres argues, the "parasite has a relation with the relation and not with the station. And it puts the relation in the form of a cantilever. The simplest diagram appears. *Static*, in English: parasite" (2007:33). Things, slightly tilted, start to move.

The third is a *spanner in the works*, something that keeps-apart, enables distinctions and differences, and yet simultaneously joins-together. Eventually, the spanner in any individual network of relations snaps and the work breaks apart. But the possibility of spanning—which depends on the physical ideality of the between—is intimately renewable: until our own vanishing we can always, as Delueze and Guattari remind us, connect different multiplicities and play with new plug-ins. The principles of design include an artistic, procedurally transversal, and pragmatic multidimensionality that embodies a sense of experimental play, conceptual and material rigor, and a re-looping; the singularities that coalesce into a certain form of the provisionally objective; and a host of transdisciplinary points of contact and eddies between different pockets of the university as well as between the university and its multiple others. Distinction without clearly bounded separation: porous membranes: vortices. Squalls and sun-devils.

Design, like *phronēsis*, makes with deliberation and it makes the possibility of making. It leaves room for a corner to appear, it waltzes along avenues, it allows things to all fall down to see what remains and what curiosities get picked up along the way to be re-cobbled into the unexpected. Design takes time and time requires a design-process that can be practiced. Design is a chronometer of the *Zeitgeist*, a register of time that necessitates original spatializations: things, performances, art, essays, debates, case studies, media productions, and knowledge itself. Liberal Learning in the laboratory that Hong Kong is neither a return to a nostalgic past nor a packaged survey of current knowledge. It is, instead, a continuing experiment with the world and a striving for deliberative practical wisdom that acts for the good of both human and non-human beings. Liberal Learning is the design of design that occurs at the unfolding edges of the contemporary global university. As we become more and more attuned to the process, there is a still distant, but approaching, vibration, a strange hum, and the staccato rhythms of what sounds like flamenco.

## Notes

There is a vast literature on neoliberalism and the financialization of higher education. See, for extremely incisive analyses, Chris Newfield's *The Unmaking of the Public University* and Randy Martin's *Financialization of Everyday Life*.

Martin Heidegger has powerfully expressed such a being-together as the crossing point of the fourfold—mortals, divinities, sky, and earth—in "Building Dwelling Thinking." His encounter with Aristotle, including the concept of *phronēsis*, is traced by Stuart Elden in "Reading *Logos* as Speech."

Without using the explicit language of design-thinking or *phronēsis*, Serres is articulating a new way of working in line with the digital atmosphere in which we live. Seeking a anciently new name for this method, he speaks of as an "*algorithmic* [or *procedural*] mode of thought … rules of order, sequences of gestures, series of formalities, yes, procedures … these all involve an activity that is very different from geometrical deduction or experimental induction" (2015:71). It is always transversal, vectorial, rather than linear. Procedural philosophy is further elaborated upon by Serres in *Ēloge de la philosophie en langue française* (1997) and I have addressed some of these issues in "Interfacing with Thumbelina" (forthcoming).

## References

Aristotle, *Nicomachean Ethics*. W. D. Ross (Trans.). Retrieved June 1, 2016, from http://classics.mit.edu/Aristotle/nicomachaen.6.vi.html

Deleuze, Gilles. *Difference and Repetition*. Paul Patton (Trans.). New York: Columbia University Press, 1994.

Dieleman, Hans. "From transdisciplinary theory to transdisciplinary practice: Artful doing in spaces of imagination and experimentation." In Nicolescu, Basarab and Ertas, Atila (Eds.) *Transdisciplinary Theory and Practice*. Lubbock, TX: The ATLAS Publishing, 2013 67–82.

Godwin, Kara. "The worldwide emergence of liberal education," *International Higher Education* (79): Winter 2015, 2–4.

IDEO. About IDEO. Retrieved June 1, 2016, from https://www.ideo.com/about/

Joyce, James. *Finnegans Wake*. London: Penguin, 2000.

Kochhar-Lindgren, Gray. "Interfacing with Thumbelina: Michel Serres, algorhythmic philosophy, and the University of Angelic invention." In Braidotti, Rosi and Dolphijn, Rick (Eds.) *Michel Serres and Procedural Philosophy: Communication, Nature, Subjectivity*. New York: Routledge (forthcoming).

Miller, Peter N. "Is 'design thinking' the new liberal arts?" *The Chronicle of Higher Education*, April 3, 2015. Reprint here.

Sachs, Jeffrey, "What is a moral university in the 21st century?" Speech at Columbia University, March 30, 2015 Retrieved June 1, 2016, from jeffsachs.org.

Serres, Michel. *Thumbelina: The Culture and Technology of Millennials*. London: Rowman & Littlefield, 2015.

Serres, Michel. *The Parasite*. Minneapolis, MN: University of Minnesota Press, 2007.

# 13

# LIBERAL ARTS EDUCATION IN THE AGE OF MACHINE INTELLIGENCE

*Daniel Araya*

Given the capacity of technology to automate labor, it stands to reason that the design of education systems is now fundamental to the future prosperity of postindustrial economies. Knowledge-based economies are said to be moving into a "Second Machine Age" in which technology is beginning to displace human labor across multiple industries (Brynjolfsson and McAfee, 2011, 2014; Kurzweil, 2006). Together artificial intelligence (AI), robotics, synthetic biology, and digital manufacturing are now poised to reshape the institutions and economic practices that anchor mass industrial societies.

At the same time, these new technologies are augmenting human capabilities and introducing new opportunities for entrepreneurial innovation across a wide range of industries (Autor, 2014). Where the Industrial Revolution leveraged machines for factory production, so today the Computational Revolution is advancing computers to augment human intelligence (Moravec, 1988; Araya and Peters, 2010). To be sure, even as the current wave of automating technologies begins to displace a variety of occupations, technology is also increasingly complementary to ingenuity and invention.

This chapter argues that the increasing pace of technological innovation now undermines any simple conclusions about the future of work and learning (Leadbeater, 2000; Blinder, 2008). It explores the value of liberal arts education as a means to both augmenting human creativity and preparing students for an age of machine intelligence. Lastly, it considers the value of "holistic" education as a foundation to a new era in which economic needs (in the traditional sense) are being transformed by technology and innovation.

## The Age of Machine Intelligence

Estimates are that there will be between 20 and 50 billion devices connected to the Internet between 2020 and 2030 (OECD, 2013, p. 10). Indeed, the application of cognitive systems—computational technologies that emulate human capabilities—is now poised to fundamentally remake postindustrial societies. As this technological revolution continues to expand and mature, it is facilitating deep structural changes in the global labor force (Economist, 2014).

What is obvious is that postindustrial societies are entering an era in which many kinds of labor are becoming much less valuable (Bekman et al., 1998; Katz, 1999; Goldin & Katz, 2008). Indeed, waves of creative destruction now threaten to unravel basic assumptions about the design and management of consumer societies (Schumpeter, 1976 [1942]). According to Ernst and Young, for example, the combination of high rates of youth unemployment across G20 countries and a broad shift in lifestyle choice are together driving the development of a rising class of young entrepreneurs (Buchanan, 2015).

While industrial labor was largely defined by repetitive tasks reinforced through standards and procedures, these tasks are now increasingly performed by software and robotics. In contrast to the perception that it is only low-skilled labor that is vulnerable to automation, theories on technological unemployment now argue just the opposite (Moravec, 1988).

Indeed, one of the main problems with educating young people for this new era is its inherent volatility. Notwithstanding the fact that the principle of machine-based automation has not fundamentally changed since the dawn of the computer era, the costs associated with automation have fallen precipitously. Innovation is now anchored to distributed production systems that leverage emergent technologies like 3D printing, AI, and robotics to drive long-term changes across the global economy (Zuboff, 1988; Brynjolfsson and McAfee, 2014). Building on AI and augmented intelligence, for example, the value of thinking and reasoning is becoming ever more closely connected to technologies that leverage human intelligence.

Human cognition is becoming embedded in algorithms that now function as agents capable operating on our behalf. Indeed, as Kelly (2014) suggests, AI is beginning to redefine human intelligence itself so that we are returning to a focus on empathy and shared social value. This is a shift from "knowledge work" to "relationship work" (Colvin, 2015), and from cultural transmission to entrepreneurial innovation. What this suggests is that machine intelligence and the automation of industrial and service-based labor is opening up new opportunities for entrepreneurs that more closely focus on humanity's higher needs, particularly personal and creative development.

This represents a broad transition beyond mass industrial society and into new stages of economy that parallel Abraham Maslow's (1954) thinking on human needs. Accordingly, human needs span a continuum from the tangible (food and water) to the intangible (self-esteem and creativity). As lower physiological needs are satisfied, higher needs for belonging and self-actualization emerge (Maslow, 1943, p. 375). Indeed, as Maslow (1943) concluded, the specific form that these needs take will vary substantially from person to person, but what we do know is that a society rooted in the highest levels of Maslow's hierarchy will be increasingly focused on individual development and collective meaning-making.

## Liberal Education in the Age of Machine Intelligence

Even as material scarcity continues to dominate our society's social values, it is increasingly clear that machine intelligence is moving to facilitate a shift in our mode of economy. One important question we might ask ourselves, today, is "What remains after we have mechanized agriculture, industry, and messaging technologies" (Lévy, 1997)? As Pierre Lévy suggests, the economy will shift toward abstract goods and services including the production of the social bond and the relational. In his view, "Those who manufacture things will become scarcer and scarcer, and their labour will become mechanized, augmented, automated to a greater and greater extent" (p. 34). Indeed, even as computers automate routine tasks, they are also amplifying opportunities for work that requires creativity, empathy, and problem solving.

In truth, technologies like machine intelligence are not only transforming our relationship to knowledge but also remaking our collective self-understanding. To be sure, Steve Jobs was fond of saying that the key to Apple's success was the marriage of technology with the humanities and the liberal arts. What he meant by this is that the best ideas emerge at the intersection of art and technology (rather than either alone). If we assume Jobs is right then we can conclude that the really important work of the future will not be technology per se, but a capacity to leverage technology for meaning-making and entrepreneurial invention.

Building on this understanding, many thinkers now argue for an enhanced focus on liberal education (Robinson, 2001; Wagner, 2012). Fareed Zakaria (2016), for example, contends that liberal education is critical to generating the cognitive skills needed for 21st century economies. Accordingly, a liberal education teaches people how to think, analyze, and learn through the integration and synthesis of complex ideas. Rather than a narrow specialization, liberal education is idealized as a multidisciplinary approach to education that facilitates aesthetics, communication, critical thinking, and storytelling.

Perhaps more than any other form of pedagogy, liberal education is fertile ground for fostering the entrepreneurial curiosity needed for creativity and conceptualization. In this way, liberal education in the Machine Age would offer a holistic approach to engaging with invention and innovation. Advocates of liberal education, for example, suggest that it provides a better foundation to critical thinking and rational judgment than science, technology, engineering and math

(STEM) alone. Rather than imparting a specific set of technical or vocational skills, a liberal education enables discursive reasoning as a means to thinking *across* disciplines. Liberal knowledge is holistic knowledge rather than simply a single discipline or specialization.

## Education and Entrepreneurship in the Conceptual Age

Beyond assembly line schools designed for the Industrial Age, what we now require are interdisciplinary programs that foster creativity for the Conceptual Age. As a 2012 Scandinavian study on improving education across Nordic countries suggests, there is an acute need to develop educational systems that stimulate creativity and meaning making (Chiu, 2012, pp. 49–50). Where schooling in the United States has become increasingly focused on standardized testing as a means to quantify education, educational thinkers are coming to understand the limits of testing in the machine age. In fact, the effort to quantify education through standardized testing is an analog of the broader automation process impacting the economy as a whole.

Calls to rejuvenate education systems in the United States and other advanced economies suggest the need for substantial investments in transforming our current industrial era education system. A key challenge moving forward, for example, is to ensure that students within postindustrial economies have the creative capacities to adapt and flourish in an era of shrinking employment. At the same time, questions remain about the future of work and learning (Palley, 2011). In fact, twenty-five million U.S. households (the bottom fifth of the income ladder) now earn just $19,500 or less per year (Kenworthy, 2013; Piketty, 2014).

As Harvard's Tony Wagner (2012) observes, the real challenge for postindustrial systems of education today is to view STEM as a means to enhancing human creativity rather than as an end in itself. Indeed, if competency within existing cultural systems was the goal of industrial education, then cultural production and the creative transformation of cultural systems will be the goal of education in this new era (Araya and Peters, 2010; Davidson and Goldberg, 2010). This would likely include a shift from the "hard" assets and capabilities of STEM to empathy, design, and entrepreneurial innovation (Satell, 2015).

To be sure, a new generation of inventors is already surfing the tide of disruptive innovation. In fact, there are 27 million entrepreneurs in the United States today, making up 14 percent of the working-age population—the highest rate recorded since 1999 (Buchanan, 2015). This makes sense. As postindustrial societies become more technological advanced and more urbanized, learning how to interact creatively within complex digitized environments is now becoming increasingly valuable.

As Steve Jobs well knew, creativity and innovation require creative collaboration *across* disciplines. Teaching students how to build theories about the world requires imagination and passion and this is foundational to a Conceptual Age. Indeed, as Pink (2006) suggests, this new era favors entrepreneurs, artists, and designers who can best leverage technology for innovation. More than simply adding in entrepreneurial training to education, this could mean changing the nature of education itself so that students are empowered to design and direct their own learning practices.

The basic idea here is that formal schooling now requires a more vigorous theory of creativity and innovation in order to reshape education systems within postindustrial societies. What is needed, in other words, is a greater investment in aesthetic vision and consilience. This means scaffolding real-world problem solving as part of the larger continuum of design, creativity, and technology-mediated collaboration. It also means embracing a holistic paradigm for learning.

This suggests the need for a fundamental break with didactic teaching and learning methods in order to transform the culture of education as "programmed knowledge" (Christensen, 1997; Christensen et al., 2008). This also means an emphasis on holistic education through transdisciplinary inquiry. Beyond disciplinary divisions, a creative education system requires seeing the world as a connected whole rather than composed of fragmented parts.

Based on the Oxford-Cambridge tradition, for example, Newman argued that a classical, liberal education reinforced a synthesis in the creation of new knowledge. Indeed, from Newman's (1891) perspective, liberal education represents a space within which all knowledge forms an interacting whole. In his view, the multiplicity of disciplines provided by a liberal education enabled students to understand and appreciate the significance of each particular branch of knowledge in relation to the rest.

While STEM education is obviously critical to economic growth, it is not sufficient to stoke innovation. Indeed, despite increasing numbers of educated students, many skilled professionals now find themselves forced into lower-skilled jobs because of the mismatch between education and market demand (Turbot, 2015). Indeed, this will mean adapting liberal arts to disruptive technologies. But it will also mean adapting technology to the liberal arts. A liberal view of education requires a return to the artistry and interdisciplinary thinking that will be the foundations to entrepreneurship in the Conceptual Age.

Indeed, even as educational reformers now focus on STEM skills, these skills will need to be more closely joined to the humanities and liberal arts. Laying out the paradoxical consequences of Moore's law, [1] for example, Rifkin (2014) argues against the common rhetoric in favor of STEM training as a means to mitigating unemployment. In his view, technological change is outpacing the capacities of a STEM labor force:

> The wholesale substitution of intelligent technology for mass labor and salaried professional labor is beginning to disrupt the workings of the

capitalist system. The question economists are so fearful to entertain is, what happens to market capitalism when productivity gains, brought on by intelligent technology, continue to reduce the need for human labor? What we are seeing is the unbundling of productivity from employment. Instead of the former facilitating the latter, it is now eliminating it. (p. 132)

At the same time, even as machine intelligence becomes more systemic and multifaceted, it will continue to open new creative opportunities. With this understanding in mind, educational strategies could begin to explicitly pair creativity with technology in order to ensure that students have the capacity to adapt to economic changes over the long-term. Liberal arts education is important to this shift because it facilitates the meaning-making process that stokes passion in students. Indeed, as Zakaria (2016) observes, the value of liberal education in conjunction with technology is its capacity to understand systems of human meaning in order to improve those systems over time. This allows for forming new perspectives beyond discrete disciplines. Indeed, this means moving beyond a narrow focus on efficient corporatized markets (neoliberalism), and toward a form of creative entrepreneurship that recognizes the need to continually remake systems of design and meaning.

More than simply adding in entrepreneurial training to education, this could mean changing the nature of education itself so that students are empowered to liberally design and direct their own learning practices. More than simply developing "start-ups," this would mean joining notions of entrepreneurship to educational programs that promote liberal notions of creativity and innovation, that is, entrepreneurial stewardship that focuses on problem solving that supports wider social value than the market alone can provide. Perhaps most importantly, it means work that requires empathy, creativity, and human interaction is now becoming critical to social and economic growth.

Rather than seeing education as a process of transmission and transaction, a liberal and holistic approach to knowledge and learning would recognize that education is greater than the sum of its parts. In fact, the original term "liberal arts" derives from the Latin word "liber," referring to the freedom to work creatively with one's own mind. Following Wilson's (1998) original thinking, for example, this suggests *consilience* or a union of the sciences and humanities within a wider, holistic synthesis of knowledge across specialized fields. Indeed, this was the very argument used by John Henry Newman (1891) in his classic work, *The Idea of a University*.

## Conclusion

Even as technology continues to automate routine labor, economic value is moving up the value chain—particularly to work that requires quality and design

(Howkins, 2001; Florida, 2002). Where computers excel at many linear functions, they are simply not as efficient or effective as human beings at tasks requiring emergent innovation—at least not yet. Indeed, even as we now stand on the foundations of a new computer era, human ingenuity remains key to the future of work and learning. It will be a society that leverages networked technology to augment humanity's collective intelligence. Accordingly, high value work is shifting to design, problem solving, and the development of novel ideas and artifacts. This suggests that educated entrepreneurs who can bridge human and machine intelligence are now critical to 21st century systems of learning and innovation (Leadbeater and Miller, 2004).

The truth is that what you know today matters far less than what you can do with what you know (Wolfram, 2010; Araya, 2014; Christensen et al., 2008). Rather than understanding education in terms of fixed objects that are transferred from one generation to the next, we need to begin to design educational systems that support liberal notions of knowledge and learning linked to design and meaning making. This suggests the need for a fundamental break with didactic teaching and learning methods in order to transform the culture of education as "programmed knowledge" (Christensen, 1997; Christensen et al., 2008). A society more closely focused on facilitating design and innovation will require a much more liberal understanding of education. It will also mean taking the long view on innovation and leveraging systems of design and meaning making across disciplines.

Looking forward, it would seem that the use and application of computing and digital media are becoming the basis for leading professions in the 21st century. Beyond Industrial-era schools that mirror the assembly lines of a fading Fordist era, what we now need are interdisciplinary programs that foster problem solving for a conceptual era. Indeed, in a world of increasing complexity, it is becoming less plausible to coerce people to become narrowly specialized through extrinsic motivation alone. People need intrinsic motivation; they need passion. A growing discussion of the need for leveraging this passion in education overlaps an argument for tighter coupling between schooling and entrepreneurship (Zhao, 2009, 2012).

To be sure, creativity is now the key driver of knowledge-based societies (Christensen, 1997). But this capacity for creativity must be rooted in a society and economy that is now being radically transformed by technology and innovation. The reality is that a "conceptual knowledge economy" rests on the liberal capabilities of entrepreneurs and innovators.

## Note

1 Moore's law is the observation that the number of transistors doubles approximately every two years. Named after Gordon Moore, the co-founder of Intel Corporation, it refers to the idea of exponential acceleration of digital technologies.

## References

Araya, D. (2014). *Rethinking US Education Policy*. New York: Palgrave.

Araya, D. and Peters, M. (2010). *Education in the Creative Economy*. New York: Peter

Autor, D. (2014). Polanyi's paradox and the shape of employment growth. NBER Working Paper No. 20485. Retrieved November 8, 2015, from www.nber.org/papers/w20485.

Bekman, E., Bound, J., & Machin, S. (1998). "Implications of skill-biased technological change: International evidence." *Quarterly Journal of Economics*, 113(4): 1245–79.

Blinder, A. S. (2008). Education for the Third Industrial Revolution. Working paper 1047, Center for Economic Policy Studies, Department of Economics, Princeton University. Retrieved November 8, 2015, from www.princeton.edu/ceps/workingpapers/163blinder.pdf.

Brynjolfsson, E. & McAfee, A. (2011). *Race Against the Machine: How the Digital Revolution is Accelerating Innovation, Driving Productivity, and Irreversibly Transforming Employment and the Economy*. New York: Digital Frontier Press.

Brynjolfsson, E. & McAfee, A. (2014). *The Second Machines Age: Work, Progress, and Prosperity in a Time of Brilliant Technologies*. New York: W. W. Norton & Company.

Buchanan, L. (2015). "The U.S. now has 27 million rntrepreneurs." *Inc.*, September 2, 2015. Retrieved November 8, 2015, from www.inc.com/leigh-buchanan/us-entrepreneurship-reaches-record-highs.html

Bureau of Labor Statistics. (2014). "Labor Force Statistics from the current Population Survey," June 9. Retrieved November 8, 2015, from http://data.bls.gov/timeseries/LNU01300000.

Chiu, R. (2012). *Entrepreneurship Education in the Nordic Countries: Strategy Implementation and Good Practice*. Oslo, Norway: Nordic Innovation Publication.

Christensen, C. M. (1997). *The Innovator's Dilemma: When New Technologies Cause Great Firms to Fail*. Boston, MA: Harvard Business School Press.

Christensen, C. M., Horn, M. B. & Johnson, C. W. (2008). *Disrupting Class: How Disruptive Innovation will Change the Way the World Learns*. New York: McGraw Hill.

Colvin, G. (2015). *Humans are Underrated: What High Achievers Know that Brilliant Machines Never Will*. New York: Portfolio.

Davidson, C. & Goldberg, D. (2010). *The Future of Thinking: Learning Institutions in a Digital Age*. Cambridge, MA: MIT Press.

*Economist, The* (2014). "Coming to an office near you: The effect of today's technology on tomorrow's jobs will be immense—and no country is ready for it." *The Economist*. Retrieved November 8, 2015, from www.economist.com/news/leaders/21594298-effect-todays-technology-tomorrows-jobs-will-be-immenseand-no-country-ready.

Florida, R. (2002). *The Rise of the Creative Class: And How It's Transforming Work, Leisure, Community and Everyday Life*. New York: Basic Books.

Goldin, C., & Katz, L. F. (2008). *The Race between Education and Technology*. Cambridge, MA: Harvard University Press.

Howkins, J. (2001). *The Creative Economy: How People Make Money from Ideas*. London: Allen Lane.

Katz, L. (1999). *Technological Change, Computerization, and the Wage Structure*. Department of Economics, Harvard University. Retrieved from http://scholar.harvard.edu/files/lkatz/files/technological_change_computerization_and_the_wage_structure.pdf.

Kelly, K. (2014). The three breakthroughs that have finally unleashed AI on the world. *Wired*. Retrieved November 8, 2015, from www.wired.com/2014/10/future-of-artificial-intelligence/.

Kenworthy, L. (2013). *Social Democratic America*. New York: Oxford University Press.

Kurzweil, R. (2006). *The Singularity is Near: When Humans Transcend Biology*. New York: Penguin Books.

Palley, T. (2011). The Rise and Fall of Export-Led Growth. Working Paper No. 675. Annandale-on-Hudson, NY: Levy Economics Institute. Retrieved November 8, 2015, from www.levyinstitute.org/pubs/wp_675.pdf.

Piketty, T. (2014). *Capital in the Twenty-First Century*. Cambridge, MA: Harvard University Press.

Pink, D. (2006). *A Whole New Mind: Moving from the Information Age to the Conceptual Age*. New York: Riverhead Books.

Rifkin, J. (2014) *The Zero Marginal Cost Society: The Internet of Things, the Collaborative Commons, and the Eclipse of Capitalism*. New York: Palgrave Macmillan.

Robinson, K. (2001). *Out of Our Minds: Learning to be Creative*. Oxford, UK: Capstone.

Satell, G. (2015). "Why the ability to collaborate is the new competitive advantage." *Forbes*. Retrieved November 8, 2015, from www.forbes.com/sites/gregsatell/2015/12/04/why-the-ability-to-collaborate-is-the-new-competitive-advantage/#5819035778b4.

Schumpeter, J. (1976 [1942]). *Capitalism, Socialism and Democracy*. New York: Harper & Row.

Turbot, S. (2015). "Is higher education equipping young people for the jobs market?" *World Economic Forum*. Retrieved November 8, 2015, from www.weforum.org/agenda/2015/06/is-higher-education-equipping-young-people-for-the-jobs-market/.

Wagner, T. (2012). *Creating Innovators: The Making of Young People Who Will Change the World*. New York: Scribner.

Wilson, E.O. (1998). *Concilience: The unity of knowledge*. New York: Vintage Books.

Wolfram, C. (2010). "Moving to the computational knowledge economy." *River Valley Technologies, ZEEBA. TV*. Retrieved November 8, 2015, from http://river-valley.zeeba.tv/moving-to-the-computational-knowledge-economy/.

Zakaria, F. (2016). *In Defense of Liberal Education*. New York: W.W. Norton & Company.

Zhao, Y. (2009). *Catching Up or Leading the Way: American Education in the Age of Globalization*. Alexandria, VA: ASCD.

Zhao, Y. (2012). *World Class Learners: Educating Creative and Entrepreneurial Students*. Thousand Oaks, CA: Corwin.

Zuboff, S. (1988). *In the Age of the Smart Machine: The Future of Work and Power*. New York: Basic Books.

# 14

# WORK, SERVICE, AND THE LIBERAL ARTS

## Campus and Community as Pedagogical Resources

*Steven L. Solnick*

A foundational argument for the liberal arts has been the importance of critical thinking as a cornerstone of productive learning and preparation for engaged citizenship. The liberal arts model in higher education—in both its American and export variants—has been variously defined by curricular breadth, self-directed inquiry, and a reliance on writing and debate.

These characteristics of the liberal arts model are often juxtaposed against a more "vocational" approach of carefully specified learning plans and competence-based milestones. In other words, the liberal arts are presented as learning to think, while vocational or professional education is associated with learning to do.

This reductionist approach is unfortunate—and not only because it undersells the value of critical thinking for vocational and professional success. It also overlooks the myriad ways in which experiential learning—beyond the boundaries of the traditional lecture, seminar or laboratory—enhances the intellectual experience and the critical lens. This chapter explores two sources of experiential enhancement to the liberal arts core available at most institutions but fully utilized by only a few: community engagement and on-campus work programs.

## Service and Service-Learning

Many small liberal arts colleges in the American system grew from roots as religiously-affiliated schools. In their earliest days, many of these institutions required regular attendance at religious services, and other manifestations of the pastoral role. Among the regular requirements at many institutions was some form of community service—conceived as a moral imperative and character-building exercise.

Community engagement emerged as a core element of the progressive education paradigm of Dewey (1916, 1938) and others. Through the progressive lens, community service provided an avenue for experiential learning—an important enhancement to the traditional rote learning model. At the same time, engagement with social issues gained through community embeddedness would drive "social consciousness" and lead to societal reform. Such sentiments began to shift community service out of the realm of religious imperative toward the realm of pedagogy.

That shift accelerated in the 1960s, as social upheavals struck campuses across the United States. The educational reform role of service-learning intersected the growing wave of student (and faculty) activism at colleges and universities (Stanton, Giles & Cruz, 1999). Many campuses began to design service-learning programs as explicit components of their "experiential" pedagogy, with some even introducing honors-level designations carrying service prerequisites or requirements (on many campuses, groups like Presidential Ambassadors may be required to have a deeper community engagement experience, and now even at the secondary level, organizations like the National Honor Society have requirements for community service).

With the expansion of formal community service programming at colleges and universities, practitioners began to examine whether the pedagogical benefit of such experiences could be empirically demonstrated (Giles & Eyler, 1999). In 1985, a number of university presidents created Campus Compact, a national organization to support community engagement programs on college campuses. By 2016, the network had grown to over public and private 1100 colleges and universities, encompassing 1.8 million students. It has launched a campaign to institutionalize a national service year, dramatically expanding on models such as AmeriCorps.

While the service-learning model at the heart of many community engagement models is increasingly valued and documented, it remains on most campuses one experiential program among many that can augment the liberal arts curricular core (e.g., international study, internships, coop programs, etc.). Few campuses have embedded service-learning at the heart of the curriculum, incentivizing faculty in arts, humanities, social sciences and natural sciences to all utilize service-learning opportunities to deepen the liberal arts experience.

## Campus Jobs and Work-Learning

While service-learning is now widely accepted as a pedagogical innovation, few campuses systematically attach pedagogical value to the on-campus jobs performed by students through work-study opportunities or other employment (beyond, of course, explicitly academic pursuits like research or lab support). These are essentially viewed as economic transactions—especially in the context of financial aid—and are rarely integrated into the college's learning model.

A group of seven "work colleges" have developed a different view of on-campus work, mandating it for all residential students and incorporating it into a work-service-learning model (details on these unique schools can be found at www.workcolleges.org). While some of these colleges treat the work mandate as a quid pro quo for free tuition (e.g., Berea College in Kentucky), others charge tuition and fees competitive with peer liberal arts institutions and offer just hourly pay to students for their labor (e.g., Warren Wilson College in North Carolina). This latter group of schools point to their work programs not as an access strategy for low-income students, but rather as a core part of their educational model. The on-campus work assignments offer learning opportunities—analogous to service-learning.

At Warren Wilson College, for instance, undergraduates staff most of the administrative and facilities maintenance roles for the campus, including land-scaping, janitorial, recycling, carpentry, painting, auto shop, and many others. They also operate a production farm with nearly 200 head of cattle as well as sheep, pigs and chickens; maintain gardens that supply vegetables to the dining halls and weekly farm stand; and maintain over 600 acres of college forests. The model has much in common with that of the Putney School in Vermont—an independent boarding school that operates a farm and incorporates a work program into its progressive education model.

In its earliest (Depression-era) days, a universal work model at a small college offered graduates a sort of vocational safety net: strong academic foundation in the liberal arts, and training in some vocational area that would increase the graduate's immediate employability after college. Many alumni of these colleges point to the strong work ethic they developed while in college, which transferred to their future careers.

In the modern era, however, with community colleges available to provide training in trades like carpentry or HVAC and state agricultural programs available for aspiring farmers, the appeal of the universal campus work as a pre-vocational program is limited. Instead, more recent (i.e., post 1990s) alumni point to problem solving, teamwork, time management, communication and leadership as "soft" skills they learned through work programs. This level of preparation should trans-late into greater post-graduate job success and satisfaction for work college grad-uates than for graduates of peer liberal arts colleges of similar scale and resources. Preliminary research conducted by the Work College Consortium provides some limited support for this claim (available on its website: "The Work Colleges Consortium," n.d.).

Beyond enhancing post-graduate employment success, however, a deeper claim would be that on-campus work can serve to augment the liberal arts pedagogy in the same way that community engagement offers service-learning as a pedagogical enhancement strategy. While empirical evidence of a "work-learning" effect is limited—in part because the effect is hard to measure and in part because hardly any schools currently link campus work programs to their curricula—the potential for this approach is probably best captured through specific examples.

## Work-Learning and Service-Learning: Examples

On-campus work and off-campus community engagement experiences can directly enhance the liberal arts values of critical inquiry, self-directed learning and intersectionality. In the examples below, work and service achieve this independently and in concert, through explicit coordination with more traditional curricular elements. Some of these examples are actual programs at Warren Wilson College, while others are hypothetical or planned programming.

*Service-Learning through Prison Partnerships:* When a campus is in close proximity to a correctional facility, service-learning partnerships can emerge quickly. The simplest version might be considered "observational": a course on the literature of incarceration might seek to engineer opportunities for students to interact with prisoners to interrogate the authenticity of the experiences portrayed in the literature. A visit to a prison in which a class meets with and/or interviews a group of prisoners might achieve this goal, but at the risk of objectifying the prisoners or—in the worst case—emulating "hardship tourism." Indeed, a risk in many college and university service-learning programs is that students' primary encounters with people from other socioeconomic categories or backgrounds is through the service-learning program, and that programming is developed "for" rather than "with" these target populations. Such programming may achieve certain moral and ethical imperatives of "service" to communities in need, but it falls short of achieving real engagement with communities of difference. As a reminder of this important distinction, many colleges and universities associated with Campus Compact have consciously retitled their service programs as "community engagement" programming.

Returning to the prison example, a marginally deeper level of engagement might be achieved through a joint activity or project that brings together students and prisoners. This might involve preparing a meal, painting a mural or maintaining a community garden. Such a joint activity can provide opportunities for deeper interaction between students and prisoners beyond the "subject-interviewer" template, and also allow the prisoner populations to have some sense of task accomplishment that supports morale or personal development.

A step further would be to blur the lines between student and prisoner by allowing both groups to study together in a college-level class taught by the college for the blended population. Students from the college participating in the program would need some special preparation to empathize with their future classmates, and the participating prisoners might need some preparation to enable them to be full partners in the endeavor since their academic preparation might be weaker. Careful negotiation with prison authorities would be essential to ensure that security protocols are observed. Nevertheless, the potential rewards of such "Inside Out" programs are many, and they open up the opportunities to students in a much wider range of disciplines ("The Inside Out Center," n.d.).

By viewing a subset of the prison population not as subjects or a target population for community service, but rather as partners in an academic endeavor, students may confront deeper pedagogical questions about how to sustain a meaningful and substantive dialogue within a sharply heterogenous group, as well as how different socioeconomic backgrounds or life experiences can shape a response to literature or social theory. Even in the sciences, such a mixed class-room may influence the direction of a course on, say, sustainable agriculture or pharmacology by reminding students and teachers alike that not all groups assign the same valence to different topics.

*Community-Derived Research:* Many service-learning programs build deep part-nerships with a network of community partners, engaged in activities such as legal aid, support for the homeless, food security, animal welfare, community gardening and a range of other issue areas. Each of these organizations is a potential gold mine of research topics for students who might find extra motivation for capstone or even semester research if they understand the potential application of their results.

Biology majors who may have developed an understanding of homelessness through a community engagement program might work with a community part-ner to develop a research agenda around optimizing the nutritional delivery to this population, conduct specific research as part of a senior capstone project and then present that research to the organization and see the results put into action. For the average student, this could be more approachable than devising a research topic purely from the academic literature, and more fulfilling if the results yield tangible social change. Alternatively, an environmental studies major might build a capstone project around redesign of a community garden, or the energy retrofit of a non-profit's headquarters—providing an immediate demonstration of the relevance of the academic work, and potentially pointing the student in a career direction.

Such intersections of community engagement and research need not be left entirely to the initiative of the students. A community engagement program office might collaborate with academic departments to build a database of research needs in the community. Such an endeavor would be an extension of a broader movement to utilize academic research to interrogate the theories of change that underpin the work of non-profits, and to utilize research to demonstrate the impact of such organizations' work (on the intersection of academic research and program assessment, see for example Banerjee and Duflo, 2011). Such a collabo-ration may have multiple benefits, showing students the practical dimensions of academic research and providing non-profits and volunteer organizations with validation of their methodologies.

*Campus as Laboratory:* Bringing the campus itself into play as a learning tool can vastly expand the canvas for experiential pedagogy. To take one example—drawn from an actual collaboration at Warren Wilson College in 2014–15—a conserva-tion biology program might collaborate with a campus landscape crew to create an artificial wetland on campus used by subsequent generations of students to learn about wetland biology. Since Warren Wilson College is a federally recognized work college, all students hold campus jobs, including most of the landscape positions (roughly 45 students working 10–20 hours per week are supervised by just 2 staff professionals).

As a consequence of this unusual staffing configuration, collaboration between conservation biology and landscaping happens at the student level, not just as a conversation between faculty and full-time staff. A class project designs the wetland conversion, supervised by a professor. The students working on landscaping (many of whom may be majoring in social sciences or humanities) study the practical steps needed to realize it, supervised by a professional landscaper. The project is realized through collaboration of these two teams, resulting in extensive peer learning among the students. The result is a lasting transformation of the campus, providing a legacy for future alumni who made it happen.

Project-based engagement of students in campus management and/or transformation yields a range of "soft" skills that complement the liberal-arts emphasis on critical thinking and self-directed inquiry. By working together in a structured environment where supervisors have pedagogical as well as professional objectives, students learn to work with team members from very different majors and backgrounds. The collaboration teaches teamwork, leadership, problem-solving, time-management and communication skills—all cited by employers as the precise qualities they look for from liberal-arts college graduates (Friedman, 2014).

*Campus as Coop*: Beyond transferable soft skills like leadership and teamwork, structured on-campus work opportunities can function like internships, directly supporting and enhancing academic majors.

One example of this is a business track currently in development at Warren Wilson College. Like many small liberal arts colleges, Warren Wilson lacks a dedicated business department, directing students instead to strong liberal arts disciplines such as economics, math or psychology. However, the campus work opportunities provide a framework for constructing an "applied-learning business track" that can overlay any academic major. Students with work assignments on the college farm might work in the farm's business office, managing both supplies and meat sales. Students working on the college's forest might opt into the more entrepreneurial crews that produce and market non-timber forest products such as mushrooms or honey. Others might support the dining hall in its sourcing and ordering of food from local farms in support of the college's Real Foods Commitment ("Real Foods Campus Commitment," n.d.). Others might be assigned to the college's purchasing or accounts receivable offices, working with vendors or bill-paying students.

All of these jobs provide valuable business-related experience, and these students might be brought together weekly from their different campus assignments for group training in basic business skills such as accounting or marketing. Coupled with a strong liberal arts major and carefully selected internship opportunities, these students can emerge with as much practical experience as students in popular coop programs at much larger universities, gained in a setting that provides for greater integration within the holistic residential college experience. In fact, since formal coop programs require a large pool of employers ready to accept 6- or 12-month employees, they are more easily established in larger universities in urban settings—such as Northeastern in Boston or Drexel in Philadelphia. Viewing campus work opportunities as part of the educational model offers an avenue for adapting a variant of the coop model to smaller liberal arts colleges located away from large employers.

*Work Opportunities as Hidden Concentrations:* Many small colleges are limited by their scale in the number and scope of majors they offer. Campus jobs can provide valuable opportunities to acquire specific skills not available through academic departments. Students providing IT support might be given targeted opportunities to learn and practice coding, for example. Or students working with the marketing department might receive practical training in copywriting or graphic design.

These opportunities are no substitute for engineering or design degrees, but that is not what students in a liberal arts program are seeking. Instead, these jobs—when viewed as part of the educational model and not simply as campus workforce—offer opportunities for students to acquire specific skills that can enhance their future career flexibility. Recent studies suggest that employers value these specific skills, especially in concert with the broad preparation and analytic capacities of liberal arts graduates (Blumenstyk, 2016).

*Capturing Experiences beyond the Transcript:* A persistent challenge in expanding the liberal arts model to include applied learning and experiential opportunities is capturing these dimensions as part of a student's record. A broad debate has emerged about how to credential competencies not reflected on the academic transcript.

Some colleges and universities have begun experimenting with certificates, or badges, for specific competencies (e.g., coding)—though there may be more urgency around this discussion for populations who have not or will not complete college. These badges or certificates can provide waystations on the road to a degree, allowing students who may need to interrupt their education to capture more value from the coursework they have completed. They may also provide greater granularity to a four-year degree, expanding on the notion of "with honors" that many colleges use to signify academic excellence.

While badges might still fit on an academic transcript, an alternative approach is to transcend the transcript completely. The rise of cloud computing has made it possible for students to create "portfolios" during their college careers that integrate traditional and applied learning experiences. These portfolios might contain academic research and also illustrate how that research was applied by a community partner. Or it might contain images or video of project-based learning on campus, or reflections on an internship or international study experience. It could substantiate for a future graduate school or employer the ways in which an economics major has acquired practical business experience in the liberal arts framework. Such portfolios have the potential to replace the transcript and the CV in coming years—think of the spread of *LinkedIn* in less than a decade. And as they become more accepted and prevalent, such tools may legitimate the expansion of the liberal arts model to include the varieties of applied learning illustrated above.

## Applied Learning: A New Frontier for Liberal Arts?

Experiential learning is not new to the liberal arts model. By expanding the scope of experiential learning to include not only innovative classroom pedagogy and service-learning but also campus work, and by considering these not as overlays to the classroom but fundamental components of the learning model, "applied learning" emerges as an exciting new extension to the liberal arts.

As more educators view community engagement and campus work as ways to learn, higher education institutions will need to respond by broadening their lenses in areas like academic records and student advising. As I note above, academic transcripts are currently struggling to reflect the full dimensionality of learning experiences for students in highly experiential programs. Looking ahead, as colleges begin to rely on these programs more heavily to provide core competencies, they will need to evolve advising systems beyond the current major-centric model. Students will need guidance not only on what courses to take, but also what internships to seek, what campus jobs are appropriate, and what community engagements might complement other learning plans.

Finally, our evaluation and assessment models will need to evolve. Current assessment rubrics baked into accreditation models are poorly suited to capture a holistic view of student learning. As colleges acknowledge all the ways that students learn, and expand their toolkit of ways they can teach, the sector will need to find new ways to assess that teaching and learning to encourage innovation and creativity.

## References

Banerjee, A., & Duflo, E. (2011). *Poor Economics.* New York: PublicAffairs.

Blumenstyk, G. (2016, June 9). "Liberal-arts majors have plenty of job prospects, if they have some specific skills, too." *Chronicle of Higher Education.*

Dewey, J. (1916). *Democracy and Education.* New York: Macmillan.

Dewey, J. (1938). *Experience and Education.* New York: Touchstone.

Friedman, T. (2014, February 23). "How to Get a Job at Google." *New York Times* p. SR 11.

Giles, D. & Eyler, J. (1999). *Where's the Learning in Service Learning?* San Francisco, CA: Jossey-Bass.

Real Food Challenge. (n.d.). "The real food campus commitment." Retrieved from www .realfoodchallenge.org/commitment (accessed June 15, 2016).

Stanton, T., Giles, D. & Cruz, N. (1999). *Service-Learning: A Movement's Pioneers Reflect on Its Origins, Practice, and the Future.* San Francisco, CA: Jossey-Bass.

The Inside-Out Center. (n. d.). "International headquarters of the inside-out prison exchange Program." Retrieved from www.insideoutcenter.org/index.html (accessed June 15, 2016).

Work Colleges Consortium. (n.d.). "Understanding and Measuring Success of Work College Graduates", Retrieved from http://workcolleges.org/sites/default/files/attachments/WCC%202012%20Brochure.pdf (accessed June 15, 2016).

# 15

# THE PROMISE OF LIBERAL EDUCATION IN THE GLOBAL AGE

*Christopher B. Nelson*

Among the many evolutions and revolutions of liberal education taking place in the current era of globalization, one occurrence stands out as particularly ironic. At the same time that the United States seems to be depreciating the uniquely American tradition of liberal arts learning in higher education, other parts of the world are starting to appreciate it.

Over the past decade or so, the number of European institutions offering something like an American-style baccalaureate program has been steadily increasing, and there is now an organization promoting such programs—ECOLAS, European Colleges of Liberal Arts and Sciences. And the American model is also beginning to gain adherents in Asia. Chester Goad, an editorial board member of the *Journal of Postsecondary Education and Disability*, told *Forbes* last year, "Just as the U.S. begins to move away from traditional liberal arts programs and turn to specialized online programs, Asia is discovering there is benefit in the creativity and well-rounded perspective that comes from a liberal arts education. Seeking to break away from their own traditionally homogenized and rigidly specialized educational system, Asian countries began in recent years to find inspiration from our system" (Klebnikov, 2015).

This newfound appreciation, as Goad intimates, comes along with conflict—the conflict between liberal education and specialized education. The desire to "break away" from the established institutional models shows increasing awareness that modern higher education has become hyper-specialized, and the divisions among the specialties have become integrated into our habits of thinking. It is now taken for granted that progress in thought is made on the front edges of specialized research. So our institutions of learning have shaped themselves into structures that foster, promote, and reward an increasingly intense focus on increasingly narrow fields of study.

Correlatively, this mindset sees general education as basic, unsophisticated, perhaps even simple-minded. It relegates general education to grammar schools, as a sort of necessary training in basic facts and elementary skills. Higher education, on the other hand, is thought of as an initiation into the mysteries of advanced thinking. It must be taught by professors who, having themselves discovered paths to the forefronts of their specialties, will lead aspiring students along those same paths.

I certainly do not reject this perspective entirely. That would be foolish. The very real advances made by the continually growing number of specialties are too obvious to deny. My intention rather is to try to show that the relentless emphasis on making cutting-edge discoveries has eclipsed another view of higher education, one that recognizes the value of specialization, but at the same time believes there is something more important in education than specialization. That view is what we call *liberal* education—education that fosters individual freedom, both in thinking and in living.

The distinction between specialized and liberal education is not new. In a way, Aristotle captured its essence in the introduction to *On the Parts of Animals* (Peck, 1937:639a2–8):

> Concerning every object of study and inquiry, whether low or high, there seem to be two ways to comprehend the matter. One is aptly called *detailed knowledge* of the subject, the other, a sort of *cultivated understanding*. For it is proper to an educated person to be able to judge adroitly whether a speaker is presenting an account well or not well. And indeed, we think both that someone of this sort is generally cultivated, and that this cultivation consists in the ability to do what has just been said.

Aristotle is describing, on the one hand, specialized knowledge, and, on the other hand, what used to be called sound reasoning, namely, the combination of training in logic, interpretation, and argumentation that allows well-educated people to tell whether anyone—even an expert in a particular subject—is arguing cogently. It is by some such ability that a scientific layman like me can study a famous paper on quantum physics by Einstein, Podolsky, and Rosen and see that their reasoning is suspiciously circular, as well as laden with all sorts of metaphysical assumptions that make their conclusions dubious.

Sound reasoning is an intellectual ability that cuts across, or rises above, specialized disciplines. Let us call such things *transdisciplinary*. Later, I will discuss another transdisciplinary ability that in our times is just as important as—or perhaps even more important than—sound reasoning. But for now, let sound reasoning stand as one example of the content of a liberal, as opposed to specialized, education—an example that was recognized as long as 2,500 years ago.

If the distinction between specialized and liberal education is ancient, so too is the conflict between them. One could argue that Socrates was put to death by people whom he, a layman, demonstrated to be ignorant about the subjects in which they claimed to specialize. So it is also nothing new that we find ourselves living in the midst of this conflict. It *is* relatively new, however, that the global community of higher education around the world is starting to address the excesses that have been caused by hyperspecialization.

America's unique tradition of liberal learning in higher education has survived the modern world's demands for ever more specialization, but it has done so under nearly constant attack from the forces of specialization since the middle of the nineteenth century. By the early twentieth century, the modern, specialized university, with it semi-autonomous departments and divisions, had already taken shape in America, and educators devoted to liberal learning were continuing their attempts to raise seawalls against the tide. This was precisely what the founders of our course of study at St. John's College, Scott Buchanan and Stringfellow Barr, were trying to do eighty years ago when they established our current curriculum in 1937. Their solution was rather extreme in the context of American higher education at the time, but it may be instructive for those around the world who are contemplating a return to liberal learning in their educational institutions.

St. John's is often called the first Great Books college. The label stuck because of the strategy Buchanan and Barr adopted to cultivate a liberal education. Their idea was to have students spend their four college years reading and discussing the works of the foundational thinkers and artists of the Western tradition. While the readings have evolved over time, not much has changed in a fundamental way at St. John's in the eight decades since. We still have a single curriculum, called simply "The Program," for all students. We offer this curriculum as the best preparation, in the faculty's judgment, for leading a life worth living, both in theory and in practice. We offer this curriculum because we think we know better than the average eighteen-year-old what a good education is. We offer it because we refuse to flatter our students by pretending that they, in their inexperience, can know what is best for their education. And we offer it because we believe that it is the responsibility of every college faculty to design what constitutes, in its judgment, the strongest possible course of study for young men and women who come seeking instruction.

At St. John's all students participate in four years of a language tutorial which studies ancient Greek, modern French, and English and American poetry. They also take part in four years of a mathematics tutorial, demonstrating together the propositions of Euclid, who first organized plane geometry into a system, and the propositions of Lobachevski, who wrote the first text on non-Euclidean geometry; they discuss Aristotle's conceptions of time and place and Einstein's entirely new notions of time and space; they study the motions of the heavens from Ptolemy to Copernicus to Newton and beyond. They do three years of laboratory science, in which they first look at the world about them and ask what they are seeing; they study chemistry and biology and ask about the organizing principles of matter and of life; they study physics, investigating the principles of classical mechanics with

Newton and the strange underpinnings of quantum mechanics with Heisenberg; they study foundations of modern biology from Darwin and Mendel to Watson and Crick while doing experiments in recombinant genetics. In addition, they sing and learn the elements of music so that they can understand, and listen intelligently to, Bach's *St. Matthew Passion*, Mozart's *Don Giovanni*, Wagner's *Tristan and Isolde*, and in order to appreciate music's power to communicate what a text alone cannot.

But all of this classroom activity revolves around the four-year-long seminar sequence, in which the students study, in very nearly chronological order, the books we are best known for reading—from Homer and Virgil to Chaucer and Shakespeare, from Cervantes and Milton to Austen and Eliot, from Tolstoy and Dostoevsky to Woolf and Conrad, from Plato and Aristotle to Descartes and Kant, from the Bible and Augustine to Aquinas and Spinoza, from Herodotus and Thucydides to Gibbon and Hegel; from Hobbes and Rousseau to Lincoln and Douglass.

A curriculum like this might seem to be extremely cost-effective. There is no need, after all, for unlimited spending on updated technology, nor for highly targeted, continually growing, costly-to-maintain specialized undergraduate and graduate degree programs, nor for far-flung and intricate administrative structures to manage institutional complexities. The needs of such a program seem to boil down to teachers, books, classrooms, and the minimum of equipment necessary to conduct scientific experiments. Such a curriculum is particularly well suited to small communities with limited resources devoted to learning above all else.

But it is still an expensive education. It's just that different choices are made about how money is allocated, with the priority being on the learning experience. We believe that learning proceeds best in discussion groups of manageable size—fifteen or sixteen students with one teacher in tutorials and eighteen or nineteen students with two teachers in seminar. This means that instructional costs are labor-intensive: such an institution cannot save lots of money by packing classes. We believe that learning proceeds best in a small community where friendships can flourish among most of the participants. This means that the buildings and grounds must be compact and conducive to small-group interactions: such an institution cannot save lots of money through efficiencies of scale. We believe that learning roots deepest when everyone's daily activities center around reading, thinking, and discussing. This means that these activities must take place in an actual physical location where every meeting of community members—even serendipitous ones—can promote learning just as much as meetings in class: such an institution cannot broaden its income stream by streaming classes on the internet.

All these considerations are best met by a small residential college, of just the kind that America has cultivated. To anyone anywhere in the world who is contemplating creating a college of liberal learning *de novo*, I recommend this model, since its outward form is perfectly adapted to its essential being. It is of course possible to construct enclaves of liberal learning within specialized universities; in America these have taken the shape of what are called "honors colleges" or "core programs." Other structures that may succeed along these lines are certainly conceivable. But such programs must be constantly on guard against encroachments; their essential being conflicts with the specialized nature of the university that contains them. Under the right conditions, however, they can survive and even thrive. For it is, of course, possible to read, study, and discuss things worth reading, studying, and discussing anywhere there are two or three gathered together with a deep desire to learn—even if conditions are not optimal.

But then there is the question of what is worth reading, studying, and discussing. At St. John's, our curriculum consists entirely of original sources. Do we think that secondary sources are not worth reading? Of course not. Indeed, some of the works on our Program are in fact "secondary" in the sense that they extend or critique works by earlier authors. In every such case, however, the later works are themselves so innovative that they are now considered "original." And our students and faculty often get together to read, study, and discuss all sorts of extracurricular material, as inclination moves and time allows. Is it absolutely necessary for liberal learning to commit solely to original sources? Surely not. And yet, I would recommend it, for a number of reasons.

First, because original sources are difficult—some of the most difficult-to-understand objects created by human beings. If people are to become proficient at sound judgment, they must cut their teeth on hard objects. Second, because they are original, both in the sense of being at the beginnings of long rivers of thought that flow out of them, and in the sense of having invented or uncovered new starting points for thinking. Third, because they transcend time, remaining always relevant because they continue to stand behind new discoveries and new thinking. And fourth, because they are elemental—not in the sense of being simple, but in the sense of being close to building blocks of thought. In addition to all this, they are also often quite beautiful.

Some think that it is a fool's errand to try to read original texts written by authors dating back thousands of years. Some might even argue that it cannot be done by modern students. On the contrary, they think, students need to be guided by experts in the languages of the authors, experts in the historical context of the authors, experts in the biographies of the authors—in short, by someone who has specialized knowledge to impart.

This is the usual way of teaching at university. The expert may indeed assign original works, or parts of them, for the students to read. Quite often, however, reading assignments are chosen from secondary sources that attempt to explain or critique or contextualize the original sources. But once the reading is done, students must attend lectures in which the works are interpreted for them by the expert lecturer. In this way, it is thought, the students gain knowledge that they could never attain unaided. But in the process their understanding is mediated by an outside authority, who all but inevitably constrains the free exploration that a student might undertake if allowed to confront the original work directly.

This sort of teaching tends to regard *detailed knowledge* as the end of learning. The facts, the ideas, the arguments that the student gleans from the expert can be tested, and then the teacher knows whether the student has learned what the teacher taught.

Liberal education does not think about teaching in this way. Of course, facts are important. Knowing things is important. But it is possible to learn lots of facts, lots of ideas, lots of arguments while not gaining the ability to approach all facts, all ideas, and all arguments with disciplined attention to their relative importance and interconnectedness. This is, so to speak, learning without learning. The result is *detailed knowledge*—perhaps even spectacularly detailed knowledge—but little or no cultivation of the transdisciplinary abilities that enable *sound judgment*. It is the intellectual equivalent of giving a man a fish instead of teaching him to fish. Now, of course it is possible to teach specialized subjects liberally, and many teachers try their best to do so. But is not easy to enlarge a syllabus, to privilege true learning over testing, to prefer genuine intellectual exploration over bureaucratic mandates, and so on.

This raises the question of what it means to teach liberally. I have already indicated that teaching liberally differs from specialized teaching in not trying to mediate the object of study for the learner. From this essential difference, four more specific differences arise.

First, liberal teaching does not attempt either to meet students at their own level or to select subject matter that seems most relevant to their current condition. On the contrary, it takes for its objects material is that far above the level of both students and teachers, so that everyone is forced to stretch their intellectual muscles and the students can see how an experienced learner—their teacher—actually goes about the business of learning. Liberal teaching also makes an effort to avoid topicality, which creates a sort of immediate but short-lived excitement, in favor of a certain remoteness in time and condition, which tends to generate sustained interest by uncovering shared human affinities over great expanses of time and by helping students to see more significance in their world by learning to look back at it, as it were, from a distance.

Second, because activism—especially political activism—is not a direct aim of liberal learning, it is not directly cultivated by liberal teaching. This is related to the previous point, since nothing is more topical or immediately exciting than trying to change the world, especially if the change is seen as being for the better. But what is at stake in liberal learning is the leisurely, long-term, deeply interested development of thought that can be brought to bear on practical matters later. "School," after all, derives from the Greek work *scholē*, which means "leisure." It is supposed to be a time set apart from practical concerns, a space in which one can examine foundations, admire wonders, contemplate openly, look at things purely. It may be that not everyone is ready for this in youth, but for those who are, it would certainly be a benefit to them and to their societies to provide the space for it.

Third, because liberal learning singles out difficult original texts as its objects of study, liberal teaching cannot accede to the fashionable, if not always explicitly stated, attitude that everything is equally worthy of study. It is true that, in the end, everything—from the most sub-mundane fleck to the most super-celestial divinity—can be of absorbing interest to the well-cultivated mind. But in the beginning, young people especially need to learn that differentiable greatness exists, that their teachers have the experience to discern it, and that they too can acquire that discernment with practice. And they need to learn to live with the conditions of excellence: that the highest things often do not have easy access; that to live a life admiring things above oneself is a source of dignity; that legitimate hierarchies give respect to all their members, whatever their status or rank; and that the greatest achievements offer themselves up both to be admired and to be critiqued.

And fourth, since liberal learning is always a search for truth, liberal teaching must make truth central to its activity. This, again, runs against the grain of modern higher education, which prefers to avoid the question, "Is it true what this book says?" Refusal to face this question makes a game out of learning—a high-level game, but a game nonetheless—the outcome of which has no permanent value for students. In liberal learning, the first approaches to the object of study may be factual: What is the author actually arguing? What does this proposition seek to prove? How does this equation capture the phenomenon? How does this musical phrase illuminate the text? But eventually someone will ask, "Do I believe this or not?" and "Do I accept or reject it because I wish to, or because the content compels me to?" It is this compulsion that constitutes the initial experience of truth, and liberal learning and teaching must make room for students to have that experience, even at the cost of "covering the material"—because liberal learning always proceeds at a leisurely tempo in deference to the deep experiences where the roots of abiding interest set themselves.

That liberal teaching has these four characteristics does not mean that it is hostile to "covering material." As I said, liberal education has no aversion to facts, ideas, or arguments. On the contrary, it recognizes them as the constituents of intellectual activity. And it certainly does not disparage detailed knowledge. On the contrary, it recognizes that one of the greatest satisfactions in life is mastering a specialized field of inquiry or a specialized activity. But it prefers to place its emphasis on learning how to approach knowledge generally, that is, on mastering the transdisciplinary abilities that make possible *self-directed learning.*

Why does liberal education emphasize self-directed learning? Because its aim is to help people become free. The purpose of liberal education is not to produce high-functioning specialists. It is to educate people who are free to search out knowledge on their own, people who are not dependent on others to tell them what they need to know, and ultimately, people who are the best judges of their own needs. As Scott Buchanan, the first dean at St. John's following the adoption of the Great Books curriculum, once wrote (Wofford & Buchanan, 1970):

> Liberal education has as its end the free mind, and the free mind must be its own teacher. Intellectual freedom begins when one says with Socrates that he knows nothing, and then goes on to add: I know what it is that I don't know. My question then is: Do you know what you don't know and therefore what you should know? If your answer is affirmative and humble, then you are your own teacher, you are making your own assignment, and you will be your own best critic.

Buchanan recognized that the spur to learning rests in the recognition of one's own ignorance.

Today's critics of liberal education decry such sentiments as high-toned but empty rhetoric—tattered remnants of aristocratic paternalism. In our modern, capitalist world, they seem to think, what every individual needs most of all is *exactly* some sort of specialty that can be bartered for the means of survival. And what society needs most of all is workers with *exactly* such specialties to provide the innovation that keeps the economic engine humming. Hawking propagandistic notions like "intellectual freedom" and "cultivated understanding"—even if they are not just antiquated fictions—is cruel and fraudulent educational malpractice, they might say, given the realities of the twenty-first century.

On the contrary, no view of higher education could be more enervating or debilitating. Freedom of thought and cultivated understanding are absolutely crucial for these times. Modern democratic societies are predicated on the freedom of the individual. Citizens of these democracies must think for themselves and make generally sound judgments, which is more likely if they have learned how to learn. Liberal democracies cannot survive without liberal education.

Moreover, capitalism cannot continue to flourish without liberal education. It needs, as its champions rightly understand, continual innovation for its survival. But liberal education grounded in original sources is a powerhouse of innovation, for two reasons. First, because the original sources comprise the historical record of *the most successful innovations in human history*. As such, they are models to be studied for what they can reveal to us about the process of making new discoveries and creating new beginnings. And second, because they demonstrate the crucial role of *imagination* in human affairs.

Imagination is the second transdisciplinary ability that I mentioned earlier, the one that may be even more important in our time than sound reasoning. Both free thinking and innovation depend on having the imagination to see alternate ways of being, to envision worlds that we do not yet see before us, to reconsider what is there, and to conceive what could be there in its place.

Training the imagination proceeds through the study of *metaphor*, by which I mean all connections of any kind among different objects, both in the physical world and in thought. The study of metaphor rises above all distinctions among academic specialties for the simple reason that any two things or ideas are related in *some* way, although it may take some ingenuity to find the points of similarity or difference. Repeated practice at developing this ingenuity results in a powerful imagination, one that reveals hidden connections, and even follows the threads of merely *possible* connections to find as yet undiscovered objects. And it is liberal education that promotes the transdisciplinary ability of imagination, by investigating metaphors wherever they occur, in literature and the arts, in mathematics and science, in politics and history.

For all the undoubted progress made by modern academic disciplines, they nevertheless constrain the imagination. The specialized methodology of each discipline insulates it from others, enclosing the specialty in the safety of its currently accepted paradigm. Each discipline has to decide what it considers a proper object, what counts as evidence, what forms of argumentation are acceptable, and so on. Imagination is not so constrained. Skilled in the study of metaphor, it can easily revise the notion of its object, quickly change course, and find new connections to speed it on its journey of discovery.

Of course, specialists too can make astounding journeys of discovery. But when they do so, it is because their imagination has been sparked by recognizing a new connection. When Darwin supposed that Nature might select traits in the manner of a livestock breeder, he sailed on the winds of imagination to a new country of thought, and transformed the science of heredity forever. When Crick and Watson conceived that chemical substances could function as elements in "codes" like those developed during the war, they built with the tools of imagination an anti-Enigma machine for the living cell, and changed the science of genetics forever.

Imagination, in fact, is the originator of disciplines, the innovator of specialties. It is only from the universe of all connections that a discipline can select its particular connections. That is to say, the special disciplines, each and every one, were established by the power of imagination surveying the universe of connections and choosing the particular connections that would apply in each specialty.

Imagination, like sound judgment, transcends all specialties. It is the generator of all innovation, including the innovation so necessary to capitalism. And it is a particular concern of liberal education. So those who reject liberal education on the ground that specialized knowledge creates innovation are cutting off their noses to spite their faces. The true sources of innovation are the transdisciplinary competencies developed by liberal education, and the emergence around the world of new institutions of liberal learning shows that the emerging global society senses a growing need for the next generation to master those competencies.

I hope these reflections help those who are planning new colleges to think about the whys and the hows of liberal learning communities. The renaissance of liberal education in the global community bodes well. It is a sign that the disadvantages of hyperspecialization are beginning to be weighed in the balance against its advantages. It is a sign that the world is striving to renew higher education, to turn toward a way teaching and learning that promotes broad engagement with the world, sound reasoning, and vibrant imagination. It is a sign that the human species may be on the path to a new way of dealing with its challenges, both economic and political.

Let us hope for this rebirth, and let us do everything in our power to midwife it. The stakes could not be higher.

## References

Klebnikov, S. (2015). "The rise of liberal arts colleges in Asia." *Forbes*. Retrieved June 3, 2015, from www.forbes.com/sites/sergeiklebnikov/2015/06/03/the-rise-of-liberal-arts-colleges-in-asia/#c0d8cedc5338

Peck, A. L. (1937). *Aristotle Parts of Animals*. (Boston: Harvard University Press).

Wofford, H., & Buchanan, S. M. (1970). *Embers of the World: Conversations with Scott Buchanan*. (Santa Barbara, CA: The Center for the Study of Democratic Institutions).

# 16

# EDUCATION FOR CITIZENSHIP IN AN ERA OF GLOBAL CONNECTION[1]

*Martha Nussbaum*

In 424 BC, the great ancient Greek comic playwright Aristophanes produced his comedy *Clouds*, about the dangers of Socrates and the "new education." A young man, eager for the new learning, goes to a "Think-Academy" near his home, run by that strange notorious figure Socrates. A debate is staged for him, contrasting the merits of traditional education with those of the new discipline of Socratic argument. The spokesman for the old education is a tough old soldier. He favors a highly disciplined patriotic regimen, with lots of memorization and not much room for questioning. He loves to recall a time that may never have existed—a time when young people obeyed their parents and wanted nothing more than to die for their country, a time when teachers would teach that grand old song, "Athena, glorious sacker of cities"—not the strange new songs of the present day. Study with me, he booms, and you will look like a real man—broad chest, small tongue, firm buttocks, small genitals (a plus in those days, symbolic of manly self-control).

His opponent is an arguer, a seductive man of words—Socrates seen through the distorting lens of Aristophanic conservatism. He promises the youth that he will learn to think critically about the social origins of apparently timeless moral norms, the distinction between convention and nature. He will learn to construct arguments on his own, heedless of authority. He won't do much marching. Study with me, he concludes, and you will look like an intellectual: you will have a big tongue, a sunken narrow chest, soft buttocks, and big genitals (a minus in those days, symbolic of lack of self-restraint). Socrates' self-advertisement, of course, is being slyly scripted by the conservative opposition. The message? The new education will subvert manly self-control, turn young people into sex-obsessed rebels, and destroy the city. The son soon goes home and produces a relativist argument for the conclusion that he should beat his father. The same angry father then takes a torch and burns down the Think-Academy. (It is not made clear whether the son is still inside.) Twenty-five years later, Socrates, on trial for corrupting the young, cites Aristophanes' play as a major source of prejudice against him.

Should a liberal education be an acculturation into the time-honored values of one's own culture? Or should it follow Socrates, arguing that "the examined life" is the best preparation for citizenship? Almost five hundred years later, in the very different culture of the Roman Empire of the first century AD, the Stoic philosopher Seneca reflected on this same contrast, creating, in the process, our modern concept of liberal education.

Seneca begins his letter by describing the traditional style of education, noting that it is called "liberal" (*liberalis*, "connected to freedom"), because it is understood to be an education for well-brought-up young gentlemen, who were called the *liberales*, the "free-born." He himself, he now announces, would use the term "liberal" in a very different way. In his view, an education is truly "liberal" only if it is one that "liberates" the student's mind, encouraging him or her to take charge of his or her own thinking, leading the Socratic examined life and becoming a reflective critic of traditional practices. (I say "him or her" not just out of contemporary political correctness: stoic philosophers of the first century AD wrote at length about the equal education of women, and defended the view that women as much as men should lead the examined life.) Seneca goes on to argue that only this sort of education will develop each person's capacity to be fully human, by which he means self-aware, self-governing, and capable of recognizing and respecting the humanity of all our fellow human beings, no matter where they are born, no matter what social class they inhabit, no matter what their gender or ethnic origin. "Soon we shall breathe our last," he concludes in his related treatise *On Anger.* "Meanwhile, while we live, while we are among human beings, let us cultivate our humanity."

In the contemporary United States and Europe, as in ancient Athens and Rome, higher education is changing. New topics have entered the curricula of colleges and universities: the history and culture of non-Western peoples and of ethnic and racial minorities within the US, the experiences and achievements of women, the history and concerns of lesbians and gay men. These changes have frequently been presented in popular journalism as highly threatening, both to traditional standards of academic excellence and to traditional norms of citizenship. Readers are given the picture of a monolithic highly politicized elite who are attempting to enforce a "politically correct" view of human life, subverting traditional values and teaching students, in effect, to argue in favor of father-beating. Socratic questioning is still on trial. Our debates over the curriculum reveal the same nostalgia for a more obedient, more regimented time, the same suspiciousness of new and independent thinking that finds expression in Aristophanes' brilliant portrait of the old education and in the defense by Seneca's contemporaries of the old-style liberal education in a time of rapid social change.

But we can defend many of the changes in traditional models of liberal education as a response to the challenge of Socrates and Seneca, and I shall argue that it is this paradigm we should consider, as we think about what is well done and not well done in contemporary reforms of liberal education. In fact, by and large, the changes that we witness are attempts to follow Seneca's advice to cultivate our humanity. Seneca's ideas of cultivated humanity and world citizenship have had a large influence on modern democratic thought, through Thomas Paine and other writers who were steeped in Stoic ideas. And these ideas have long been at the root of our aspirations, as we construct a higher education that is not simply pre-professional, but a general enrichment of and a cultivation of reasonable, deliberative democratic citizenship.

Today's universities are shaping future citizens in an age of cultural diversity and increasing internationalization. All modern democracies are inescapably plural. As citizens within each nation we are frequently called upon to make decisions that require some understanding of racial and ethnic and religious groups in that nation, and of the situation of its women and its sexual minorities. As citizens we are also increasingly called upon to understand how issues such as agriculture, human rights, ecology, even business and industry, are generating discussions that bring people together from many different nations. This must happen more and more, if effective solutions to pressing human problems are to be found. But these connections often take, today, a very thin form: the global market that sees human lives as instruments for gain. If our institutions of higher education do not build a richer network of human connections it is likely that our dealings with one another will be mediated by the defective norms of market exchange. A rich network of human connections, however, will not arise magically out of our good intentions: we need to think about how our educational institutions contribute to that goal.

The new emphasis on "diversity" in college and university curricula is above all, I would argue, a way of grappling with the altered requirements of citizenship in an era of global connection, an attempt to produce adults who can function as citizens not just of some local region or group but also, and more importantly, as citizens of a complex interlocking world—and function with a richness of human understanding and aspiration that cannot be supplied by economic connections alone. In this attempt, the humanities—often viewed as useless and equally often viewed with suspicion, as scenes of subversion—play a central role.

The systems of university education in [most countries outside the US] have a disadvantage from the point of view of implementing my proposals. All colleges and universities in the United States offer approximately two years of "liberal education" (sometimes also called "general education") in many subjects before asking students to focus primarily on a major subject for another two years.[2] They do this out of the conviction that higher education is not simply preparation for a career, but a general enrichment of citizenship and life. Thus every undergraduate, whether focused on business or mathematics or art history, will take whatever basic required courses the university sees fit to require. This of course is not the situation [around the world] where for the most part students simply study one or perhaps two subjects, and are admitted to the university in order to pursue that subject. Moreover, professional courses such as law and medicine in the United States are offered only as second degrees, after the candidate has already received a bachelor's degree in some other subject, whether history or philosophy; in [most countries] students enter such courses directly. So here is another source of humanistic richness in the professional education of US students that is absent from most [non-American] universities.

It is particularly difficult for a [higher education] system structured in the [monodisciplinary] way to integrate new forms of study, such as women's studies and the study of race. Most students do not want these to be their major subject, because they do not lead to many job opportunities. Most often, they are sought out, in the US, as either basic required courses or so-called "elective courses," that is, courses where the student has some latitude to roam outside the major subject. In Europe it has been exceedingly difficult for programs in these areas to get established. In both England and The Netherlands, I know that people in women's studies feel extremely marginal at most major universities, because the structure of degree programs does not include them, or, if it does, few students want to make the major commitment of doing an entire degree in that area. But short of that, students have little access to those subjects, and the programs are typically more helpful to faculty doing interdisciplinary research than to students.

Ultimately, I believe, the universities [around the world] will need to think about adding a segment of general "education for citizenship" to the curriculum, in order to realize the goals that I shall outline here. I shall return to that theme in my conclusion. But now let me proceed with the ideas themselves.

In *Cultivating Humanity*, I have argued that three capacities, above all, are essential to the cultivation of humanity in today's interlocking world. First is the capacity for critical examination of oneself and one's traditions—for living what, following Socrates, we may call "the examined life." This means a life that accepts no belief as authoritative simply because it has been handed down by tradition or become familiar through habit, a life that questions all beliefs and accepts only those that survive reason's demand for consistency and for justification. Training this capacity requires developing the capacity to reason logically, to test what one reads or says for consistency of reasoning, correctness of fact, and accuracy of judgment.

Testing of this sort frequently produces challenges to tradition, as Socrates knew well when he defended himself against the charge of "corrupting the young." But he defended his activity on the grounds that democracy needs citizens who can think for themselves rather than simply deferring to authority, who can reason together about their choices rather than just trading claims and counter-claims. Like a gadfly on the back of a noble but sluggish horse, he said, he was waking democracy up so that it could conduct its business in a more reflective and reasonable way.

This norm of deliberative democracy has not been fully realized in our modern democracies, any more than it was in ancient Athens. As I write this, the American controversy about the election continues, and one may observe the extent to which mere rhetoric and the attempt to sway public opinion dominates over all attempts to reason clearly and well. Good reasoning can be found on both sides, and at many levels. But so often the dominant concern of both journalists and politicians is for how things "play," for "spin," rather than for the quality of ideas and arguments.

There are some philosophers, notably Alasdair MacIntyre, who see in our situation a defect of modernity itself, and who hold that things were much better in ancient Greece, when we had a secure grasp of an end for human beings imposed by authority on all citizens. I think that MacIntyre is quite wrong here, both about the Greeks and about us. The Greek democracy had just the same problems that we have: that is why Socrates' mission was necessary. Nor does the solution to those problems require abandoning the Enlightenment's commitment to self-critical reason, or the commitment to pluralism and toleration that is at the heart of our modern ways of life. Political deliberation can proceed well in a pluralistic society—if citizens have sufficient respect for their own reasoning and really care about the substance of ideas and the structure of arguments. The responsibility for instilling these values lies with our institutions of higher education.

I believe that for this reason instruction in philosophy is an indispensable part of higher education. Of course it can't be just any type of philosophy course. Large lecture classes are not very much use, because the main purpose is to give students practice in analyzing and constructing arguments in a Socratic fashion. What is crucial is plenty of opportunity for interchange between faculty and students, and many writing assignments, carefully evaluated with ample comments. More or less useless, in my view, are required courses where lectures are given to a huge number of students, who have no opportunity to discuss or to write papers and evaluation is based on a multiple choice examination. This is not Socratic philosophizing, this is unhelpful regurgitation.

Many American universities and colleges, however, have been able to construct curricula that require all students to take one or two courses in philosophy. (Often this is an excellent source of employment for talented Ph.D. students, who are either teaching assistants in such courses or in some cases teach sections of the courses on their own.) Let me mention just one example of the effects of such required courses, a student named Billy Tucker at a business college named Bentley College in Waltham, Massachusetts. Tucker went to Bentley because he planned to focus on marketing and did not want a more general academic education. On the other hand, the college wisely requires two semesters of philosophy from all students, and hires enough faculty to keep class size around twenty-five students per faculty member.

Tucker encountered a very gifted teacher, originally from India, named Krishna Mallick. Mallick began with the trial and death of Socrates. (I met Tucker at my fitness center, where he was working behind the desk, reading Plato's *Apology* and *Crito*.) She also showed a film about Socrates, and the combination really grabbed the imagination of this young man, intelligent but lacking in confidence about his own intellect. He thought it was so odd that Socrates did not escape from prison when he had the chance, but died for the activity of arguing. This example stung his imagination, and he got more and more interested in the course, which continued by presenting the basics of formal logic, so that students could then discover examples of valid and invalid reasoning in newspaper editorials and political speeches. Tucker did really well on this, and was amazed to discover that he actually had a good mind—he had thought he was not that kind of person. Finally, the course assigned students roles in debates about issues of the day that were to be staged before the class. Tucker was puzzled to discover that he was assigned to argue against the death penalty, although he actually supports it.

Tucker told me that this experience gave him an entirely new attitude to political debate: he had never understood that you can argue on behalf of a position that you do not hold yourself. Now he is more likely to see political argument as a process of searching for good answers, rather than just a way of making boasts and establishing your status. Now he knows how to ask what assumptions both sides share, where their differences really lie, and what the structure of each argument is. As you can guess, I think that this result is exactly what Socrates was after, and an exceedingly important result, in a democracy where most people learn their norms of political rhetoric from the rhetoric of talk radio. I believe that such abilities can be cultivated in many different types of classes, but that philosophy does the best job of educating the mind in this way—if taught with sufficient attention to the student's starting point, and with sufficient imagination and creativity. The important thing is that students need to be made active, and I must emphasize that the proposals I am making are no good at all in the absence of resourceful creative teaching that really respects the mind of the pupil.

But now to the second part of my proposal. Citizens who cultivate their humanity need, further, an ability to see themselves as not simply citizens of some local region or group but also, and above all, as human beings bound to all other human beings by ties of recognition and concern. As I have already said, the world around us is inescapably international. Issues from business to agriculture, from human rights to the relief of famine, call our imaginations to venture beyond narrow group loyalties and to consider the reality of distant lives. As Seneca and the ancient Stoics knew, we very easily think of ourselves in group terms—as Americans first and foremost, as human beings second—or, even more narrowly, as Italian-Americans, or heterosexuals, or African-Americans first, Americans second, and human beings third if at all. We neglect needs and capacities that link us to fellow citizens who live at a distance, or who look different from ourselves. This means that we are unaware of many prospects of communication and fellowship with them, and also of responsibilities we may have to them. We also sometimes err by neglect of differences, assuming that lives in distant places must be like ours and lacking curiosity about what they are really like. Cultivating our humanity in a complex interlocking world involves understanding the ways in which common needs and aims are differently realized in different circumstances. This requires a great deal of knowledge that American college and university students rarely got in previous eras, knowledge of non-Western cultures, of minorities within their own, of differences of gender and sexuality.

As I have said, Americans face particular dangers in this area. On the one hand, we have been thinking about internal minority traditions for a long time, and to some extent we have succeeded in understanding our nation as a multicultural society, where the contributions of different groups all make a difference. I shall return to that point later. But on the other hand, Americans, unlike most citizens of Sweden, are tremendously ignorant of the other nations of the world. They have little factual knowledge and little curiosity. Institutions of higher education have a crucial role to plan in combatting these cultural vices. So as I describe this part of my proposal, I shall focus on teaching involving non-Western cultures, although I shall later return to the role of learning about internal minorities.

Education for world citizenship has two dimensions: the construction of basic required courses that all students take (part of the "liberal education" or "general education" component of a US university education) and the infusion of world-citizenship perspectives in more advanced courses in the different disciplines. Let me give one example at each level, making my description concrete enough to give you an idea of the actual classroom experience.

At Scripps College, in Pomona, California, the balmy climate and the lush campus sometimes make studying difficult. As a visitor from Chicago, I feel like getting outside as quickly as possible. Nonetheless, the freshman class, consisting of 250 women, crowds the lecture hall, with eager energy and expectation. Their freshman core course is about to meet, to discuss feminist criticisms of the international human rights movement as a false Western type of universalism, and responses that other feminists have made to those criticisms, defending the human rights movement against the charge of Westernizing and colonizing. (That's what I am there to do.) Called "Culture, Values, and Representation," this course, required of all first-year university students, replaced an earlier required course on Western civilization course that had gotten tired and diffuse. It studies the central ideas of the European enlightenment—in political thought, history, philosophy, literature, and religion. (The staff is drawn from many different departments; instructors take turns giving lectures, and each leads a section.) The study of the Enlightenment is then followed by critical responses to it: by formerly colonized populations, by non-Western philosophy and religion, by Western postmodernist thought, including feminist thought. The course then turns to responses that can be made to those criticisms.

This course obviously does not provide a systematic investigation of even one non-Western culture, but it sets the stage for inquiry and questioning. Its clear focus, its emphasis on cross-cultural debate and reasoning, rather than simply on a collection of facts, and its introduction of non-Western materials through a structured focus on a single set of issues, all make it a valuable introduction to further questioning on these issues. Above all, the course has merit because it plunges students right into some of the most urgent questions they will need to ask today as world citizens: questions about the universal validity or lack of validity of the language of rights, the appropriate way to respond to the legitimate claims of the oppressed. I like this course so much that I have imitated its structure in a seminar that I will soon be conducting for leaders of business and industry at the Aspen Institute in Colorado.

Pedagogically, this course gives a good model of how to deal with large class size without diluting instructional quality. The lectures themselves, of course, do not involve much faculty–student interaction—although a dramatic and problem-oriented lecturing style can do a lot to involve students and prevent passivity. But there is at least one discussion section every week, led by a faculty member, and the sections have around 15 students. There are also very regular writing assignments. Students thus are rendered active participants in the working out of the ideas of the course, and the open-ended structure of criticism and reply indicates to them that these are ongoing problems in human life that they will have to approach as best they can, rather than closed issues to which some knowing intellectual has found a solution. The spirit of questioning carries over into the informal life of the campus. Because all students take it, discussion of its questions fills the dining halls and residences.

Another important aspect of the course's success that needs comment is its interdisciplinary character. Faculty from many different departments are brought together and given financial support to work on the course during the summer, exchanging ideas and getting one another's disciplinary perspectives. Such financial support for development of new ideas in a deliberative interdisciplinary framework is crucial to making the course as rich as it is.

Now let me turn to a program that aims to affect more advanced courses in each of the disciplines. Again, I begin with a description of what faculty are actually doing.

At St. Lawrence University, a small liberal arts college in upstate New York, the snow is already two feet deep by early January. Cars make almost no sound rolling slowly over the packed white surface. But the campus is well-plowed, even at Christmas. In a brightly lit seminar room a group of young faculty, gathering despite the vacation, talk with excitement about their month-long visit to Kenya to study African village life. Having shared the daily lives of ordinary men and women, having joined in local debates about nutrition, polygamy, AIDS, and much else, they are now incorporating the experience into their teaching—in courses in art history, philosophy, religion, women's studies. Planning eagerly for the following summer's trip to India, they are already meeting each week for an evening seminar on Indian culture and history. Group leaders Grant Cornwell from Philosophy and Eve Stoddard from English talk about how they teach students to think critically about cultural relativism, using careful philosophical questioning in the Socratic tradition to criticize the easy but ultimately (they argue) incoherent idea that toleration requires us not to criticize anyone else's way of life. Their students submit closely reasoned papers analyzing arguments for and against outsiders taking a stand on the practice of female circumcision in Africa.

Again, notice that the success of this program requires interdisciplinary discussion and financial support. The unique travel component was very important to these faculty, but is probably not absolutely indispensable. What is indispensable is the time to sit together and read and work together, learning how the problems of a region of the world look from historical, economic, religious, and other perspectives. Each faculty member will ultimately go on to incorporate this knowledge into the standard course offerings in his or her field. Thus, Economics now offers a course on "African Economies." Art History offers a course focused on representation of the female body in African art. Philosophy offers a course in cultural relativism and the critique of relativism. Biology offers a course in AIDS and the African experience. These courses enrich standard course offerings in each of the departments.

These same two levels need to be considered when we consider what students should learn about minorities and previously excluded groups in their own nation. Once again, the basic courses that all students take should contain a new emphasis on the diversity of the nation's own population.

Thus in many American universities discussions of US history and constitutional traditions now contain a focus on race, the changing situation of women, and the role of immigration and ethnic politics, that would have been previously unknown. At the same time, courses in each of the disciplines must increasingly incorporate and are incorporating these perspectives. Literature courses increasingly focus on works by women and expressing the experience of excluded racial minorities; economics, art history, biology, religious studies—all these can find ways of confronting students with the reality of a multi-ethnic and multicultural society. Even in disciplines as traditional as the Greek and Roman Classics, we now study the lives of women in the ancient world, and the role of slavery in ancient economies, something that both promotes a richer understanding of the past and facilitates good deliberation about modern problems.

As I remarked earlier in countries where university curricula have a firm disciplinary focus it will not be easy to incorporate the "general education" part of my proposal. That may happen over time, but it is possible right now to think of ways in which each of the separate disciplines may prepare students more adequately to see themselves as citizens of a multicultural and diverse society, in a multinational interdependent world.

This brings me, in fact, to the third part of my proposal. Citizens cannot think well on the basis of factual knowledge alone. The third ability of the citizen, closely related to the first two, can be called the narrative imagination. This means the ability to think what it might be like to be in the shoes of a person different from oneself, to be an intelligent reader of that person's story, and to understand the emotions and wishes and desires that someone so placed might have. The narrative imagination is not uncritical: for we always bring ourselves and our own judgments to the encounter with another, and when we identify with a character in a novel, or a distant person whose life story we imagine, we inevitably will not merely identify, we will also judge that story in the light of our own goals and aspirations. But the first step of understanding the world from the point of view of the other is essential to any responsible act of judgment, since we do not know what we are judging until we see the meaning of an action as the person intends it, the meaning of a speech as it expresses something of importance in the context of that person's history and social world. The third ability our students should attain is the ability to decipher such meanings through the use of the imagination.

This ability is cultivated, above all, in courses in literature and the arts. Preparing citizens to understand one another is not the only function of the arts in a college curriculum, of course, but it is one extremely important function, and there are many ways in which such courses may focus on the requirements of citizenship.

Many courses in literature and the arts cultivate this sort of imagination, and many standard and familiar works thus prepare students to understand the situation of people different from themselves. But there is also reason to focus on the incorporation of works that confront students vividly with the experience of minority groups in their own society and of people in distant nations. The moral imagination can often become lazy, according sympathy to the near and the familiar, but refusing it to people who look different. Enlisting students' sympathy for distant lives is thus a way of training, so to speak, the muscles of the imagination.

This point was vividly put by Ralph Ellison, one of America's great novelists, in his novel *Invisible Man*. In an Introduction to a reissue of the novel in 1981, Ellison explicitly links the novelist's art to the possibility of American democracy. By representing both visibility and its evasions, both equality and its refusal, a novel, he wrote, "could be fashioned as a raft of hope, perception and entertainment that might help keep us afloat as we tried to negotiate the snags and whirlpools that mark our nation's vacillating course toward and away from the democratic idea." This is not, he continues, the only goal for fiction; but it is one proper and urgent goal. For a democracy requires not only institutions and procedures, it also requires a particular quality of vision, in order "to defeat this national tendency to deny the common humanity shared by my character and those who might happen to read of his experience" (xxvi).

Let me show you a bit of how Ellison's novel does this, by commenting on its opening paragraph. A voice speaks to us, from out of a hole in the ground. We don't know where this hole is—somewhere in New York, it appears. It is a warm hole, and full of light; in fact, there is more light in that hole, we are told, than on top of the Empire State Building, or on Broadway. The voice tells us that he loves light, and he can't find much of it in the outside world. Light confirms his reality. Without light, and that is to say virtually always in the world above, he is invisible, formless, deprived of a sense of his own form and his "vital aliveness."

> I am an invisible man. No, I am not a spook like those who haunted Edgar Allan Poe; nor am I one of your Hollywood-movie ectoplasms. I am a man of substance, of flesh and bone, fiber and liquids—and I might even be said to possess a mind. I am invisible, understand, simply because people refuse to see me. Like the bodiless heads you see sometimes in circus sideshows, it is as though I have been surrounded by mirrors of hard, distorting glass. When they approach me they see only my surroundings, themselves, or figments of their imagination—indeed, everything and anything except me.
>
> Nor is my invisibility exactly a matter of a biochemical accident to my epidermis. That invisibility to which I refer occurs because of a peculiar disposition of the eyes of those with whom I come in contact. A matter of the construction of their inner eyes, those eyes with which they look through their physical eyes upon reality.

Ellison's novel concerns a refusal of acknowledgment, a humanity that has been effaced. From its very opening, however, the work itself goes to work undoing that refusal of recognition, alluding as it does so to its own moral capacities. The refusal to see the Invisible Man is portrayed as a moral and social defect, but also, more deeply, as a defect of imagination, of the inner eyes with which we look out, through our physical eyes, on the world. The people around the Invisible Man see only various fantastic projections of their own inner world, and they never come into contact with the human reality of his life. *Invisible Man* explores and savagely excoriates these refusals to see, while at the same time inviting its readers to know and see more than the unseeing characters. "Being invisible and without substance, a disembodied voice, as it were, what else could I do? What else but try to tell you what was really happening when your eyes were looking through?" In this way, it works upon the inner eyes of the very readers whose moral failures it castigates, although it refuses the easy notion that mutual visibility can be achieved in one heartfelt leap of brotherhood.

The novel's mordantly satirical treatment of stereotypes, its fantastic use of image and symbol (in, for example, the bizarre dream-like sequence in the white paint factory), and its poignant moments of disappointed hope, all contribute to Ellison's democratic end, linking the novel's sources of pleasure to its sources of insight.

One could go on much further about this wonderful work. But my point is that we need to educate the eyes of our students, by cultivating their ability to see complex humanity in places where they are most accustomed to deny it.

Defeating these refusals of vision requires not only a general literary education, but also one that focuses on groups with which our citizens' eyes have particular difficulty.

Although one may certainly add a literary component to courses in many different disciplines, from law to philosophy, I think that here the "liberal education" part of the US system has a special strength, enabling all students to get a common imaginative awakening through confrontation with carefully chosen literary works. It is very difficult to see how students bound for careers in business and industry, for example, will get such a training from courses in those disciplines alone. Our campuses educate our citizens. This means learning a lot of facts, and mastering techniques of reasoning. But it means something more. It means learning how to be a human being capable of love and imagination.

We may continue to produce narrow citizens who have difficulty understanding people different from themselves, whose imaginations rarely venture beyond their local setting. It is all too easy for the moral imagination to become narrow in this way. Think of Charles Dickens's image of bad citizenship in his novel *A Christmas Carol*, in his portrait of the Ghost of Jacob Marley, who visits Scrooge to warn him of the dangers of a blunted imagination. Marley's Ghost drags through all eternity a chain made of cash boxes, because in life his imagination never ventured outside the walls of his successful business to imagine the lives of the men and women around him, men and women of different social class and background. Scrooge is astonished at the spectacle of his old friend wearing this immense chain. "I wear the chain I forged in life," he tells Scrooge. "I made it link by link and yard by yard. I girded it on of my own free will, and of my own free will I wore it." Trying to deny what he is hearing, Scrooge, terrified, blurts out, "You were always a good man of business, Jacob." "Business," the Ghost dolefully intones. "Mankind was my business. Charity, mercy, benevolence were all my business." (Here in Dickens's own Christian way he is directly alluding to Seneca's ideas of cultivated humanity, and to related ideas of mercy and benevolence.) Then, turning to Scrooge, the Ghost asks, "Don't you feel the weight of the chain you bear yourself?" "My chains!" Scrooge exclaims. "No no." And then, in a smaller voice, "I am afraid."

Scrooge got another chance to learn what the world around him contained. During that fateful night he got what we might call a belated liberal education, traveling to homes rich and poor, to a lighthouse on the sea, to the poverty of his own clerk's home only a mile or so away in Camden town in North London, but a very long mile indeed, the mile that divides rich from poor. We need to produce citizens who have this education while they are still young, before their imaginations are shackled by the weight of daily duties and self-interested plans. We produce all too many citizens who do drag cash boxes around with them, whose imaginations never step out of the counting house. But we have the opportunity to do better, producing Socratic citizens who are capable of thinking for themselves, arguing with tradition, and understanding with sympathy the conditions of lives different from their own. Now we are beginning to seize that opportunity. That is not "political correctness," that is the cultivation of humanity.

## Notes

1 This article was originally a lecture based on the book *Cultivating Humanity*, and was published in the international journal *Studies in Philosophy and Education*.
2 Strictly speaking, the course of study is rarely linear in this way. Usually students begin study of the major subject early, in the first or certainly the second year; and in the third and fourth years they do not study only one thing, but continue to take some basic required courses and other "elective" (optional) courses outside their major.

## References

Dickens, C. (1843). *A Christmas Carol.*
Ellison, R. (1995). *Invisible Man.* 1947. New York: Vintage.

# ABOUT THE EDITORS AND CONTRIBUTORS

## Editors

**Daniel Araya** is a researcher and advisor to government with a special interest in technological innovation, public policy, and education. He is a Hult-Ashridge Research Fellow with the Hult Center for Disruptive Innovation in San Francisco and a Sharing Cities Policy Fellow with Shareable. He is a regular contributor to various media outlets including Futurism, The Brookings Institution, and Medium. He is also a film producer and writer and holds a doctorate from the University of Illinois at Urbana-Champaign. His newest books include *Augmented Intelligence* (2017) and *Smart Cities as Democratic Ecologies* (2015).

**Cathy N. Davidson** is Distinguished Professor at Director of the Futures Initiative at the Graduate Center of the City University of New York. Davidson previously taught at Duke University for more than two decades. From 1998 to 2006, she also served as Duke University's (and the nation's) first Vice Provost of Interdisciplinary Studies. She has published more than twenty books, including *Now You See It: How the Brain Science of Attention Will Transform the Way We Live, Work, and Learn* (2011). A frequent speaker on institutional change at universities, corporations, nonprofits, and other organizations, she writes for the *Harvard Business Review*, *Wall Street Journal*, *Fast Company*, *Chronicle of Higher Education*, *Washington Post*, and *Times Higher Ed*, among others. In 2011, President Obama appointed her to the National Council on the Humanities. Dr. Davidson received her MA and PhD in English from the State University of New York, Binghamton, and did postdoctoral study in linguistics and literary theory at the University of Chicago.

**Peter Marber** is an acclaimed writer and teacher specializing in globalization, human capital, and emerging markets. He currently teaches at Harvard University and is conducting research at the University of Cambridge, Faculty of Education. Prior to Harvard, Marber taught at Columbia University's School of International & Public Affairs and Columbia Business School for more than 20 years. An author of more than 100 articles and columns on global topics, he has authored or edited five books. His newest titles include *Higher Education in the Global Age* (with Daniel Araya, 2013) and *Brave New Math: Information, Globalization and New Economic Thinking in the 21st Century* (2015). He is a frequent commentator on global happenings for the *Wall Street Journal, Financial Times, Barron's* and other media outlets. He serves on various boards for Columbia University, New America, World Policy Institute, and the Emerging Markets Trade Association. Dr. Marber holds degree from Johns Hopkins, Columbia and Cambridge.

## Contributors

**Mark Archibald** is Assistant Director at the Henry B. Tippie College of Business, University of Iowa.

**Kara A. Godwin** is an international consultant and a research fellow at the Boston College Center for International Higher Education. With special interest in liberal and innovative education, her research focuses on university learning, teaching, and curriculum; international development; public policy; and internationalization. Her forthcoming book, Changing Tides: The Global Rise (and US Decline) of Liberal Education, analyzes the expanding global interest in liberal arts education. Dr. Godwin has worked with Northwestern University, the Norwegian Agency for Development Cooperation, Olin College of Engineering, The Economist, the Rhode Island Board of Governors, and Amsterdam University College. She holds a PhD from Boston College, a master of science from Northwestern University, and a BA from Augustana College.

**Cindy A. Kilgo** is Assistant Professor of Higher Education at the University of Alabama.

**Bruce A. Kimball** is a professor in the School of Educational Policy & Leadership at the Ohio State University. Dr. Kimball pursues research on the emergence of "free money" ideology, fundraising, and endowments in American higher education and was a Guggenheim Fellow in 2012. Kimball is the author of *Orators and Philosophers: A History of the Idea of Liberal Education* (1986), *The 'True Professional Ideal' in America: A History* (1992), *The Condition of American Liberal Education: Pragmatism and a Changing Tradition* (1995) with Robert Orrill, *The Inception of Modern Professional Education: C. C. Langdell 1826–1906* (2009), and *Voices from the Liberal Arts Tradition: A Documentary History* (2010). He earned his bachelors at Dartmouth College and his doctorate from Harvard University.

**Gray Kochhar-Lindgren** currently consults at the University of Hong Kong, on leave from the University of Washington. Through cross-disciplinary and cross-genre connections, his work focuses on questions of philosophy, cities, spectrality, non-modern networks, literature, global noir, and the 21st-century university. A Fulbright Scholar, Dr. Kochhar-Lindgreen has authored numerous articles and several books including *Kant in Hong Kong: Walking, Thinking, and the City* (2014), *Philosophy, Art, and the Specters of Jacques Derrida* (2011), *Night Café: The Amorous Notes of a Barista* (2010), *TechnoLogics: Ghosts, the Incalculable, and the Suspension of Animation* (2005), *Starting Time: A True Account of the Origins of Creation, Sex, Death, and Golf* (1995), and *Narcissus Transformed: The Textual Subject in Psychoanalysis and Literature* (1993).

**Grant Lilford** is Professor of English, and Chair of the Division of Christian Studies and Humanities. at Brewton-Parker College in Mount Vernon, Georgia. An author of several scholarly articles, Dr. Lilford previously taught at the University of the West Indies-St. Augustine, the University of Zululand, University of Botswana, Uganda Christian University, and North Carolina State University. He holds a BA in Africana Studies and English Literature from Vassar College, an MA from the University of Sussex, and a PhD from the University of Cape Town.

**Jesse H. Lytle** is the Chief of Staff at Haverford College, representing the President and the College on a wide range of business and institutional issues. Before coming to Haverford in 2012, he held administrative, research, and teaching roles at Amherst College, the University of Pennsylvania, and Mount Holyoke College.

**Graham N. S. Miller** is a doctoral candidate in Higher Education and Student Affairs at the University of Iowa.

**Peter N. Miller** is Dean of the Bard Graduate Center in New York, where he has taught since 2001. He previously taught at the University of Chicago and University of Maryland. Dr. Miller has won numerous fellowships and has written or edited several books including *Defining the Common Good: Empire, Religion and Philosophy in Eighteenth-Century Britain* (2004) and *Peiresc's Europe: Learning and Virtue in the Seventeenth Century* (2000). He holds degrees from Harvard University and University of Cambridge.

**Christopher B. Nelson** has been president of St. John's College in Annapolis, Maryland, since June 1991. He is an alumnus of St. John's (BA 1970) and a graduate of the University of Utah College of Law (JD 1973), where he founded and directed the university's student legal services program. An author of numerous articles and columns, Nelson is a national spokesperson for the liberal arts, participating actively in the American conversation about higher education.

**Neema Noori** has been an Assistant Professor in the Department of Sociology and Criminology at the University of West Georgia since 2008. He received his PhD in Sociology from Columbia University in 2006. After completing his dissertation, Dr. Noori taught for three years in the Department of International Studies at the American University of Sharjah in the United Arab Emirates.

**Martha Nussbaum** is an American philosopher and the current Ernst Freund Distinguished Service Professor of Law and Ethics at the University of Chicago, a chair that includes appointments in the philosophy department and the law school. Nussbaum is one of America's leading social scientists, and she is the author or editor of a number of seminal books, including *The Fragility of Goodness* (1986), *Sex and Social Justice* (1998), *The Sleep of Reason* (2002), *Hiding From Humanity: Disgust, Shame, and the Law* (2004), and *Frontiers of Justice: Disability, Nationality, Species Membership* (2006).

**Ernest T. Pascarella** is the Professor and Mary Louise Petersen Chair in Higher Education at the University of Iowa. Dr. Pascarella has been identified as one of the most cited scholars in the world's leading higher education journals.

**Steven L. Solnick** is the seventh president of Warren Wilson College. From 2002–2012, he was Ford Foundation Representative in Moscow and New Delhi. Before joining the Ford Foundation, Solnick was associate professor of political science at Columbia University, where he also was coordinator for Russian Studies at the Harriman Institute. He previously was research associate at Harvard University's Russian Research Center and Center for International Affairs. Solnick holds a bachelor's degree in physics from the Massachusetts Institute of Technology, and a doctorate in political science from Harvard University. He also has a BA (First Class) in politics and economics from Oxford University, where he was a Marshall Scholar. In July 2017, Solnick will become the Head of the Calhoun School in New York City.

**Charlene Tan** is an associate professor at the Policy and Leadership Studies Academic Group, National Institute of Education, Nanyang Technological University. A former history school teacher and a philosopher by training, she has published widely on the philosophy of education, comparative education, and critical thinking, with a particular focus on education in Singapore and China. She has held visiting appointments at the University of Oxford, University of Cambridge, and Beijing Normal University. She holds a doctorate from the National University of Singapore. Her forthcoming book is titled *Educational Borrowing in China: Looking West or Looking East* (Routledge).

**Marijk van der Wende** was the Founding Dean of Amsterdam University College (2007–2015) and previously held professorial positions at VU University Amsterdam (2006–2015) and the University of Twente (CHEPS) (2001–2008). She was a visiting scholar at the University of California at Berkeley, Harvard University, Boston College, and Shanghai Jiao Tong University. She holds BA degrees in teaching and pedagogy, and MA and PhD degrees in educational sciences, from the University of Amsterdam and the University of Utrecht, respectively.

**Daniel H. Weiss** is president of the Metropolitan Museum of Art and was previously the 14th president of Haverford College. A leading advocate for the residential liberal arts college, Dr. Weiss served from 2005 to 2013 as president of Lafayette College, where his tenure was noted for a strategic plan that led to an increase in the size of its permanent faculty, revision of its Common Course of Study, and the development of new interdisciplinary programs across the curriculum. Previously, Dr. Weiss was a professor of art history at Johns Hopkins University, where he went on to serve as Dean of the Zanvyl Krieger School of Arts and Sciences. He earned both an MA and PhD in the History of Art from Johns Hopkins as well as an MBA from the Yale School of Management. He is the co-editor of *Remaking College: Innovation and the Liberal Arts* (2013).

# INDEX